Tony Thompson is a journalist who has written on crime for the *Independent*, the *Guardian* and *GQ*. He has spoken to current as well as ex gang members: he has travelled extensively to track the roots of the gangs. He has bargained for guns in Woolwich, spent evenings at illegal Triad and Yardie gambling dens, and drunk beer with wanted contract killers.

He is currently news editor for *Time Out* and lives in London.

Gangland Britain

Tony Thompson

CORONET BOOKS
Hodder and Stoughton

First published in Great Britain in 1995
by Hodder and Stoughton

First published in paperback in 1996
by Hodder and Stoughton
A division of Hodder Headline PLC
A Coronet paperback

15 17 19 20 18 16 14

British Library Cataloguing in Publication Data:

Thompson, Tony
Gangland Britain
1. Organized crime – Great Britain
2. Gangs – Great Britain
I. Title
364.1'06'0941

ISBN 0 340 60825 0

Typeset by Palimpsest Book Production Limited,
Polmont, Stirlingshire
Printed and bound in Great Britain by
Mackays of Chatham PLC, Chatham, Kent

Hodder and Stoughton
A division of Hodder Headline PLC
338 Euston Road,
London NW1 3BH

Acknowledgments

The vast majority of the sources, confidants and informants who have assisted me in the preparation of this book are too shy to be mentioned by name. In the case of law enforcement officials, to name all would put lives and investigations at risk, but you know who you are and I am for ever grateful.

As for those who have supported and stood by me through a hellish eighteen months of frantic research and writing, I would especially like to thank, in no particular order, John Knight, Ann Geeves (and Paul and Oliver!) and Honey Salvadori.

I am also grateful to a handful of fellow hacks, particularly Angus McKinnon, Duncan Campbell, Denis Campbell, Andy Kershaw, Yvonne Ridley, Lee Marshall, Nigel Green, Brian Hilliard, Yves Lavigne, David Kaplan, Lucy Kaylin, Gillian Scott, Catherine Pepinster, Brian Freemantle and Dominic Wells, Anita Chaudhuri, Sid Smith and everyone else at *Time Out* for putting up with me during the most difficult stages.

Finally, extra special thanks to my parents, Aicha Idmessaaoud, Richard Reyes, Caroline Dawnay, Humphrey Price (without whom none of this would have been possible), and Dawn Bates.

Contents

Introduction

In writing *Gangland Britain*, my chief aim has been to take the reader on a journey into that underworld and to lay bare the methods and motives of the modern-day gangster.

It is a world which, over the last decade, has changed out of all recognition. The sixties-style family firms still rule in many parts of the country, but today the big money is being made by a handful of ruthless, stateless, high-tech gangs which collectively make up an increasingly formidable global mafia.

Britain has proved highly attractive to this new monolithic threat. Partly because our police are unarmed, our racketeering laws non-existent, our death penalty extinct, and our prison sentences comparatively lenient. But mostly because of an ever-improving communications infrastructure, a rich appetite for drugs and sizeable ethnic communities from all corners of the globe among which the criminal fraternity can hide.

It wasn't until 1992 that a national body monitoring the activities of organised crime in an empirical way, the National Criminal Intelligence Service, was set up. But for observers of the international scene, it was too little too late.

The best estimates suggest that the current domestic turnover of professional crime is somewhere between £20 billion and £40 billion each year, making it at least the country's fourth-largest industry. By far the greatest proportion of this wealth is earned by the key organisations detailed in the pages that follow.

Wherever possible, I have based my information on facts gleaned from members, former members, and associates of the gangs themselves – they are, after all, the only people who truly know what is going on. As far as possible, this information has been corroborated and confirmed by other sources.

This book was never intended to be an exercise in finger-pointing – while some names do appear in print for the first time, others remain anonymous. Many of those who agreed to talk to me provided fascinating insights into the workings of international organised crime, but also implicated themselves in everything from drug trafficking and fraud to firearms offences and multiple murder. I am too thankful for their information to betray their trust. Furthermore, to do so would be little short of signing my own death warrant.

Now to deal with the complaints.

For those who feel the book has too much of a London bias, this has not been deliberate but merely reflects the fact that 70 per cent of crime in Britain is carried out in the capital. For those who feel I have glamorised the underworld, this is to an extent unavoidable. No matter how many multi-million-pound drug smugglers end up behind bars, there will always be others who say: 'I could do that, I could have what he had, but they'd never catch me.' The attraction of living on a rock-star income, even if you do have to spend half your time watching your back, is a powerful one.

For those who feel the book is sexist, that too is a reality of the underworld. Despite occasional media interest in girl gangs and the fact that there have been female-run Mafia and Triad syndicates, most crime is male-dominated and women are most often relegated to the role of accessory.

For those who regard the book as being xenophobic, I can only say that the ethnic divisions outlined within are another stark reality. Without exception, each individual mafia has emerged because of specific social, economic and geographic factors within its mother country and, as expatriate communities have been set up abroad, so the gangs have followed.

It should, however, be pointed out that in every case, organised criminals make up only a fraction of a percentage of the population – this book does not seek to tar every Jamaican, Colombian, Sicilian or Asian with the same brush, it merely focuses on the tiny underworld element within each group.

I cannot, however, pretend that the book is fully comprehensive. Nor does it contain a conclusion or provide possible solutions as to what should be done to counteract the threat of organised crime.

It is simply an account of the current state of play in the British underworld, a potted profile of the people who inhabit it, and a fleeting glance at the lives they lead.

Tony Thompson

Chapter One

Heirs to the Krays

The Fall and Rise of Traditional British Organised Crime

'. . . how many guns have we got here? Thirty?
Thirty-five? I could get a man to hold
every single one of these if I need to.
You know what that is? It's a
fucking army, that's what.'

South London underworld arms dealer talking to the author

At first he was deadly serious. But then there was a hint of a smile, followed by a mischievous chuckle and now a full-blown laugh. Max may have killed six people, but he's lost none of his sense of humour.

He's laughing so much that his huge shoulders are bobbing up and down, making froth spill out of the neck of his beer bottle. Max takes another sip and struggles to compose himself – he's dying to tell me about 'the one that got away', one of the lighter moments in his life as a professional hitman.

'It's a silly story,' he says with a grin. 'It was a favour for a friend, a crippling job. Two of us went up to Lancashire to empty a couple of barrels into this bloke's legs . . . I was only getting a grand for it – normally I wouldn't get out of bed for that much but, like I say, it was for a friend, and the geezer did deserve to get it . . .' The smile holds steady.

'Anyway, we got there, took out the sawn-off, kicked down the door and burst in. Only it was the wrong bloke! I came so close to shooting him I can't tell you! It turned out we'd been given the wrong house number – the bloke we wanted lived next door.

'But then we were fucked. I mean, you can't exactly say, "Oh, sorry, mate, we'll just pop next door and blow your neighbour's kneecaps off", can you? We had to leave it and come home . . .'

What the 'geezer' had done to warrant such punishment, known in the trade as a 'frightener', was to double-cross an associate of one of London's leading crime families, taking delivery of a hefty batch of amphetamine powder but running off without paying for it.

To Max, it's just another amusing anecdote, an everyday story of simple gangster folk, but taken in a wider context, it's a perfect illustration of how the drugs trade has dramatically changed the face of professional organised crime. The precious little honour and loyalty that existed in the days of the Krays and Richardsons has long gone, while the 'accepted' level of gangland violence has escalated beyond all comprehension.

Drugs, along with the emergence of the supergrass, the increased likelihood of being shot dead by armed police while on a 'job', and improvements in banking security, have drastically altered the way in which the modern British villain goes about earning his daily bread.

Where once there were specialist safe-breakers, drivers and lookouts, diversification is now the key and the individual members of a modern firm are likely to have their fingers in a number of lucrative pies including car ringing, cheque fraud, counterfeit currency, VAT fiddles and illegal gambling, as well as the staples of robbery, extortion and the new big thing, drugs.

But while the backdrop may have changed, the essence of London's underworld remains essentially the same. The old-style families still exist and still rule their respective territories with absolute ruthlessness, the major difference being that today none has the aspiration to control all crime in the capital as their sixties counterparts did.

Far from being part of some carefully thought-out, bloody battle for overall supremacy, the periodic pub murders and doorstep shootings that men like Max are hired to carry out are simply the inevitable end-product of inter-family feuds, disputes and double-crosses.

At the time of writing, there are six major crime families in London, each with its associated firms and individual hard-men willing to lend their support whenever needed. There are also dozens of smaller, independent firms with no particular allegiance to anyone.

One of the families is based in Deptford and is involved in a wide range of activities, especially the supply of cannabis and speed. Another, whose members have particular skills in armed robbery and car theft, use the money they make to fund huge drug deals. Their legitimate business front — handy for laundering their spoils — is a pub in their home manor of Woolwich.

In north London, three brothers, known for their resolute hardness as much as for their business acumen, use the clubs and restaurants they own to help disperse the proceeds of the vast drug trafficking network they control. The brothers are sophisticated and established enough to be able to deal directly with representatives of the South American cartels in order to bring cocaine into the country. They also arrange the smuggling of enormous quantities of cannabis and speed to feed the highly lucrative holiday nightclub market. If you find yourself offered drugs in Ibiza, Tenerife or Majorca, the brothers will almost certainly have supplied it. Of late, the Adams have grown spectacularly rich on the back of the conflict in Bosnia, making use of the many UN convoys to move coke across the borders with ease.

Most of the time the families co-exist in relative harmony — at a gangster wedding three years ago, members of five of the six families attended — but occasionally there are disputes, such as the series of impromptu gun battles on the streets of Islington, north London, in January 1990 between the Adams and the Reillys. Or the far more serious feud between the Arifs and associates of the Brindles which, in the last four years, has led to the deaths of at least ten people (and the wounding of a dozen more), all of them victims of contract killings.

Similar families and firms rule towns and cities across the rest of the country. For example there are the Harrisons in Newcastle, the Duresses and the Showers in Liverpool, the Porters in Birmingham and the Goochie and Doodie gangs in Manchester. Meanwhile, in Glasgow, the battle to be top dog in the city's £100 million-a-year heroin trade has become increasingly bloody following the demise of the Thompson clan. But London has always been and looks set to remain home to the country's criminal élite.

Sixty per cent of all the armed robberies in Britain take place in the capital. More surprisingly, the Flying Squad estimates that around 75 per cent of high-value armed robberies that take place elsewhere are committed by Londoners.

But while 'going over the pavement' remains a way for aspiring gangsters to prove their mettle, these days it is more often seen as a way of acquiring the stake money to invest in bigger and better things rather than as an end in itself. The fact that the number of armed robberies increased dramatically during the late eighties has more to do with a new breed of opportunist robbers than organised gangs.

Working alone and often armed with replica guns and occasionally inspired by television programmes like *Crimewatch*, which make it look easy, they target the new open-plan banks, post offices and betting shops, often settling for a hastily grabbed handful of notes rather than trying to clean out the safe.

With a few notable exceptions, the age of the old-style armed robber ended at around 6.40 a.m. on the morning of 26 November 1983. That was the day on which a gang of men burst into a warehouse at Heathrow, poured petrol over the groins of the security guards and, cigarette lighters at the ready, theatened to set them alight unless they opened the vaults.

The gang had initially been after the million or so pounds in cash stashed in the warehouse safe, but when one of the guards failed to remember his part of the combination, the gang decided to settle for the consignment of gold that had arrived late the previous evening.

The strongroom contained around 6,800 bars of gold weighing more than 3 tons. The total haul was worth more than £26 million, and from that day on, the heist became known simply as Brinks-Mat.

To all intents and purposes, it was just the sort of crime that

London villains had been committing, with varying degrees of success, for decades. Traditionally, the spoils of such jobs would have found their way to the pubs and clubs of east and west London a few days later. But in the case of Brinks–Mat, the public outcry and the sheer size of the police operation forced those involved to become far, far smarter. And they did.

Twelve years after the crime, not one single gold bar has been found, dozens of strong suspects are still at liberty, and only £3 million of the total haul has been recovered.

A special task force, set up to track the money-laundering operation, found it led to the Channel Islands, the British Virgin Islands, American offshore islands, and into Florida and Miami. Robbery Squad officers found themselves coming across the first examples of criminal diversification as the trail took them into drug deals and fraud, and the first examples of international cooperation as the trail led to links between Italian, French, Spanish and American gangsters.

The squad was one of the first to tackle the new breed of gangsters who are now common among the upper echelons of professional crime. Whereas top villains of the past had merely lived quite comfortably from the proceeds of crime, the Brinks–Mat breed had phenomenal wealth which allowed them to live millionaire lifestyles complete with boats, mansions and multiple bank accounts awash with hundreds of thousands of pounds.

A lifestyle that could easily slip between the pages of *Hello!* magazine is what every professional criminal now aspires to. And for those without the specialist contacts or guts or the knowledge needed to pull off major frauds or blags, the easiest and most lucrative trade that crime has to offer is drugs.

And inevitably, whenever drugs appear on the scene, their two close cousins – guns and hitmen – are never far behind.

Max doesn't kill or hurt people on a full-time basis. It's unlikely that anybody does. Ostensibly, he runs a small building firm in the north of England but spends a good deal of time in the capital where his face and track record are well known to most of the firms and families that, from time to time, make use of his services.

'I had a little job to do in Tenerife,' he says. 'There was a nightclub owner over there who had upset some people rather badly. I'm not quite sure what the gist was, whether it was drugs or whatever, but there was a contract out on him for twenty grand.

'They came to me and said they already had someone out there with a firearm, all they needed was a man to go and pull the trigger. If I'd've said no, they would have got it done anyway.

'I got hold of a yearly passport in a false name and went out there for a week. Now, with Tenerife being an island, I couldn't do it on the first day – they'd have just sealed the place off. I had to leave it as late as possible. I had photographs of the guy and knew where the bar he owned was so I decided to spend my time hanging around there.

'I went to the club a few times, just drinking socially, then I got chatting to the actual owner, the guy I was there to kill. I started expressing an interest in doing a bit of work in the bars, talking along those sort of lines, so by the time the last day came, we were quite pally and I'd stay behind with him each night after the bar shut, drinking and chatting.

'On the last night, I stayed late and gradually the staff filtered off, all the barmaids had gone home, and it was just the two of us left. We were both pretty tanked up so I suggested we took the jeep I'd hired for the week and went off for a tear round the island.

'He was well pissed up, he was going, "Yeah, fucking great", so off we went. Now in Tenerife, you've only got two main roads that link the place together. And once you get out of the actual towns, it's just desolate, just volcanic rock.

'So we were in the jeep on this road, the TF7 I think it's called, and I drove him halfway to Santa Cruz and then pulled over – for a piss is what I said – he wanted one too so that made

it easy. While he was in the bushes I just walked up behind him
. . .' At this point Max forms his hand into the shape of a gun and
twitches his fingers a few times. His face is expressionless.

'I dragged him further into the bushes, got back in the jeep,
back to the hotel, next morning I booked out and I was on the
plane before anyone even found him.' There is a long silence
while the gravity of what Max has been talking about sinks in.

Struggling for an appropriate question, I finally ask him how
he felt, killing someone after getting to know them like that.
'It's not like he was a friend and then someone asked me to
do it. Someone asked me to do it first. It's just a job. It's just
like you coming here to do this interview. There ain't no bad
dreams, no remorse, no guilt. Nothing.

'I like to know I'm doing things for the right reason. If
someone was a really nice guy, I probably wouldn't . . . well, I'd
think about it a bit more. I've just done this job in Birmingham
and that was a real arsehole drug dealer. People like that just
piss me off. I wanna put 'em down anyway.

'I always ask, I always want to know. A lot of people wouldn't
but that's just me – I like to know why I'm putting a bullet
in someone. If I feel justified in doing it, then I'm justified.
I wouldn't go and work for an arsehole and shoot a nice guy,
but I'll do it the other way round.'

I ask about the money – £20,000 sounds like a lot, even for
killing someone. It turns out the firm involved paid slightly over
the odds as Max had to travel. The average is roughly £10,000,
still not exactly small change. 'It is quite a lot, but people will do
it for a lot less than that nowadays. I mean, you can go down the
road and get some coke-head teenager to do it for five hundred
quid, but will he do it properly?'

Properly? Max gives hypothetical examples to illustrate the
differences which I've exchanged with real ones. The killing on
3 August 1991 of the youngest member of the Brindle family,
twenty-three-year-old David, was by Max's reckoning a rank
amateur affair.

Two men wearing ski-masks burst into the Bell pub, just off

the Walworth Road, and fired several shots at Brindle, hitting him once in the back as he tried to get away. Four others in the pub were hit by gunfire and pensioner Stanley Silk, who was standing next to Brindle at the bar, also died. The men ran out, started up a car and made their getaway. Had they been professionals, says Max, they would have waited outside the pub in a car. When Brindle emerged, one would have walked up and asked him for the time. As Brindle looked at his watch, he would have been shot twice in the head. The car would pull alongside, the killer would jump in and the pair make their escape.

Better still, says Max, the killer would be riding pillion on a motorcycle driven by his accomplice. The full-face helmet would hide his identity completely, and when it comes to making a speedy escape around town, two wheels are far better than four.

Professionals also use better equipment, says Max, going on to talk about guns the way a championship golfer might talk about his clubs. 'I know a lot of people go for these automatics nowadays, but the trouble is they leave shell cases all over the place. Too much forensic.

'You get a nice thirty-eight revolver, snub-nosed, it's very small, very compact, very powerful. It'll rip through people. You get some nice nickel- and lead-tipped bullets, white plastic-nosed ones or hollow-point . . . you don't want full metal jacket – they leave nice clean holes – you want to do as much damage as possible.'

Max is a crack shot, having completed and passed a police firearms training course, though to explain how he did so would betray his identity. He points to a man across the bar and explains how he could fire six shots and hit the bloke's head every time from where he is sitting, some thirty feet away. But when he's 'on a job', he likes to get in close.

'You don't want to take a chance. You're better off doing a couple of body shots then a couple to the head. There's no way anyone's going to walk away from that.'

Do you check them to make sure they're dead? 'Oh no,

they're dead. No doubt. As soon as someone dies from a gunshot, they instantly piss and shit themselves. You know what you've done.'

And what about hurting people? Breaking arms, blowing away kneecaps? 'I don't really bother nowadays,' he says, taking a long draw on his beer. 'It's just not worth the hassle. If it's personal to me, I'll do it, but otherwise you're talking about five hundred quid to do someone's legs in which is nothing. Now, if you get done for that, you're looking at a shit-load of bird just for doing someone's legs. You're mugging yourself off if you do it.

'I personally earn over two grand a week, so what's the point of putting myself on the line for five hundred quid, it's not even half a week's wages!' A friend who has been listening in on the conversation now pipes up: 'But ya do, don't ya, ya do . . .' And Max is back to laughing again.

I had first met Max two weeks earlier while visiting Andrew, an underworld arms dealer who, after months of gentle persuasion, had agreed to let me take photographs of his arsenal.

Sitting on Andrew's pastel-blue sofa drinking tea while his girlfriend rushed around with a dustcloth – 'I don't want people thinking we live in a pigsty' – Max happened to drop by.

The two of us made small-talk about his building firm in the Midlands while Andrew struggled into the living room with a large crate of heavy-duty welding gloves. Each glove contained a gun, and right at the bottom was Andrew's current favourite, a brand-new Uzi submachine-gun.

As Andrew emptied the crate, his excitement grew. 'How many guns have we got here?' he panted. 'Thirty? Thirty-five? I could get a man to hold every single one of these if I needed to. You know what that is? It's a fucking army, that's what.'

Max and I studied the collection, picking out a few for the picture. The variety was daunting. Brownings, Webleys and Walthers. But surprisingly, the one gun that Max got really excited about was a single-shot Derringer – the kind of gun that women in Western films wear in their garter belts.

Max placed the gun in the palm of his massive hand and clenched his sausage-like fingers. It vanished from view and a knowing smile appeared on his face. 'Lovely little thing this,' he cooed. 'How much do you want for it, Andy?' At the time it seemed a strange choice for the six-foot-plus, eighteen-stone man-mountain that Max was. Now I know better.

In 1954, there were four armed robberies in London. In 1994, there were on average four armed robberies in London every single day.

Nobody knows for sure how many guns there are in criminal hands, but the availability is considerable and increasing rapidly. Once reserved for the top gangsters, highly sophisticated weapons are now available to virtually anyone who wants one. And, according to Andrew, that's everyone.

'Whatever area of the crime game you're in these days, everyone wants a gun,' he says. 'Right from burglars and muggers to pimps and fences. Even drug dealers – not the big players but the kids with market stalls selling ten-quid bags of grass – they're all tooled up too.'

The evidence for this is all around. Last February, a humble bag-snatcher, spotted and chased by security guards from the Regent Palace Hotel in west London, turned, pulled out a handgun and opened fire. A week later, a bus conductor demanding a fare from two men on the upper deck of a Routemaster in Oxford Street found himself looking down the barrel of a sawn-off shotgun as they voiced their objection.

The price of a gun on the black market ranges from £150 to £300 for an old revolver, up to around £700 for a newish, semi-automatic handgun, and up to £1500 and above for a machine-gun or assault rifle.

For up-and-coming criminals who don't want to risk carrying a gun when they are not 'working', weapons are commonly hired from dealers like Andrew. The terms vary but in general involve a returnable deposit plus a fee. If the gun is fired, the deposit is retained and the renter is obliged to dispose of the weapon. The reason for this is that no one wants to pick up someone else's history. With advances in forensic techniques, it is relatively easy for the police to match bullets and shells to a particular gun, so an unlucky armed robber might find himself charged with a murder he knew nothing about.

Should the police ever get round to dredging the Thames close to Bermondsey, they'll find out what happens to such weapons.

According to research carried out by the National Criminal Intelligence Service, the two main sources of weapons for the black market are thefts from legitimate certificate-holders and a trade carried out by bent gun dealers.

But hundreds of other guns come direct from the Continent where gun laws are often fairly lax. In Belgium, for example, it is possible for a British citizen to purchase a pump–action shotgun – heavily restricted in the UK – simply on production of a passport. Such guns are regularly smuggled back into the country. 'Only a fool would try and come back through Dover,' says Andrew. 'Liverpool, that's the best bet. They're pretty slack there.'

Known methods of bringing weapons into the country include dismantling them and posting the bits separately to safe houses or placing different parts in different suitcases in an attempt to fool the X-ray detectors. Guns are also hidden in freight or foodstuffs. Others are said to be concealed among deliveries of a particular foreign newspaper.

A current favourite, particularly among Yardie gangs, is the Glock 17L 9mm semi-automatic. This state-of-the-art weapon is, with the exception of the barrel, constructed from high-tensile plastic making it far lighter, quieter and more durable than conventional firearms. More importantly, it doesn't set off those troublesome airport metal detectors.

Yet more guns pour on to the black market through what is officially classified as 'leakage' from military sources. The Home Office has never issued figures – and never will – for the number of weapons lost, damaged or stolen during military exercises, but the public houses close to, say, Aldershot are said to be a frenzy of activity after tours of duty and training exercises, though this has declined somewhat with the ending of the Cold War.

Criminals also exploit two major legal loopholes in order to maintain their firepower. The first of these involves ammunition. While a full firearms certificate is required to purchase live rounds, no licence is needed to purchase shell cases, powder, firing caps and bullets.

It is therefore possible, using a machine that can be purchased by mail order, again without a licence, to make live rounds from the comfort of your own home. In recent years, various police experts have testified that this situation was acceptable as there had never been any evidence of criminals taking advantage of it, and because it would be virtually impossible to enforce restrictions on the sale of components. But in the first four months of 1994, raids on three underworld armouries uncovered bullet-making equipment, and there were at least two murders in which 'home-made' ammunition had been used.

The other loophole involves deactivated weapons – genuine guns that have been made safe by firearms dealers and certified by the Home Office. These were introduced as a sop to the gun lobby in the wake of new legislation after the Hungerford massacre which made it illegal, even for licence-holders, to obtain semi-automatic weapons.

Deactivated guns, which range from machine-pistol to anti-aircraft weapons, have holes drilled in their barrels, metal rods welded into their ammunition chambers, and part of the firing mechanism removed.

While this is usually sufficient to ensure that most guns can never be fired again, one particular type of weapon – a machine-gun that works on the 'blowback' principle, a type that includes Uzis, Sten guns and various East European automatic pistols – is so crudely constructed that it can easily be restored to full working order. This was evidenced with near-fatal consequences when Detective Sergeant Michael Stubbs of the London Flying Squad was shot in the head with a Czech-made

Skorpion submachine-gun wielded by armed robber Stephen Farrer towards the end of 1993.

At the time, the press concentrated on the fact that it was the first time a machine-gun had been fired at the police in Britain. It was, in fact, also the first time a deactivated gun had been fired at the police.

In answer to a parliamentary question in May 1994, the Home Secretary revealed that in the previous year two murders and fourteen shootings had been carried out with deactivated weapons. New legislation has now been introduced which, by increasing the amount of work that needs to be carried out on a weapon before it can be classified as officially deactivated, will nullify the threat. However the law only applies to new weapons so there are still thousands of deactivated guns in circulation which have the potential to be converted.

And even without these loopholes, there is still no shortage of black market weapons, or underworld armourers. 'It's only the amateurs who rent,' says Andrew. 'They only do little jobs – post offices, betting shops. If you're planning something big, you're better off with your own gear. All the big families and firms have their own armourers. You don't want too many people knowing your business, that's how you end up inside.'

Many of the weapons within even the top firms are surprisingly old. A high proportion of the handguns used in armed robberies and street battles are British service weapons such as Webley revolvers, dating from the thirties and forties, which were kept in private houses as souvenirs of past conflicts. But, as a result of more recent conflicts, the balance appears to be shifting.

'Since the Falklands and now with this Bosnia thing, I don't know how but all of a sudden the market is getting flooded with loads of foreign, good, high-quality guns,' says Andrew enthusiastically. 'But not blagging guns, fucking war guns. There's all these night-sights and laser guidance things, bazookas and Kalashnikovs – everyone's got one now so you'd be a dickhead not to get one yourself.'

This kind of talk, according to underworld observers, is a requiem for a gangland tragedy. Thirty, twenty, even ten years ago, a gun was a tool of the trade. You carried it while you were working, used it if you were brave enough and felt you had no option, then stashed it when you were finished.

Today, the gun is virtually a fashion accessory and bravery comes pre-packaged in the form of neat white lines of powder on a mirror. In the old days, a pro wouldn't even have a small drink before going on a job. 'Now people get charlied up, think they're it and start shooting,' says Andrew.

'All that stuff [drugs] they use nowadays makes them confident, brave, raring to go. Someone's only got to plant the seed and they're off. People used to be known as hard-men. They'd win a reputation by having lots of tough fights and coming out on top. Nowadays, if you're that good, you just get shot. There are no more hard-men any more, just nutters.'

The link between British organised crime and the business of drug trafficking is a surprisingly recent one. Up until the mid-seventies, the majority of Britain's cannabis was being moved by well-educated sorts from good backgrounds – men like Howard Marks and Charles Radcliffe who had almost accidentally expanded their supply operations beyond their circle of friends and went about their work in a *Boys' Own* fashion.

But as the decade drew to a close, gangs of former armed robbers – who had hitherto despised anything to do with drugs – began moving in on the scene and taking it over. Between 1977 and 1980, the amount of cannabis resin seized by British customs officials trebled.

There were a number of factors behind this change in attitude and increase in criminal involvement. Firstly, during the mid-seventies cannabis had started to replace tobacco as the primary prison currency, and many of the old anti-drugs school of villains found themselves having their first, tentative toke while behind bars.

Having realised that they didn't immediately turn into child molesters or suffer from paranoid psychosis, they started to see the drug in a new light. The profits were high, the risks were low, and the market seemed insatiable.

The second factor came to the fore in the summer of 1978 when the Spanish government ended its hundred-year extradition treaty with Britain. Originally drawn up by Benjamin Disraeli with the specific intention of preventing British runaways from finding sanctuary in the sun, the Spanish decided it was unworkable, paving the way for the birth of the infamous Costa del Crime, the poor man's Brazil.

Over the next three years, more than one hundred of Britain's most wanted men beat a retreat to a luxurious exile. Few became homesick. The weather was warmer, the houses were bigger, the cars were always convertible and the police didn't recognise you, let alone trouble you.

There were British pubs selling British ale, restaurants serving roast beef and Yorkshire pudding lovingly prepared by British chefs, and even British prostitutes advertising them-selves in the back of *Sur* newspaper. This, at last, was the life they had yearned and strived for.

After a while, though, many found something was missing. The highlight of the week became the visit to the local supermarket or the day when the next video of *Coronation Street* arrived.

But what the expats disliked most of all was when friends from London came to visit. They'd explain how quickly the underworld was changing, how much better they were to be out of it. How they'd never keep up with the young turks. In a phrase, they were 'gone at the game'.

But the expats had an ace up their sleeves. With Morocco just a fast speedboat ride from the Costa del Sol, Spain was, and still is, the biggest port of entry to Europe for North African hashish.

In those early days, the area was ideally suited to the task. Smugglers could slip out of the many harbours between

Malaga and Marbella almost undetected among the hundreds
of pleasure craft. They could easily outrun the Spanish police's
comisarias which hadn't been upgraded for years and, as a final
bonus, drug profits could be (and continue to be) laundered
thorough Gibraltar's plentiful offshore banks.

At first they took a purely financial interest, putting up
the money for a stake and doubling their investment in a
matter of days. But then they started to get more involved,
more greedy.

The biggest 'firms' employed Moroccan middle-men who
would haggle for a good price in the Rif mountains where the
marijuana grows on discreet farms, hidden from prying eyes by
cedar forests, or meet representatives of the growers in plush
Tangiers hotels.

There would also be a team of boatmen, drivers and heavies.
Rarely would quantities of less than half a ton be considered.

To stay one step ahead, the method of smuggling would be
varied. Sometimes small boats would be used; sometimes panels
of hashish would be stashed inside lorries in 'friendly' Moroccan
warehouses. The vehicles would be loaded with perishable goods
such as oranges, frozen fish or fresh flowers and then sealed
shut with Transport Internationale Routière (TIR) bonds which
ensured they sped through customs checkpoints with little or no
interference.

Other teams would simply fly their consignments direct from
the Rif to small airfields in quiet Spanish provinces while others
still would rely on visiting friends and relatives to strap a few
kilos to their bodies and breeze through customs with the
holiday crowd.

By the early eighties, there was an efficient, British-controlled
cannabis-smuggling network moving approximately four tonnes
of high-quality resin back to dear old Blighty each year. The
local police had little chance of infiltrating the network – few
of the firms hired Spaniards – and by the time they started to
make inroads, the firms had already moved on.

In the early eighties, the South American cocaine barons

started to target Europe, the American market for the then upmarket drug having become saturated. Spain, with its common language and large Colombian population, quickly became the main port of entry. The traffickers received a boost in 1983 when changes to the Spanish criminal law decriminalised the possession of cocaine unless the amount involved greatly exceeded an individual's personal needs (it wasn't recriminalised until 1992).

Scouts sent out by the Colombians quickly made contact with the satellite British underworld which soon adapted part of its cannabis-smuggling network to accept South America's finest export. Between 1980 and 1984, the amount of cocaine seized in Spain increased fourfold. The amount seized in Britain rose by exactly the same factor.

(Heroin, then as now, was seen as a 'dirty junkie's drug'. Even today, none of London's main crime families will tolerate it within their ranks. In April 1980, a *Sunday Times* story about organised crime muscling in on the cannabis scene noted: 'The only consolation for police and customs is that gang activity does not appear to have made serious inroads into Britain's heroin traffic . . .' In fact organised crime was deeply involved in the heroin trade; it just wasn't British organised crime.)

The re-establishment of the Spanish extradition treaty in 1985 did little to stem the flow of drugs – by then, British villains were competing with dozens of international gangs including Arab gun-runners and Turkish heroin smugglers. Much of the expat element soon gave way to a younger, hungrier mob.

Today, characters like The Enforcer, The Whistler, Mad Dog and Kickbox Stevie call the tune. They play for higher stakes and are not afraid to show disrespect to the old school. Former Great Train Robber Charlie Wilson found that out in August 1990 when he was executed in the garden of his Marbella mansion. Two years later The Enforcer, a sixteen-stone hard-man from Rochdale, hospitalised none other than Ronnie Knight of Security Express fame in a dispute over a 'business' transaction.

The new breed took over and developed the drug scene.

In the case of cocaine, many switched to importing the stuff direct from Colombia themselves; in the case of cannabis, others found new sources and routes, such as smuggling cannabis from Afghanistan across the Soviet Union via Moscow and Leningrad to Britain.

Back in the UK, having seen the popularity of the dance scene and its dependence on drugs, others got involved in the manufacture of LSD, amphetamine and most recently Ecstasy, offering a new generation of youngsters the same summer of love as their parents had experienced twenty years earlier. (In some cases, the parents would help out and father and son would eventually appear together in the dock.)

When it came to supplying drugs to clubs and rave parties, developing an interest in nightclub security services turned out to be a key area. If you control who goes in or out of a club, you control who deals the drugs and can therefore ensure that you get a cut of every pill, tab or snort sold.

With this in mind, gangs of modern-day hard-men began setting themselves up as security firms, often with alarming results. Strikeforce Surveillance, for example, became notorious on the rave scene before it disbanded in 1990. Its reputation for aggressive tactics was sealed when, during an outdoor party at Reigate, Surrey in September 1989, the sixty-strong Strikeforce team hired to 'guard' the event attacked police trying to arrest a drug dealer. The bouncers, armed with baseball bats, knives and CS gas canisters, left sixteen police officers injured.

Another firm, Rats Securities, run by Brixton-based Vincent Atkins, who has convictions for assault and wounding, gained a reputation for taking on the heavy jobs that no one else would tackle and advertised itself as featuring '12 highly trained kick-boxers, all over 6ft tall, who will go anywhere, anytime to do anything.' It too has now disbanded.

Even without controlling the drugs, the contracts were incredibly lucrative. A firm like Rats would charge £200 per doorman (although the bouncers themselves would receive only

£50) with up to twenty-five being needed for a typical rave. Often, the firm would cover two or three events each week.

Competition for contracts, not surprisingly, was fierce. When the widely feared Panther security firm from Harlseden lost a £3000 deal to guard a reggae gig at their local community centre, they took their revenge on the rival Jumbo Defence Force who took their place.

The JDF, who had travelled up from south of the river and knew nothing of Panther's reputation, had been warned that their rivals would attend the gig and had been told not to search them. But a scuffle started when Harry Mundy, a JDF bouncer, failed to recognise Panther Virgil Adams and began to frisk him. The Panthers, led by Andrew Marshall and Sam Campbell, launched a frenzied attack on Mundy, hacking at his groin and legs with a knife and ten-inch bayonet, inflicting wounds so severe that surgeons were forced to amputate one of his legs.

Marshall and Campbell then spotted Phillip Williams, a local man who was living with Marshall's ex-girlfriend. They chased him, pinned him up against a wall and slashed at him repeatedly. He died on the way to hospital.

Today, the outdoor rave scene has mostly died down, but the controlling influence of the doormen remains, as one DJ who asked not to be identified explained.

'Most of the clubs in London are paying protection money; they have to be somebody if they're not. People don't know it's going on because no one shows off about it any more. But it's still there.

'There are organised firms that go around and do it. Lots of times, I've been working and a load of blokes have come in and said to the manager, "Right, we're your new partners. Either we take half of everything, or we smash this place to fuck and you'll be left with all of nothing."

'It's the doormen that run the drugs too. It makes sense really. How else can they search everyone at the door but people still get in with guns and drugs and stuff. They usually confiscate any drugs they find and give them to one person to sell. I've even heard of cases where a dealer's managed to slip past so the doormen give some punter twenty quid and they go round asking everyone for an E until they find the dealer. Then the bouncer grabs them.'

Tony Tucker, Patrick Tate and Craig Rolfe, the three Ecstasy dealers found brutally executed in a Range Rover in a lonely Essex lane in December 1995 had all worked as bouncers (Tucker had even once been a minder to boxer Nigel Benn) before moving up a league into the supply business.

The trio were also known to have attempted to take over a number of clubs in the Basildon area and had been responsible for a series of 'stings' against rival firms, though it is not clear which of these activities led to their deaths.

Tackling this criminal infiltration of the security industry is a delicate business. When the Labour MP Ian McCartney began campaigning for the vetting of nightclub bouncers to stop the protection rackets, he and his family began receiving death threats. In one case, his wife received a card confirming an appointment for plastic surgery, although she had never been in touch with the clinic. In another, the family received bereavement cards although no one had died. McCartney also received an unsolicited visitor at the House of Commons whose description matched that given to the police by an informant who tipped them off that a contract had been taken out on the MP.

Of course, not all bouncers are involved in selling drugs or protection rackets, but few can claim to be completely removed from the underworld. Ever since the Krays bought Esmeralda's Barn, clubs and crime have been inexorably linked. Clubs are either run by gangsters, or patronised by them. Increasingly, they are where deals are struck, where business is settled, where 'work' is planned and where post-job celebrations are held.

The bouncers are an integral part of this, particularly as back-up 'muscle' is often taken direct from their ranks. Ensuring everything runs smoothly for the gangster element is a top priority. Fall foul of the unwritten law, and bouncers can all too easily find themselves in the line of fire.

Marcus agrees to speak to me only on condition that I don't identify the men who are trying to kill him.

The head of a Margate-based doorman agency, Marcus was working a club in Cliftonville one Saturday night in May 1993 when he spotted one of his staff arguing at the doorway.

A man outside was shouting and swearing aggressively, demanding to be let into the club, but the doorman was standing firm, refusing to allow him past unless he paid the entrance fee. Marcus takes up the story.

'I went over to try to keep the peace and calm the situation down but the guy was coked out of his head and wasn't having any of it. His eyes were wide, pupils dilated and he was saying: "Who the fuck are you?" He told me to keep my nose out of it and kept insisting he'd already been in the club earlier, even though his hand hadn't been stamped.'

What Marcus did not know at the time was that the man was telling the truth. He had indeed been inside the club that night, having arrived earlier in the evening with a London 'face' – the son of one of Britain's most notorious villains. Marcus himself had seen the 'face' and let him in, waving through his friend without bothering to register his looks.

Having got drunk and 'charlied up', the guest had then left the club alone. Without his famous escort, he seemed like just another Joe, hence his difficulty in getting back in. Had he had his wits about him, the mere mention of the name of the 'face' would have done the trick. Instead, Marcus had no reason to believe the man was anything other than just another lairy youth trying to get in for nothing.

'The guy wasn't being calmed down at all,' Marcus continues. 'So I said to him: "If that's the way you are, you're not coming in at all", and I pushed him out the door. The next thing I knew he'd hit me with his right hand, a hook round the side of the head. So I grabbed him by the throat with my left and hit him hard in the face which sent him flying across the pavement.

'He was so high, he got straight up and came charging back at me for another go. The second time I grabbed him bodily and I picked him up and threw him across the pavement about twelve feet.

'Apparently he broke his ankle when he landed but he was so far out of it, he didn't even realise it himself. He got back up again, limped back to the door and started calling me a wanker and this and that, saying he was gonna get me shot, that I was gonna die and that I didn't know who I was messing with. But you get that all the time when you're working the doors so you don't take a lot of notice.

'He then went to take another swing at me so I brought my foot up and kicked him straight in the stomach. Dropped him. Completely. Took the wind out of him. He fell to the pavement in a heap and I said, "Right, that'll shut you up for a while."'

It was then that his friend, the 'face', came downstairs from the nightclub above. 'I suddenly realised who the other bloke was. He said, "Who's done this to my mate?" I've gone, "Let me explain what happened." He just shook his head and said, "I'm not interested."

'He never said a thing more. He just looked me up and down, took in everything that he could about my appearance, picked his mate up, got in a taxi and left. No threats. And when people don't do that, when people don't threaten you, it's actually far more frightening.'

The following morning, Marcus received a telephone call from the club's owner – a friend of the father of the face – who informed him that, not to put too fine a point on it, he was now on the wanted list.

'He said he was going to try and sort it out and went up to London for a couple of days to talk to the blokes involved. He came back saying it was sorted – that the family weren't happy about it but that because of their friendship with him, they were going to let it go.'

If it sounded too good to be true, that's because it was. Three months later, Marcus was working the door at a fairly rough pub close to Margate when he received a a telephone call.

Just as he moved away from the double doors where he was standing, a man burst in with a sawn-off shotgun and fired off both barrels. 'The blast was aimed at knee height,' he says, 'as if they wanted revenge for me breaking the guy's ankle. At the time I wasn't really sure if it was related. I thought it might have been something to do with the troubles in the pub.

'But then a few weeks later, on Bonfire Night, I had another little visit. I'd actually taken the night off. Normally I'd be going to work about nine in the evening, but this particular night I was taking my girlfriend out. At about quarter to eight I went to leave the house to buy a bottle of wine at our local off-licence down the road.

'There were fireworks going off all over the place, loads of noise and everything. As I went out to get into my car – and I'm fairly observant anyway because of the nature of my job – I noticed two blokes on the other side of the road. As soon as I came out, they turned and looked at me. They didn't look comfy, didn't look right. They were walking down a main road but they didn't look like they was going anywhere. They were just ambling along which, if you're on a main road, you don't normally do.

'They kept looking over at me, I kept looking back. One was very, very tall with blond hair, the other a lot shorter with dark hair but unshaven. Both were in their mid to late twenties and at first I thought they were probably trying to case the house to burgle it.

'Anyway, I got in my car and had just started to reverse off the driveway when I saw these two guys run across the road. I looked round to check the traffic and when I looked back, I saw them on my side of the road, about twenty feet away from the car.

'Then I saw them whispering at each other and looking at me and pointing. Then all of a sudden I saw the right hand of one of them, the shorter guy, go under his cardigan and produce a gun. I only saw the silhouette but I knew exactly what it was. By the time I'd taken in what it was and had thought through some of the possibilities of why he had it, the bloke had raised the gun up and come running at the car. Now a lot of people have said that they were just trying to warn me. Believe me, if they was just trying to warn me, they could have done it from twenty feet away. They could have just pulled the gun out and shot a few rounds off.

'I know that the guy ran at the car with the sole intention of getting up to the window and shooting me. Now I don't know how much damage he was planning to inflict but as far as I was concerned it was gonna be fatal.

'So I just slammed the car into first gear, put my foot down and drove straight up into the middle of the road away from them. I heard four or five shots fired and my rear tyre blew out. I just carried on down to the off-licence, got the bloke to phone 999.'

(Amateurs, Max would have said. At this point, I can't help wondering how he would have handled the job. Marcus would just have got into the driver's seat when there would have been a tap at the window. 'Excuse me, mate, I'm looking for . . .' Four bangs. End of story.)

'It took the police half an hour to arrive,' says Marcus, shaking his head. 'This is on a 999 call where someone's been shot at, and when they did turn up, they were unarmed. What's the point? They were totally, totally useless.

'I made a statement but then I withdrew it. I knew they weren't going to find the blokes who did it and if they went around knocking on doors, they were just going to annoy people. Instead, I had a word with a bloke who's got a big firm up in London. I think that helped. I've not been told it's over so I don't know for sure. I still look over my shoulder every day.'

The 'bloke' in London was a certain Dave Courtney, a well-known figure in the underworld. The head of a major firm of doormen, he has a string of convictions for grievous bodily harm and assault. His name has also been linked to various robberies and thefts though he has yet to be successfully prosecuted for such a crime.

Above all, he is known as a hard-man, the sort that most sensible people would cross the street to avoid. For example, in 1980 he was sentenced to three years for attempted murder after attacking five waiters at his local Chinese restaurant with their own meat cleavers.

In October 1990, Courtney, who at the time was starring as an extra in the television series *The Paradise Club*, found himself on the front page of the *Sun* following an alleged fight over nightclub security contract rivalries. One hundred and sixty bouncers had watched him and another man fight a vicious bare-knuckle fight which ended with Courtney having part of an ear and the end of his nose almost bitten off.

Recovering in hospital, Courtney refused police protection, claiming the injuries were caused by a dog: 'I don't think the fucking dog is gonna find out what ward I'm in and come round to bite me again,' he told them. No charges were ever brought in connection with the fight.

The underworld is awash with Courtney stories, from raids on his clubs where the police seized enough drugs, weapons and other evidence to fill five bin liners to epic battles seemingly in every town in the country. Many such stories are undoubtedly apocryphal, but one that checks out occurred at a certain London nightclub which Courtney patronised.

One night, a dozen or so members of a rival firm arrived and announced that they would be taking over the club. Courtney arrived a little later with a friend and the manager ushered him into the office to meet the new owners.

Courtney objected to the takeover, only to be told he was somewhat outnumbered. Courtney then produced a gun and with typical wit replied: 'I think me, Smith and Wesson can handle you lot.'

One close acquaintance, a certain Reginald Kray, describes him as: 'One of the old school in principle and character ... I would trust him with my life. There has been ample evidence in the past of his abilities as a fighter, he has a big following and is recognised throughout London as a main figure . . . I value him as a very close friend.'

So close, in fact, that when the other half of the terrible twinsome, Ronnie, passed into the next world in March 1995, it was Dave Courtney's firm that was chosen to guard the body, arrange security for the funeral procession and, following the unwanted attention of some young souvenir hunters, stand watch over Ronnie's grave.

But the Courtney of the past is gone. Now thirty-seven, he believes the time has come to make the change to a more legitimate profession. He is currently in the process of reinventing himself as an agent for the entertainment business, putting the violent past behind him.

This change of attitude is immediately evidenced by his new calling cards. Originally they read: 'A very dodgy bastard. Anyone, anytime, anywhere.' Now they read: 'A very flash cunt but a nice flash cunt.'

For as long as he can remember, Dave Courtney always wanted to be a gangster.

His introduction to a life of crime began in 1971 when, in an attempt to instil discipline and find a suitable outlet for the boy's excess energy, his headmaster sent him along to the local boxing gym.

The young Courtney took to the sport at once. He learned to hook, to upper-cut, to slip and to duck. He learned about courage, about pain, failure and success. More importantly, though, he learned that, while all men may be created equal, they don't necessarily stay that way.

Occasionally at the gym, numerous shadowy figures would arrive who created something of a commotion. Training would stop and the staff and older boxers would flutter around the guests like butterflies, cracking open bottles of champagne and spirits as if a long-lost cousin had returned to the fold.

The men would always be immaculately dressed. Whatever the fashion of the day, they always wore sharp, hand-made Italian suits and silk ties. Their wrists and fingers would be weighed down with a mass of glittering gold, their hair groomed to perfection, and by their sides would be an ever-changing selection of beautiful women.

They arrived in the biggest, newest cars available and parked them prominently so that everyone could see them. Whenever money was called for, they would pull out brick-thick wads of notes, throwing them around like confetti. The men were always flush but on some occasions more so than on others, as if their wealth came in fits and starts. It didn't take Courtney long to find out their trade.

The men were south-east London's premier villains of the day. Armed robbers, safe-crackers, hijackers and the like – men of honour whose chosen profession was considered wholly justified and acceptable. In those days, the word criminal was reserved for rapists and child molesters. Robbery was merely theft with persuasion.

To Courtney, the men were heroes and role models. By the time this gutsy fighter had reached his mid-teens he had represented both club and country and become a favourite of the gangsters.

'At fifteen, I knew exactly what I wanted to do,' he says. 'I knew exactly what kind of life I wanted to live and what I was going to have to do to get it. I knew I had the bottle to do what they were doing and I had the right attitude – I don't run away, I don't grass people up and I can be trusted. It's almost as if I was born to be a gangster.'

After dozens of amateur fights, Courtney turned professional, supporting himself in the early days by working as a dustman. After eight bouts, he realised that, far from becoming a wealthy world champion, he could never be anything more than a standard circuit fighter, taking on all-comers in an effort to get by. Instead, Courtney went underground, competing in seventeen unlicensed bouts, then as now the preferred entertainment of the underworld. He soon began organising contests of his own, using boxing colleagues to work as bouncers and sowing the seeds of a future business. Progress was rapid – providing doormen turned out to be so lucrative he switched to running his own agency full time.

There was also plenty of work from the boxing-gym crowd, much of which he won't talk about but which included evicting squatters, repossessing cars and general strong-arm work – rent-a-clump, as Courtney calls it.

'When you run an agency you've suddenly got two hundred blokes willing to do whatever you say and, without meaning to, you suddenly find you're some kind of threat to others. Trouble becomes almost unavoidable and the higher up the ladder you go, the worse the trouble gets.

'Whereas a smack in the mouth might do for a "normal" person, when people think you can handle yourself, they decided you need a good kick-in. And so it goes on until people think the only way to stop you is to have you topped.

'You've got to live with the fact that someone out there wants to do something like that to you. But the rewards of this life are so high, you put up with it – I go abroad a good few times a year, I've got a nice house, nice car. I risk my liberty to live the way I do and I've been to prison a few times, but I love my life and I wouldn't change a day of it.'

To people like Dave Courtney, to live any other way would be crazy, the idea of having a nine-to-five job absurd. But the advantages are considerable. Like the Dire Straits song says, you get your money for nothing and your chicks for free. Temptation is everywhere.

'I get it every day, every single day. Everything from prostitutes to stolen horses to drugs, firearms as well as jewellery, video cameras – you name it. And even if I don't want it myself, people are always asking me for things as well. Without meaning to, you become some kind of middle-man.'

Today, Courtney looks every inch the gangster, albeit one cast from a mould dating back some twenty years. He never travels without his own brick-thick wad, is laden with glittering heavy metal, including a solid-gold miniature knuckleduster on a gold chain around his neck. He currently drives a pristine silver 1957 Jaguar, though he changes cars regularly to keep one step ahead of the Old Bill.

'I was brought up with the old school. In those days it was almost honourable to be a gangster. You could almost stand up at school and say my old man's a bank robber and everyone would have clapped, and said "good on him".

'Nowadays, you can say that most people who are involved in crime are really involved in drugs. Villainy revolves around money and there's no better, easier, quicker way to make money than drugs. And I should know. People who wouldn't have touched drugs a few years ago are well into it. The stigma's gone. No one looks down on it.

'But once you're involved in drugs, you start coming across serious drug users who spend half their time out of their nuts. These people would rob their own grandmothers to get money for a deal so they've got no qualms about shopping their dealers.

'I don't consider myself a coward but the idea of dealing in gear scares the shit out of me. Because it doesn't matter how clever or how careful you are, it's all down to someone grassing you up. And to risk my liberty on the hope that no one will ever grass on me frightens me.

'Fifteen years ago, if someone was a grass he would have the shit kicked out of him when he was in prison. Now you go to prison and you have whole wing-loads of grasses.

'If the first supergrass had been shot, like he fucking should have been, it would never have become a trend. And now everyone's at it. If you had told me fifteen year ago that there would be a programme on prime-time telly for grasses, I'd never have believed it. But you watch *Crimewatch* and they say, "If you know anyone who's done anything, give us a call and we'll nick them and give you loads of money."

'For people like me, it's like trying to imagine that in fifteen years there will be a programme just for paedophiles, that's how disgusting it is.

'Then there's the way the sentencing is all fucked up. I know a bloke, Wolfie, who got three and a half years for running rave parties. He was only eighteen. I know of rapists who don't do that sort of time. And you get blokes doing multi-million pound frauds and they do two years in Ford open prison. It's a joke.'

It is partly this frustration and partly the realisation that few men like Courtney live to a ripe old age which has led to his decision to quit the crime game, though it's turning out to be far from easy.

'I love the lifestyle and I want to keep that, but I want to get rid of the danger element. I don't want to have to walk around looking over my shoulder all the time. I can only ever enjoy myself 95 per cent, I always have to keep one eye open.

'After 18 years of messing about in this game, the most important lesson that I've learned is that your past always catches up with you, so you need to leave as many people smiling as you can. After all, it's hard enough fighting against the police without fighting against one another.

'I know how to get power. I've also studied how people with power got it. I don't want to make the same mistakes that they did. There are usually only three things that get you out of the game: a woman, prison or a bullet. I'm hoping to find a new one.

'But it's also very hard once you're in this walk of life to step out of it because all your friends are into the same things and it's too scary to have a close friend who isn't. If you're on the wrong side of the fence law-wise, you can't tell another person the sort of things you're up to, you have to stick with people you feel safe with.

'If you suddenly wake up and decide I don't want to be like this, you can't. It's impossible to get out of. It's addictive. It's living life in the fast lane when everyone else looked like they were living life in the bus lane.'

But Courtney believes he has found a way out. Working the

old crime/entertainment link, he has launched himself as a record producer and talent agent. He already has dozens of acts on his books, all of which are controversial and more than likely to be banned from anything other than the club circuit. An example? A pair of black twins with husky, come-to-bed voices who rap about topics like the Kray twins and the exploits of some of London's lesser-known villains.

Riding shotgun with Dave Courtney as he goes about his day-to-day business provides a fascinating first-hand picture of the modern-day underworld. He may want out of the crime game, but not everyone he knows is aware of it yet and there are still plenty of loose ends to be tied up.

First stop is a 'fixer' in Surrey where Courtney buys two bullet-proof jackets. Two of his bouncers have become involved in a protracted dispute with a local gang of thugs and are expecting a drive-by shooting outside the central London nightclub where they work.

Next we head off to see one of London's largest fences. With Dave as a guide, underworld doors which would normally remain firmly shut magically open up. In this case, Dave has called in advance to explain about my book and that he'd like to show me the operation. A few minutes later we're weaving through the streets in his gleaming Jag. I'm expecting a small terraced house, full of unopened boxes of electrical goods and a shifty weasel of a man running the show. I'm in for a surprise.

We park outside a parade of shops on a run-of-the-mill High Street and make towards one with a spartan selection of goods in the window, obscured by mesh shutters. We press a buzzer and, having checked our identity, the owner lets us in. Once inside, everything seems reassuringly familiar. The shelves are neatly if sparsely stocked with a wide range of quality brand-name clothing, and in a cabinet under the till there is a rack full of watches and jewellery.

The only thing out of the ordinary is the astoundingly cheap prices, but then everything is stolen. The proprietors, a couple of likely lads with ponytails in their mid-twenties, receive goods from all over the capital and beyond.

As well as acting as go-betweens for burglars and buyers, they are also involved in the actual setting up of jobs, using their retail contacts to advise, often for a price, on the movements of lorries, new stock in warehouses, and so on.

If a job for which the fences have provided the intelligence comes off, they get to buy the goods at a preferential rate. And from their shop, it finds its way to market stalls all over the capital and beyond.

All around there are bargains galore. Along one wall are £300 jackets going for £100 (less if you buy in bulk). There are designer trainers, sportswear, shirts, trousers – everything the well-dressed villain might require. Behind the counter is a box of nearly new car stereos. 'Stolen from nearly new cars that is,' quips Courtney.

Many people find it hard to believe that such blatant premises could exist purely for the fencing of stolen property. Even senior police officers in the capital were sceptical until a group of detectives persuaded them to fund a little shop of their own as part of the Operation Bumblebee anti-burglary initiative in March 1994.

In just three weeks the shop, in Walthamstow, east London, was visited by almost four hundred criminals who deposited stolen goods valued at more than £500,000. One ram-raid gang brought in designer clothes worth £80,000, while a single teenage thief brought in thirty car radios in less than twenty-four hours.

Throughout the rest of the day with Courtney there are numerous cryptic phone calls as well as a couple of instances where I'm excluded from being too deeply involved in the action. 'Sorry, Tone, this is serious business,' he would say, ushering me into another room.

It was on one of these occasions that I got chatting to another member of Courtney's team, the wheeler-dealer known as Big

M. Like Dave, M would like out of the game, but his preferred path is more typical – he wants to do one big job to set him up for life and then retire.

He never wanted to be a criminal; it just turned out that way. You could almost say that society was to blame. 'I was fully employed up until the age of twenty-five, first as a qualified electrician and then as a butcher,' he says.

'I got married, had two kids and started working all hours to try to make ends meet. I launched my own electrical business and worked all day and all night at it, but all I got was a hernia. When I came out of hospital, I tried again but it just didn't work. No matter how hard I tried, I just couldn't get what I wanted out of life by doing the right thing.'

Seeing he was struggling, a former schoolfriend – a member of one of the south London crime families – offered him the chance of making a bit of cash on the side.

'He was in a firm but I didn't see it like that. He was just a friend to me. I started off doing a bit of [getaway] driving for him and then I got into drugs. First time, I went to France, dossed about for a week or so, and then drove back in this car that had fifty kilos of cannabis resin stuffed into it.

'I got ten grand for the first run. My original idea was to do three runs, get thirty grand, buy a little car front business and set up a future. But it didn't work out like that. I got caught the second time and served four years in prison in France.

'My wife divorced me while I was inside and that totally fucked my head. I know there's plenty more fish in the sea, but I ain't got no rod. I tried full-time employment again but it still didn't work. The first Christmas I was out, I had eighty quid and I struggled to buy my children presents. I couldn't provide how I wanted to provide.

'But I didn't go out and take it from somebody, I earned it, albeit in a different context. I don't have a lot of respect for the law these days. I got nicked for a dodgy tax disc I put on my ex-wife's car a while ago. The police raided her house and were saying: "Your husband, he's a big-timer, he's this and he's that and we're going to get him", and I was thinking, fuck, it's only a bleeding tax disc, it's not like anyone's been killed. The law just suits itself, so I suit myself.

'Nowadays I just think, fuck the world, I'm just going to enjoy myself. These days I buy and sell. If you had something on you, I'd buy it, if you wanted something, I'd get it for you and sell it on.'

Big M reaches into his pocket and pulls out a wad of notes and some jewellery. 'This is from the Robin Hoods – they're all the burglars and that. Someone sets them up, finds the places for them to rob and then we buy the stuff at our prices.'

. He flashes a grotesque bracelet, spinning it in his hands. It's heavy, solid gold with animal shapes hanging off it in all directions. 'In the shop, that's about six hundred quid. I got it for eighty and I'll sell it on for one-fifty.'

He also has a tiny diamond-crusted brooch in the shape of a racehorse. 'This one is worth fifteen hundred quid. I bought it for four and I'll sell it on for five. Last week, I earned three grand.'

I ask Big M to look into the future and tell me what he sees for himself. 'In five years' time, I will have a house, I will have a car, I will have a boat. I will be having a nice time and I will have some form of future for my children.'

And will you still have £3000 a week coming in? 'I'll get a business, a car front, it's a good base for other things. And maybe a club.' And will you be legitimate? Big M grins. 'I'll go fully legal as soon as I get the chance.' We both smile. I heard it and he said it, but neither of us believe it for a moment.

My day as a gangster's sidekick ends, not surprisingly, at a club, which purports to offer 'South London's best Sunday rave' with a warning that the 'management reserve the right to do whatever they want!'

Standing at the bar, listening to the thumping beat of techno-house and surveying the dance floor, I spot a slightly tubby, grey-haired man sitting in a corner by the stairs, nursing a beer. He turns out to be Harry Haward, better known as Flash Harry, a notorious face of the sixties.

I introduce myself, hoping for an opportunity to find out what really happened at Mr Smith's nightclub in Catford, south London, on 7 March 1966. That night Harry's brother, Billy, along with other members of the Haward firm, got into a rumble with some of the most feared men of the day.

The opposition included Eddie Richardson, younger brother of Charlie, Mad Frankie Fraser, 'the most dangerous man in Britain', and Jimmy Moody, the man who twenty-five years later shot David Brindle in the Bell pub in Walworth and was himself shot dead in an Islington pub in June 1993.

By the time the night was over, one of the Haward firm, Richard Hart, was shot dead while Richardson, Fraser, Billy Haward and another man, Harry Rawlins, were left badly injured. There are dozens of different versions circulating about what happened, but sadly, Harry isn't willing to cast light on any of them. 'Leave the real men alone,' he advises.

Undeterred, I try a somewhat more innocuous question, shouting to be heard above the synthesised beat. 'What do you think of the music, Harry?' 'Fucking crap,' comes the reply.

Big M is at the club, wheeling and dealing as usual. He pulls out a huge wad of cash and passes over a £50 note, asking me what I think. I'm confused until he points out that the note is actually a counterfeit. It is near-perfect. Even comparing it with a genuine note I am hard pressed to tell the difference.

'They're good,' says M, 'but most people are too suspicious of fifties these days. Tens and twenties are coming – that'll be good, much easier to get rid of.'

I ask M to explain how counterfeit currency fits into modern-day crime. 'Because of the quantities I buy, I can get these fifties for four quid a note,' he says. 'I sell them on for seven and then they get sold on again for a tenner each. Then some poor bastard tries to use one in a bank and gets done for it,' he giggles.

'The blokes who do these, they are churning out loads of

different currencies. Their dollars are brilliant. They went over to the States for a couple of weeks last month with twenty-five thousand dollars' worth. They made a fortune. What you do is buy loads of stuff for two or three dollars and pay with a twenty. Then you get loads of genuine change.'

Counterfeit money is becoming increasingly important to the gangster. Not only does it allow him to maintain his lifestyle without having to work too hard, it also enables him to save money on drugs. The second-largest collection of counterfeit dollars bills, after that circulating in America, can be found in Colombia.

The amount of counterfeit currency produced in Britain, together with traveller's cheques, pension books and similar items, has rocketed over the past four years. In 1989 just £100,000 worth of counterfeit was seized. In 1990 the figure was £500,000. By 1992 it had risen tenfold to more than £5 million. In 1993 it topped £15 million, the following year more than £25 million worth was recovered while in April 1995, a single seizure in a grubby lock-up garage in the East End led to a record seizure of £18 million worth of fake £50 and $100 dollar bills.

This dramatic rise is chiefly due to the introduction of colour photocopiers and laser scanners which eliminate the need for a highly skilled engraver to carve a copy of the note on to a printing plate, opening up the market to a far wider range of villains.

Although new banknotes issued since this time have an improved range of security features, research has shown that the general public has a very poor knowledge of them and is therefore more likely to be easily deceived. Some of the forgeries are so convincing that even bank employees have difficulty spotting them. The much-vaunted metallic strip can be reproduced by using a black line covered with white opaque ink, or simply by printing foil on each side of the note, while watermarks can be added by hand using white spirit. A 'used' look can be obtained by rubbing the notes with talcum powder.

The increasing use of vending machines has also led to a sharp rise in the number of fake coins in circulation, something that crooks of yesteryear would have found simply uneconomic to attempt.

The technology has also lent itself to producing fake and doctored passports, driving licences, MoTs, pension books and all manner of documentation, opening up a whole new world of money-making possibilities for the most enterprising of villains.

Dave Courtney finally makes it to the bar where I'm standing – it's taken him at least half an hour to get from one end of the club to the other. Every other step, he has to stop because someone wants to shake his hand, give him a hug or buy him a drink, which is partly explained by his popularity and partly by the fact that everyone wants him as a friend – he's not known as the underworld's Yellow Pages for nothing.

No sooner is he standing beside me than a fresh-faced bloke in his early twenties with a ponytail appears, wanting to discuss business. This time, Dave takes him to one side and has a quick word, explaining who I am, what I'm doing there and that he'd like me to ride shotgun.

Because of his trust of Dave (as opposed to anything to do with wanting to co-operate with a book on the underworld) the bloke, let's call him Julian, reluctantly agrees and the three of us retreat to an ante-room behind the sound system.

There are two proposals. The first involves an outstanding £22,000 business debt which Julian would like Dave to 'assist' in collecting. 'I just want to frighten him at first, see if he plays along. If not . . . I want to get someone to do the business.' The second involves the opportunity to buy a stake in an £85,000 consignment of Ecstasy due to be shipped into the country the following week. Courtney suggests a few names and numbers then Julian goes away happy.

An hour later, he searches me out among the crowd. It turns out he's fascinated by the idea of a journalist writing about crime by actually hanging around with criminals. His eyes are huge dark coals, and his manner unnaturally excited – he's taken Ecstasy or at least speed but is still coherent enough to want to talk.

The heat of the dance-floor is getting too much for me so the two of us go upstairs to chill out near the entrance. A few people wave at Julian on their way in or out – he's a well-known figure on the club drug scene – but when one particular sandy-haired man arrives, Julian beckons him over, whispering to me to let him do all the talking.

'Hi Barry,' he says. 'How's tricks? This is Tony, he does a bit of driving every now and then.' He then turns to me. 'Barry's in the game too,' he says with a wink. 'But he's seriously busy.'

Barry can't resist the bait. 'Not just now though, Jules,' he says, almost sadly. 'We've had to slow things down a bit. You know we did twenty-seven post offices in eighteen months! The Old Bill are well suspicious, got a couple of us under heavy-duty surveillance.'

I whistle through my teeth, trying to sound empathetic rather than shocked and doing my best to look like a getaway driver. Barry continues, 'Poor old Mick won't go out of the house any more. He's completely lost it. He just sits there with the scanner [tuned to the police frequency] on and a gun on top of the telly waiting for them to knock at his door. Totally paranoid.'

Barry goes on to give a few more details of the armed robberies he and his gang have taken part in and regales us with a couple of anecdotes – for instance, the time they broke into a club and couldn't resist a casual drink behind the bar not realising that the alarm had gone off and the police were on their way.

By this time I'm less surprised at the willingness with which gangsters will talk about their work, provided they think they're in safe company. The point is that career criminals live these incredible lives full of danger, bravado and machismo, but for the most part they can't talk about it. When they come together they swap tales of their deeds in the same way most other people would talk about the latest films they have seen or the dinner party they went to at the weekend.

During a break in the conversation, Barry pulls out his wad – not notes this time, but tax discs (genuine ones, stolen along with an authorisation stamp during one of his post-office excursions), valid for eight months and a bargain at only £20 each. When we decline, he reaches into his other pocket and pulls out a plastic bag stuffed with about fifty beige tablets and makes his way to the dance-floor.

Later, Julian tries to explain to me the reasons behind his own ventures into drug dealing.

'The problem is there is a big demand for drugs, therefore there has to be a supply. There are people out there with a problem, and people without a problem who just take the stuff for fun.

'If the government really wanted to do something about crime, they would do something about reducing the demand for drugs which would affect supply. Instead they are trying to tackle it the other way round.

'They want to get away from the problem. The problem is this society is fucked up on drugs, they don't want to admit it and as a direct result, you find people like me who come into the business, earn some good money out of it and fill that gap. There's that gap that's got to be filled. Supply and fucking demand! Somebody's got to do it. Minimum risk, minimum fucking everything.'

It's nearly 3 a.m. when I leave the club. Barry button-holes me in the corridor on my way out. 'So if we need a driver, it's down to you, is it?' he asks. I nod nervously, deciding this would not be a good time to break cover. 'Yeah ... get me through Julian.'

The Brinks-Mat job may have been one of the first examples of true international co-operation between British and foreign criminal gangs but, thanks largely to the drugs trade, such joint ventures are now commonplace.

As Superintendent Neil Dickens, the man in charge of co-ordinating the country's regional crime squads, puts it: 'It never ceases to amaze me. I don't know a single top villain who can speak a foreign language, yet they manage to do business with people all over the world.'

But as an ever-increasing number of criminals move up the scale and play for higher and higher stakes, inevitably there are some who simply cannot cope with the pressure of it all.

In the early hours of 29 December 1991, while sleeping in the bedroom of her shabby south London council flat, Rosemary Trenchfield heard a scuffle in the hallway followed by 'a bang, like a cap gun'.

She ran out to find her stepbrother, Patrick Thomas, lying on the carpet, blood pouring from a single bullet wound to his right temple. He was still alive as Rosemary rushed to the phone to call an ambulance, but dead by the time she got back.

Patrick – Pat to his friends – was much liked on the Turnham Road estate in Brockley. Neighbours remember him as polite and respectful, the sort who always had time to say hello and never caused any trouble.

'He was really nice,' said one. 'Not flashy or loud – not one of those lads that think they're really tough or bad. Just a decent bloke.'

Virtually everyone on the estate expressed surprise at the manner of Thomas's death. In life he had done little to attract attention and gave the impression of being content to live life in the slow lane. He seemed happy to share a flat with his stepsister, her husband and daughter, work periodically as a barman and car dealer, drive around in his ten-year-old BMW and drift from day to day with no real plans or ambitions.

In a typical snapshot taken by a girlfriend, he stands looking slightly unsure of himself, hands clasped nervously, head cocked to one side with a reticent, faraway smile on his face. A dreamer.

But all this was jut a cover. At the time of his death, Thomas had more than £150,000 in various building society accounts spread throughout the capital. For behind the quiet façade, Thomas was an ambitious career criminal, specialising in armed robbery and drug dealing.

Although not a Mr Big, he had rapidly worked his way up the ranks to such an extent that he had become an 'honorary' member of the pub-running Woolwich-based crime family.

Two weeks before his death, Thomas's carefully contrived persona had helped get him acquitted of possessing more than £30,000 worth of high-quality cocaine. However, his co-defendant, David Summerville, with whom Thomas had spent eight months on remand at Belmarsh prison, had ended up with seven years.

At first, it seemed that Thomas had been killed for revenge – having beaten the drugs rap by shifting the blame, he had paid the price of freedom. But as the investigation proceeded, police realised that the stakes had been much, much higher.

In May 1990, Thomas had been a key member of a firm that had pulled off the biggest single robbery in history. The conspiracy involved dozens of gangsters from more than twenty countries with links to the Mafia, Colombian drug cartels, and the IRA.

Thomas, it soon became apparent, had simply got in way over his head.

At its launch on April Fool's Day, 1992, the National Criminal Intelligence Service, Britain's non-operational equivalent of the FBI, announced that it had produced a database containing the names of the top fifty criminals in the country.

These were the 'super offenders' – men who rarely went out to commit crimes themselves but used their contacts and influence to organise everything from major bank robberies and drug deals to frauds and money laundering. Most of those on the list lived in luxury and, such was their skill at distancing themselves from their offences, only a minority had any criminal convictions.

Early in 1990, four of the men on the list met in a discreet wine bar in the City of London. One felt he had an idea for a scheme that, if successful, would eclipse everything they had previously achieved. In criminal parlance, it was The Big One.

The idea had been inspired by the news on 4 January that a City of London messenger had accidentally dropped £4 million worth of bearer bonds while *en route* to the Bank of England. They were later found floating in the gutter by a passer-by.

Bearer bonds and their close cousins, certificates of deposit, are essentially cheques drawn on the government, major banks and large commercial organisations which are used to transfer large sums. Each carries the standard banknote phrase about promising to pay the bearer on demand and, in the right hands, the notes are as good as cash.

At the start of the decade, around £30 billion worth of bonds and certificates was being marched round the streets of London by a bunch of elderly messengers. For the syndicate, it seemed like a crime just waiting to happen.

With careful planning (and possibly an inside tip-off) they believed it would be a relatively simple matter to snatch a bundle mid-delivery. But the approach was critical. Most of the finance houses had arrangements to cancel bonds if they arrived more than an hour late. If there was any indication that a professional gang was behind the theft, the bonds would be impossible to trade.

The job had to look like the work of an opportunist who had absolutely no idea what he had his hands on. It had to look like a random mugging. The search was on, and Patrick Thomas was soon identified as the ideal candidate. He accepted, flattered to have moved up yet another rung on the criminal ladder.

Over the next few months, the syndicate used its global crime connections to set up a complicated system based in Switzerland to dispose of the bonds. They were due to be flown out to Zurich and sold through a 'friendly' broker; the proceeds would quickly be 'lost' in the electronic jungle of the international banking system.

At 9.38 a.m. on 2 May 1990, fifty-eight-year-old John

Goddard, a messenger for Sheppards, a City-based money-broking firm, was walking along a small alley called Nicholas Lane when he was approached by a black man in his late twenties. The man held a knife against Goddard's throat, demanded his briefcase, took it and ran off.

The following morning, the headlines were promising. 'Opportunist snatches £292 million in paper money,' reported *The Times*, going on to explain that it was unlikely the thief would benefit from the crime.

'The Bank of England said last night they believed the robber was purely an opportunist . . . had the robbery been carried out by a gang familiar with the money markets, there could have been substantial losses.'

But within the syndicate there were problems. The laundering scheme in Switzerland had fallen apart before any of the bonds could be disposed of. Word was sent out to known fraudsters and villains who would have been able to launder the bonds to get in touch with the syndicate.

One of the first groups to express an interest was a satellite of the New York Mafia. They were already involved in a similar scam, having acquired $7 million worth of bonds from an American finance house which they were attempting to launder in Britain. It seemed a good idea to attempt to work the traffic the other way as well.

The Mafia's British contact was Keith Cheeseman, a semi-successful con-man from Luton. He had access to some of the stolen British bonds through south London businessman Raymond Ketteridge, and sent a few to his American go-between, Texan Mark Osborne.

Soon, Osborne found himself being introduced to Tony Dipino, another Mafioso who had expressed an interest in buying the British bonds to launder the proceeds of an enormous drug trafficking deal. The pair met up in Mulligans bar on 42nd Street on 31 July 1990 and Osborne handed over ten certificates, each with a face value of £1 million.

Once the sale was concluded, Dipino had a surprise up his

sleeve. He wasn't a Mafioso but an undercover agent for the FBI, and Osborne was under arrest. With true American spirit, Osborne opted to become a co-operative witness and allowed the FBI to tape his telephone calls to Britain, pretending the sale had gone ahead.

The file of conversations soon piled up: Osborne calling Cheeseman and being told to put the proceeds 'somewhere safe'; Cheeseman warning that the remaining bills were 'red blanket hot'; Ketteridge complaining that he had not yet received money for the first lot of bills.

Then, on 16 August 1990, Osborne disappeared, turning up five days later in Houston, Texas with two bullets in the back of his head. Someone, it seems, knew he had talked.

But Osborne was not the only informer. Somewhere along the chain between the syndicate and the bonds, someone else had blabbed. For during the summer of 1990, the City of London police had a series of 'lucky' breaks which enabled them to recover more than £150 million of the stolen bonds; £77 million were found during a 'routine check' at Heathrow, another £80 million in Cyprus, plus smaller amounts in Scotland, the Netherlands, West Germany and Singapore.

On 7 September 1990, a man with an Irish accent using the name Anthony Gallagher delivered a package to Aero Peru's cargo office in Miami for delivery to Peru. Singled out for inspection on suspicion that it might contain money for laundering, the package in fact contained £71 million of the stolen bonds. It emerged that the IRA had got involved in disposing of the bonds and was in the process of trading them with Colombian drug barons based in Peru in exchange for drugs and cash.

As one detective put it. 'There are so many people involved in this it's unreal. Everybody seems to want a piece of the action.'

But back in London the members of the syndicate were far from happy. As well as the bonds, they had lost more than £200,000 in set-up costs and, perhaps more importantly, their standing as London's criminal élite had been severely compromised. The informant would have to be found and revenge seen to be done.

In March 1991, Patrick Thomas and David Summerville were in the process of cutting up a kilo of virutally pure cocaine when armed police burst into their Greenwich flat.

In true villain style, Thomas viewed it as a temporary setback, an occupational hazard. He was certain he could convince the jury that all the drugs belonged to Summerville.

But while on remand, something happened which rapidly ate away at those feelings of security. On 26 October 1991, while he was reading a copy of the *Today* newspaper, a headline caught Thomas's eye: '£290m clue to headless corpse.' The story told how a mutilated body found in woodland near Bolney, Sussex, had been identified as belonging to Keith Cheeseman.

The head and hands had been removed to make identification as difficult as possible, but the story went on to say how police felt that Cheeseman's death fitted in to recent events: he was on the run from the FBI and his partner had been murdered the previous year.

In fact, Cheeseman was alive and well. The day after the 'corpse' was found, he was spotted having dinner with his ex-wife, Kerry, in Kent. But for Thomas, reading the story was like reading his own obituary. Overnight his personality changed. He became withdrawn, sullen and prone to extreme mood swings.

Cheeseman was dead. So was Osborne. Thomas was convinced he would be next. Even his acquittal at Southwark Crown Court on 11 December failed to lift his mood. Thomas returned to live with Rosemary, but things went from bad to worse.

Almost immediately he became involved with a couple of minders he had employed to take care of his business interests while he was inside on remand. He was left bruised and with a slightly cut face.

On 23 December he attempted to make a withdrawal from one of his false building society accounts, but the cashier became suspicious and demanded more proof of identity. Thomas panicked and ran off. A few days later, he became even more depressed after his girlfriend and daughter visited him but refused to stay overnight.

On the morning of Saturday, 28 December Thomas was spotted climbing the stairs by a neighbour. 'I said hello but he just waved at me and said nothing,' she said later. 'He didn't seem himself at all.'

That afternoon, Thomas embarked on what was to become a massive bender. He met up with friends in the Sands public house in Blackheath and crawled around a few others, ending up at the Greycoat Boy in Greenwich at 11.30 p.m. All day long he'd been mixing his two favourite tipples – a shot of Jack Daniels followed by a snort of cocaine.

Just after midnight, Thomas and friends visited some West End nightclubs where he took a couple of Ecstasy tablets as well as continuing to drink and snort.

In the early hours of Sunday morning, he attempted to get into the Ministry of Sound club at the Elephant and Castle but freaked out when a bouncer tried to frisk him. 'It seemed he had something hidden in the small of his back,' said a friend, 'and didn't want it to be found.'

Thomas returned home alone just before 5 a.m. Minutes later he was dead.

After an extensive eight-month investigation into the death of Patrick Henry Thomas, Detective Inspector Dave Bowen, the man leading the murder inquiry, reached his verdict. 'It is my opinion and that of my fellow officers that Patrick Thomas committed suicide.'

At the inquest, witnesses said that Thomas's stepsister Rosemary had told them that she had seen a gun at his side as he lay in the hallway but had hidden it – at this point Thomas was still alive and she didn't want him going away for a firearms offence when he'd only just got off on remand.

A close friend of Thomas's, Cassius Walker, stormed into the centre of the court and demanded to know why Rosemary had told so many people about the gun but had not told the police. 'I am not saying she killed him,' Walker said, 'but why is she lying?'

There was also the discovery of a second bullet lodged in the front door of Thomas's flat which ballistic experts confirmed came from the gun that had killed him. However, witnesses remember only one shot on the night. The implication seemed to be that Thomas had possessed the gun for some time and had test-fired it earlier that week in the house; that he had the gun with him on the night he died – hence his freaking out while being frisked by the bouncer – and that in a fit of depression, he had killed himself when he returned home.

The name of Raymond Ketteridge, the man Cheeseman claims supplied him with the stolen bonds, doesn't appear on the NCIS list of the top fifty criminals, though it does feature in the top two hundred and also on numerous police intelligence reports.

His only conviction dates back twenty-three years, yet Ketteridge somehow can't shake off the 'minor criminal mastermind' tag. His name has been linked to several major frauds and robberies and he has served nearly two years on remand in France and Turkey for offences that he was later acquitted of.

He was said to have been one of the ringleaders of the £40 million Swissbank fraud in 1988, and is still wanted by the FBI for his alleged role in the bonds robbery. Police in Houston, Texas, would also like to talk to him about the death of Mark Osborne.

An attempt to extradite him in July 1991 fell through when, on the first day of the trial, the Crown announced that it would not be 'in the public interest' to proceed. This is legal shorthand for the fact that the prosecution case was based on the evidence of an informer whose identity would have been revealed had the case gone ahead.

Ketteridge is therefore a free man but dare not travel outside the UK. He has been told that even before he gets off the plane, a fresh extradition claim will be lodged against him.

Meeting with the man himself proves to be a surprising experience. He chooses a plush west London restaurant and arrives, mobile phone in hand, wearing a Barbour jacket, looking every inch the modern city gent.

Grey-haired and stocky but thoroughly affable, he is not at all what you expect from someone who supposedly mixes it with the big boys. But that's just what Ketteridge does. According to his version of events, his numerous brushes with the law are nothing more than a police vendetta and a case of guilt by association.

He drops a few names of well-known London villains. 'I grew up with these people,' he says. 'We were all brought up in the East End together. Now a lot of the people from there have problems and turn to a life of crime, but these people are my friends. It doesn't mean I do business with them. I've been legitimate for the last twenty years.

'Naturally, there are one or two things I've been involved in,' he says grudgingly. 'But I'm not going to talk about them for obvious reasons.'

What he will talk about is his alleged role in the biggest robbery in the world. According to Ketteridge, the whole thing was set up by two police informers, one of whom Ketteridge had previously counted as a friend, purely so that they could claim the reward money.

It is not, says Ketteridge, his voice on the FBI tapes, simply someone using his name in order to put the police off the scent of the real villains.

He is a member of the old school and the experience has shattered his faith in the concept of honour among thieves. 'I can understand someone turning grass to save themselves if they're facing a long stretch, but to set up a job just so you can grass on it . . .' He shakes his head in despair. 'I think the blokes who did this should be injected with AIDS. That's what they deserve.'

On the day he returned from a four-day fact-finding visit to

Italy, where he met the chiefs of the anti-Mafia units, the Metropolitan Police Commissioner Paul Condon warned that the biggest threat to law and order in the capital came not from the international crime syndicates but from the old-style gangsters.

'They are the sort of people who, fifteen years ago, were the top-flight armed robbers; people who are prepared to kill and if that means shooting a security guard or a policeman, they will not think twice,' he said.

In fact he was only half right. While the old school are still a threat, they are a dying breed. Already there are signs that new, fantastically lucrative crimes that require younger heads and fresher minds are beginning to sweep into the underworld.

Computer memory chips and processors – biscuit-sized plastic slabs worth several thousand pounds – are already being described as the dope of the nineties because the trade is proving so popular. Theft from automatic cash machines, achieved using sophisticated technology to make blank copies of cards, now tops £5 million each year, a phenomenal amount considering that only a handful of gangs specialise in it.

In 1991, Scotland Yard set up a dedicated Mortgage Fraud Unit to investigate the emerging crime which now costs an estimated £4 billion each year and is rising. Mainstream white-collar crime is also growing. In 1993 the Serious Fraud Office was investigating sixty cases totalling £6 billion, but admits that this is only the tip of the iceberg, with hundreds of defrauded institutions unwilling to report thefts because they fear losing customer confidence.

Then there are brand-new areas, including the criminal disposal of toxic waste, the blackmail of major organisations by threatening to sabotage their computer systems, and the manufacture of new and ever-more potent synthetic drugs.

What is of greatest concern is that all this activity is tied up with increasing co-operation between British and foreign syndicates. The learning curve is a sharp one, with the heirs to the Krays and those that followed them learning from the mistakes of hundreds of years of involvement in organised crime.

Meetings between supposedly rival British groups to carve out new territories and combine resources can only be a few years away. Ruthless, able to travel worldwide with ease, backed up by the latest technology and willing to kill to maintain the status quo, this fledgling British Mafia may yet turn out to be a major force in international organised crime.

As Albert Pacey, Director-General of the National Criminal Intelligence Service, told the Home Affairs Select Committee inquiry into organised crime during an oral evidence session in July 1994, 'There is no one Mr Big, but there are plenty of Mr Big-enoughs.'

Chapter Two

Big Me Up

The Yardies and West Indian Organised Crime

'The cops don't bang
The law don't hang
Lock 'em up, not lang'

*Yardie rhyme on the benefits of operating
in Britain as opposed to the USA: unarmed police,
no death sentence, and shorter prison terms.*

It's 3.15 a.m. and I'm standing on the edge of a smoke-filled Birmingham dance-floor with Digga, a notoriously violent Yardie gangster, who's attempting to teach me his favoured technique for ripping off other drug dealers.

'You have to play the fool,' he says fervently, 'make the guy think you're an arsehole, a total fucking idiot.' By way of example, Digga slips effortlessly into a nervous, stumbling staccato voice with a convincing English accent, flicking his eyes from side to side and jerking his body for added effect.

'"I want to buy some drugs but I'm scared. I don't want to go down to Brixton, I might get robbed. I don't trust those guys down there. I don't want no bullshit. Honest to God, man. Me and my friends, we put our money together, I don't want to lose it . . ."'

The idea, explains Digga, is to convince the dealer that you pose no threat so that he's willing to take you back to his main stash. No one with any brains goes out with more than a couple of rocks of crack or a few grams of cocaine at a time, partly as a safeguard against being robbed and partly because, if they're caught, they get done for simple possession (average £100 fine, even for crack) rather than supplying (average three-year sentence).

Digga's voice returns to normal. 'By now he's got you down as some foolish fresh bwoy. Thinks you're didgy. Yannerstan? He asks how much you want and you say five ounces, more than he's gonna carry. Ten grand's worth. Anything. That makes him excited. He wants you to buy, he wants to do the deal. Deep within, you wants to rob him then! But you have to play the fool some more.

'You keep talking fast, fast. You don't let him know where you're from. You say Moss Side, Nottingham, Swindon, Aston, anywhere but the truth. You flash a bit of money to show him you're serious, let him feel like he's in control, like you're scared of him. Like you respect him.

'Eventually the guy takes you back to a place, offers you a drink or a smoke.' Digga's voice speeds up as his excitement mounts. 'You reach into your pocket to pull out the money . . . but you pull out your piece instead! Then before he knows what's happening, *bam*, your gun is at his head and ya start talking *tough*!'

The Jamaican accent intensifies and Digga pushes a rough trigger-finger against my temple. 'Ya move an ya *dead* man. Me put shot in ya face *now*! This will be a new pussy hole for ya, blood clot . . .'

Digga smiles and his eyes mist over. He's no longer teaching, he's reminiscing. '. . . then you push the man into the airing cupboard and take *everyting* you see. Come downstairs *fast*, woosh, your bwoy is in the car outside, engine running, foot on clutch and away, waaah. Sweet, man.'

In Yardie circles, the notion of honour among thieves doesn't even have folklore status. It's not so much a myth as an outright fantasy with no basis in the past or present reality. 'On the front line,' says Digga, 'life is rough. If you see fifty men out there, maybe ten is selling crack, ten is high and the other thirty is just pure thief. You don't dare trust no one. Not even man you think is your friend.'

Instead, most Yardies embrace a philosophy of life that revolves around stealing people's money, taking their drugs by force, shooting first, asking questions later, and sleeping with a loaded automatic under your pillow, just in case.

And it's that absolute ruthlessness, combined with an insatiable, reckless greed and a total disregard for life, which has led to the Yardies, in the space of ten years, becoming one of the most feared of all the international criminal syndicates, despite being the smallest, least organised and least sophisticated.

Much of their notoriety has come about because of the typically *Grand Guignol* nature of many of their crimes, such as the cold-blooded murder of PC Patrick Dunne in October 1993 by a trio of laughing gunmen who had just brutally executed small-time dealer William Danso, chasing him around his living room firing at least seventeen shots at him.

Or the case of the aunt of a young dealer, kidnapped by Eldon Brown and his half-sister Evelyn 'Fat Pam' Mason, who had been ripped off to the tune of £10,000 by the woman's nephew, Tony Dawson. The woman was subjected to a forty-hour torture session which included being stabbed, beaten and forced to perform oral sex. She eventually escaped by throwing herself out of a fourth-floor window, breaking her pelvis, ankle and three vertebrae.

Or the case of Mark Burnett, a suspected drug dealer whose trademark was his extensive 'cargo' – £4000 worth of gold chains around his neck. His downfall came after he accidentally stood on the toe of a notorious and widely feared Yardie while at the packed Podium nightclub in Vauxhall in October 1991.

Although everyone who had entered the club had been thoroughly searched, the Yardie, seething with rage, drew a gun and began firing. One bullet struck Burnett's thigh, severing his main artery, and he bled to death in minutes. Two other ravers were also wounded.

There were almost two thousand people in the club at the time – 350 claimed to have been in the toilets when the shooting took place. Hundreds more gave the police false names and addresses, and of the few who did not and of the 270 who were immediately arrested, none could recall seeing anything out of the ordinary.

Or the case of Gary 'Tyson' Nelson, a 26-year-old self-employed security guard who fired five shots at Gary Kewell simply because he had tried to overtake Nelson's BMW. One of the three men charged with the murder of PC Dunne (the charges were later dropped due to the lack of evidence but the Crown Prosecution Service has stressed that the men may be charged again if further evidence comes to light) Nelson was also said to have been responsible for shooting at known drug dealer Mohammed Massoquoi five times following an argument in a Brixton nightclub. He had previously been acquitted of possessing a firearm with intent to endanger life following an incident in north London in which two Yardies were convicted of shooting at a police officer. Bizzarely, Nelson, who had a string of convictions for violent offences stretching back to his teens, whose reputation was so great that even the IRA terrorists with whom he was on remand allowed him to use their telephone cards for free and whose strength was so great that he once broke free from a prison straitjacket, shared his south London flat with his mother.

From comparatively humble beginnings in prostitution and cannabis dealing, Yardies now dominate the crack trade in the inner cities through their cottage industry of fortified drug 'factories'. Many of these are situated in abandoned council flats which are then fitted with steel gates or New York jambs – a baulk of timber wedged between a steel-reinforced front door and the opposite wall – to frustrate attempted raids or robberies. The more established venues even have surveillance cameras.

The best police estimates suggest that at least 50 and perhaps as much as 90 per cent of the crack trade in major towns and cities throughout Britain is in the hands of Jamaican criminals. And as the number of crack seizures has rocketed, so has the level of violence.

Since 1986, there have been at least fifty-seven Yardie-linked murders along with countless woundings, serious assaults and rapes. Most of the victims are members of the black community or other Yardies. Impromptu gun battles are also increasingly common: in parts of London, Birmingham and Manchester the police now tell the public not to bother handing in the used shell cases they regularly find in the streets – there are simply too many for them to deal with.

In the summer of 1991 gunshots were so common on Brixton's Railton Road that every time a car backfired, residents dived for cover. After a month of almost daily shooting incidents, including a gun battle close to a children's playground, four hundred locals petitioned the police to demand action. The number of patrols and beat officers was increased, but the problem simply moved on to Clapham – the manor of PC Patrick Dunne.

Shortly after the murder of the community policeman, one man living nearby wrote to the *Independent* to complain about how the Yardies had taken over Clapham's Landor Road, openly touting pump-action shotguns. Another, a local mini-cab driver, told the *Guardian* how he regularly ferried the leading gangsters around with pistols and shotguns across their laps as they sat in the back of his car.

This willingness to display and use guns has virtually forced other criminals, black and white, to do the same, or risk being ripped off or shot dead by their Yardie counterparts. Between 1993 and 1994 there was an unprecedented sevenfold increase in the number of assaults involving guns in the London area.

This in turn has led directly to an increase in the number of armed response vehicles in many major cities; the issuing of bullet-proof jackets for officers on standard beat patrol; and the Commissioner of the Metropolitan Police predicting that, by the end of the decade, it is likely that the entire UK police force will be fully armed.

In some areas, most notably Manchester's Moss Side, the Yardie-led gun culture has spread through an entire generation. Many of the youths caught up in the scene, like wannabe nineteen-year-old dealer Julian 'Turbo' Stewart, have taken to wearing bullet-proof jackets (as do Moss Side's ambulance men). It saved his life when he was the victim of a drive-by shooting, but his pursuers simply changed tactics. A few weeks later, in January 1994, he was cornered on his mountain bike and shot in the head at point-blank range – revenge for his own bungled attempt to execute a rival.

Increasing witness intimidation in Yardie court cases, particularly in Manchester and parts of south London, has led to calls for improved after-care schemes or US-style protection programmes for those who decide to testify. Until then, instances of ID parades where witnesses point out a man suspected of a shooting only to come back the next day and say they've made a terrible mistake and want to withdraw will continue.

This ability blatantly to commit crime and seemingly get away with it means that the Yardies have provided role models for dozens of British-born black − but also white and Asian − youngsters who now cast aside the idea of a conventional career for the quick and spectacular rewards that crack dealing can bring.

Crack itself has been blamed not just for an increase in drug-related crime but for a parallel increase in the violence associated with such crime. Incidents such as the murder of John McTurk, a social worker, attacked with a broken bottle by crack-head burglar Paul Flint, or the case of Francis Casey, the teenage crack addict who went on a three-week spree of frenzied attacks on nineteen elderly people, ending with the murder of an eighty-eight-year-old spinster whose face he repeatedly stamped on, are becoming disturbingly common.

In 1993 in London alone, there were ten murders and twenty attempted murders linked directly to the crack trade.

The drug has also created a new underclass of addicts far more desperate for their next fix than any cocaine or heroin junkie could ever be. City councillors in Liverpool have warned that children as young as thirteen are turning to prostitution and selling themselves for as little as £5 a time in order to fund their habits. In London, Birmingham and Nottingham, addicted prostitutes eschew the risk of AIDS, offering unprotected sex for just a few pounds over the odds.

Far from being confined to deprived inner cities, crack has been found in significant quantities in Amersham, Cheltenham, Norwich, Peterborough, Swindon and Worcester, to name but a few, with a corresponding increase in violence and crime reported by local police in each area.

For an organisation often referred to, almost dismissively, as the epitome of 'disorganised organised crime', the impact of the so-called 'black mafia' on the face of Britain's inner cities and beyond has been utterly astounding. And the indications are that it's going to get much, much worse.

There are no old Yardies: the average life-expectancy of a fully fledged member of the clan is just thirty-five. Digga's childhood friend, Tuffy, missed out by one year.

'If Tuffy had listened to people, if he had listened to me, things would be fine,' says Digga, shaking his head slowly. 'He'd be here right now. But he wouldn't stop. He was robbing people all over the place. He got greedy. Too greedy. He was out of control.'

Tuffy's real name was Mark McGibbon, but British detectives knew him best as Christopher Alexander Bourne. As one of the most senior Yardies ever to visit these shores, there was a time when Tuffy commanded the respect of hundreds, a time when he couldn't walk into a club without the DJ wanting to 'big him up' – shouting his name out over the record in recognition of his status. But then he got too big for his boots.

It wasn't always that way. Those who remember Tuffy from his childhood years recall him as a smallish, almost insignificant character who was bullied at school and unloved at home: the boy least likely to do anything of merit.

But during his teenage years he quickly discovered that the gun gave him the power and esteem he so craved, and he fell into a criminal apprenticeship in Kingston's violent street gangs. There he learned to hold up soda trucks, rob banks and shoot security guards who got in his way.

In 1978, Tuffy was sentenced to two counts of life imprisonment (reduced to fifteen years on appeal). By 1985 he had been freed on parole much to the chagrin of the cops who had helped put him away, and a year later he joined the increasing exodus of Jamaican criminals spearheading the expansion overseas.

Christopher Bourne first featured on British police intelligence reports shortly before September 1989 when he was deported back to Jamaica after being caught in possession of a large amount of high-purity cocaine in Manchester. Two months later he attempted to re-enter the country on a false Jamaican passport but was caught and held in a detention cell at Gatwick. He escaped.

In January 1991 he was arrested for distributing forged banknotes and, after spending a year in prison, was deported to Jamaica once more in January 1992. But Tuffy was nothing if not persistent. He made at least six more valiant attempts to enter the country illegally at Gatwick and Heathrow.

According to police and immigration sources, he failed each time. However, Digga recalls seeing Tuffy in Manchester in the summer of 1992 while other friends report seeing him at regular intervals throughout that year in both Britain and Jamaica.

One, who himself first arrived in the UK in October 1992, recalls how Tuffy helped make him feel at home. 'When he found out I'd just arrived, he reached into his wallet, counted out a thousand pounds and handed it over as a kind of "welcome to Britain" present. He was obviously doing very, very well. Money was nothing to him.'

But almost everyone close to him knew that most of Tuffy's money was coming straight out of the pockets of other dealers, and warned him to be careful. His once-loyal supporters and bodyguards were becoming increasingly concerned. Because Tuffy was robbing anyone and everyone, they had all been tarred with the same brush. Some felt they might just as well paint targets on their backs.

Despite the contrary testimony of friends, immigration officers believe it wasn't until 5 February 1993 that Tuffy finally eluded them. He had switched tactics, attempting to get into the UK via Birmingham airport. But such was his notoriety that he was recognised as being barred by the sole immigration officer on duty. But when an arrest was attempted, Tuffy vaulted over the control barrier and sprinted his way to freedom.

Once back in London, Tuffy expanded his operations, robbing whole crack houses as well as individual dealers. His name was linked to a spate of shootings on the Chalkhill estate in Wembley where at least six dealers where shot in the knees, IRA style, as a warning not to be so slack in handing over their supplies in future.

Tuffy also robbed a man known as Juggernaught – a senior Yardie from a rival gang who has lived in Britain for more than ten years. While others revered Juggernaught, Tuffy 'dissed' him bad, making him plead for his life on bended knees while stripping him of his cash, gold chains and drugs.

By early May 1993 Tuffy was revelling in his position as one of the most feared men in London. He knew he'd made dozens of enemies but he didn't seem to care. However, he'd failed to realise that the people who feared him most were those closest to him. Tuffy, his friends decided, would have to go.

The previous month, Tuffy's 'intelligence officer' had told him about a crack house based in a council flat at 54 Vassel Road, Brixton which was being run by twenty-six-year-old Raymond 'Emma' Grant, a local Jamaican tailor and also a long-standing member of the Spanish Town Posse.

A raid was quickly planned and the subsequent haul – two kilos of cocaine and crack, around £10,000 in cash and a number of thick gold chains – was enough to ensure that when Tuffy was told on 30 May that the den had restocked and was ready for robbing once more, he couldn't get there quick enough.

'But it was a set-up, he was met by gunshots,' says Digga. 'He had his piece out but there was too many man there. They trapped him between the wall and the steel door. There was four against one. Everyone was shooting at him. His own people too. He had no chance.'

Three bullets were embedded in his chest, two more passed straight through him, and a further ten were recovered from the wall against which he had stood. At least four different guns had been fired at him. Tuffy managed to escape from the flat and tried to run down the road, but he collapsed and bled to death having only travelled a few yards. His own gun was found nearby.

One of the first on the scene was ten-year-old Robert, one of Tuffy's three children with a south London 'baby mother', Marcia. With five children of her own and looking after another of Tuffy's from a previous relationship, Marcia puts a different perspective on the gangster's life.

'People may see him as wicked and bad but he was good to me and the kids loved him – they truly adored him. To me, Tuffy's more alive than the five children's real father.'

But some of the letters that he left behind show that Tuffy's violent streak was very much in evidence. 'I have to write you this letter 'cause I'm being cruel to you without cause and that's not my heart's desire . . . this morning was worse than ever. I hit you again after I gave you my word. It's like I'm killing you . . . '

Tuffy's story is nothing out of the ordinary. A frighteningly similar character can, most days, be found at his 'headquarters' in the basement of a shop in Brixton, from where he rules over his drugs and guns empire with a rod of iron.

Mr A (he cannot be fully identified for legal reasons) is one of London's biggest crack dealers. He is believed to have organised the shooting of Winston Delgado – a member of a rival gang who was attempting to bring cut-price cocaine into the country, in 1991. He has twice been charged and, thanks to intimidating witnesses, twice acquitted of murder himself but has killed at least two more times.

Furthermore, his close associates and members of his gang have been involved in at least six more murders since 1990. Mr A also runs a bogus but lucrative security company, owns a mobile phone shop, has a passion for dog fighting with a fearsome collection of unregistered pit-bull terriers, and seems to have little or no fear of arrest.

'If any of what you say is true,' he told me when I put some of these allegations to him over the telephone, 'I wouldn't be able to walk around freely like I do. People would be after me.' Mr A then suggested we meet up at a secluded address for him to 'explain' the kind of business he was really involved in. I declined.

This terrible trio represent the shape of things to come so far as the Yardies are concerned. As more and more people are attracted into the big-money world of crack dealing, so the opportunities for rip-offs, the disputes over territory and the inevitable bloodshed will continue.

With Turkish, Nigerian and Asian syndicates now moving into crack in a major way, the next five years will see the Yardies battling it out to keep hold of the number-one slot. They are unlikely to lose.

The somewhat improbable but widely accepted notion that Jamaica, an island with a population of just 2.5 million, all but invented drug-related crime came about long before anyone coined the term Yardie or discovered crack cocaine.

A ramshackle criminal minority had been exporting tons of the island's most potent brand of cannabis – sensimillia – to London, New York and Toronto since the early sixties. However, police in all three cities practically ignored the trade as there was no evidence of links to major crime and precious little, if any, violence.

According to British law enforcement briefings of the time, some Jamaicans, particularly the pacifist Rastafarians, were known to be indulging in low-key cannabis dealing, but the profits were minuscule compared to those earned through heroin trafficking which was seen as a far more sinister threat.

During the seventies in the Handsworth area of Birmingham, for example, an informal coalition developed between local law enforcement and the area's Rastafarians. The police agreed to turn a blind eye to the small-scale ganja smuggling and dealing operations in return for the Rastas helping to keep heroin dealers out of the area.

Rastafarians hold marijuana as a sacrament (they have identified it as the 'herb for the service of man' of Psalm 104
and elsewhere in the Bible) and require a regular supply for
numerous religious rituals and festivals. Its illegality quickly led
to the development of a sophisticated underground distribution
and smuggling network first in Jamaica and then beyond as the
movement spread. At first, this was a purely non-commercial
venture, but the increasing popularity and therefore increasing
market value of sensimillia outside the Rasta community led to
an inevitable change.

In 1975, an ounce of ganja costing around US$4 in Kingston
could be sold for around US$80 in New York and even more in
London. And while the Rastas themselves were not particularly
interested in developing the market, they soon found themselves
infiltrated by those who were.

These newcomers, many of whom were fugitives from
Jamaican justice who had adopted the Rasta look as a form
of disguise, took advantage of the police apathy towards the
group to develop the drug trade virtually unhindered. And by
the time the authorities realised what was happening, it was
already too late.

The first warning bells sounded across the Atlantic. Between
1974 and 1976 at least fifteen Rastafarians were shot dead in
New York, sparking dramatic headlines in the local papers.

While police there were concerned, the violence seemed
limited to a small section of the community, possibly tied
up with religious fundamentalism and not much of a threat
to society as a whole. But the situation was considered serious
enough to warrant further investigation, albeit on a limited scale.

A confidential report compiled by the New York City
Police Department in 1977 (though not issued until 1983)
showed how the problem of 'Rasta Crime' in the Brooklyn,
Bronx and Queens districts of the city had 'been completely
underestimated. Not only were Jamaicans identified as totally
dominating the cannabis trade, they had also expanded their

operations to include assault, extortion and the smuggling of illegal aliens.

And far from being non-violent, the dealers had sent the local homicide rate through the ceiling, ruthlessly executing both one another and anyone else who happened to stand in their way. The report was an early glimpse of all the elements that would later become Yardie trademarks.

'Their major source of income is derived from the illegal sales of guns and narcotics,' said the report. 'Many crimes go unreported due to the victims' fear of reprisal against themselves or family members still on the island of Jamaica. Most [of the criminals] are armed and will kill to avoid detection or apprehension. They pose a definite threat to any police officer they come into contact with . . .'

Indeed, law enforcement agencies around the world testify that there is something uniquely vicious and chilling about Jamaican criminals – no other islanders in the Caribbean have such a reputation – and the roots of this behaviour are buried, not too deeply, within the complex social and economic history of the island over the last thirty-odd years.

After winning its independence from Britain in August 1962, Jamaica entered a new era of political consciousness and conflict with the two main contenders – the right-wing Jamaica Labour Party led by Edward Seaga and the socialist People's National Party led by Michael Manley – adopting extreme tactics in order to secure votes.

The sprawling tin-shack slums of the capital, Kingston, were the main target, first for blatant gerrymandering and then equally blatant bribery. The local MPs fought for their seats by guaranteeing the desperately impoverished residents substantial financial aid in return for their support.

Soon, voting a party to power wasn't so much about the broader issues of lower taxes and trade deficit as the specific, personal matters of whether your home got connected to the water and electricity supply, whether the road got a coating of tarmac, and whether a doctor would open a practice in the neighbourhood. In essence, politics suddenly became an issue worth fighting for. Worth fighting about.

This in itself might not have been too problematic but for a number of aggravating factors. The first of these had occurred a decade or so before independence when hundreds of thousands of Jamaicans had left the island's ghettoes to set up new lives for themselves in Britain, America and Canada. More often than not, any young children were left behind to be brought up by relatives.

Lacking close parental guidance (seven out of ten ghetto children were born to single-parent families), living in appalling conditions, and facing unemployment rates in excess of 80 per cent (compared to the official island rate of 16 per cent), life held few attractions for this generation of disaffected street youth.

But the teenagers found they could gain respect, power and considerable influence by becoming 'enforcers' for their chosen political parties, using strong-arm tactics to help 'convince' the floaters which way they should cast their votes.

(Such tactics were and continue to be effective because most Jamaican elections are incredibly close. In 1967, for example, the JLP won with 224,180 votes. The PNP polled 217,207.)

Yet this too might not have been overly troublesome, had it not been for the rise of the gun.

Jamaica's declaration of independence was sandwiched between the 1961 US-sponsored invasion of Cuba's Bay of Pigs and the Cuban missile crisis of October 1962. Once the Soviet missile sites had been removed from Cuba and the US naval blockade disbanded, Jamaica – just ninety miles away – assumed key strategic importance. President Kennedy wanted to ensure at all costs that the island's extremists didn't push it into communism while his Soviet opposite number, Khrushchev, wanted to ensure the exact opposite.

Soon, Jamaica's warring political factions were receiving clandestine support, mostly in the form of guns and other weapons. (The PNP's gunmen also received extensive guerrilla-warfare training at secret bases in Cuba while the CIA placed agents on the island to support its own cause. The JLP leader soon became known as Edward CIAga.)

Prior to independence, electoral violence had been limited to a few fist fights and the occasional stabbing, but once the guns arrived each new election heralded a fresh outbreak of urban warfare as opposing gangs sought to 'dispose' of one another.

In the run-up to the 1967 poll, eleven people died, while in 1972 the body count rose to forty-nine. In between there were numerous riots, fracas and ever-more violent clashes between opposing gangs of supporters.

Both political parties spent hundreds of thousands of dollars constructing flagship housing estates – Tivoli Gardens for the JLP and Arnett Gardens, better known as Concrete Jungle, for the PNP – supposedly a vision of what life would be like for all if the respective parties were voted to power. Instead, they simply helped make the divisions between the two even clearer.

By the mid-seventies, the gun culture was firmly entrenched and downtown Kingston had been carved into a series of 'garrison constituencies', each led by a local 'Don' who controlled gangs of teenage enforcers known as posses – a tag taken directly from the spaghetti Westerns that were massively popular in Jamaica at the time and which did much to legitimise the violence.

For the enforcers the risks were high, but so were the rewards. As well as respect and status, those on the winning side were also given flats on prestige estates like Tivoli and other perks. 'Better ten years of a good life than fifty of living like a dog,' they would say.

However, the effect on Jamaica itself was catastrophic. Gun crime became so rife that the government introduced a unique judicial institution – the Gun Court – along with a new law enabling any person found guilty of possession of an unlicensed firearm or even a few bullets to receive a mandatory life sentence.

But the initiative had little effect. The battles continued to rage with such ferocity that even the innocuous-sounding slum areas that formed the main war zones were forced to take on more appropriate names. The McIntyre housing estate in Brown's Town became Dunkirk, Smith Lane became Tel Aviv, and Duhaney Park became Angola.

The violence was soon virtually continuous. Even between elections, rival political death squads would hunt down one another's top gunmen, leading many to flee first to the mountains and then to America, Canada and Britain.

Once safely abroad, they hid among the growing black and Rastafarian communities, returning to Jamaica periodically on false passports to commit murders with relative impunity. In the run-up to the 1976 election, eventually won by the PNP, these awayday killers pushed the death toll up to 113. With Seaga's long run ended, the JLP gunmen found themselves not only targeted by death squads but also painfully short of funding. Dozens left the island and, once safely abroad, saw in the burgeoning cannabis trade a way of financing their battles and putting the JLP back on top.

One of the first to make the break, and the virtual pioneer of Jamaican organised crime in Britain, was Robert Blackwood, also known as Bowyark and Rankin Dread. He had been a notorious enforcer and the right-hand man of Claude Massop, a Don who ran the JLP 'garrison' in the Rema district until he was killed by the police in mysterious circumstances in the late seventies.

Bowyark's name had been linked to the murder of at least twenty-nine PNP and drug-dealing rivals and a further four policemen, but bringing him to justice proved problematic. By the time one of the cop killings came to trial, three of the witnesses had been murdered and a fourth had 'lost his memory'. The charges were dropped.

After Massop's death, Bowyark assumed control of Rema but, after being involved in a shoot-out with two police officers, decided to jump bail and 'go foreign', obtaining a false passport and fleeing to London under the name of Errol Codling in 1978.

An attempt to extradite him from Britain in 1979 failed and he settled into his new life. His six fake passports recorded a host of travels – Miami, New York, Bristol, Sheffield, Birmingham and Dublin – cities where he would set up drug deals and distribution networks, staffing his outfit with trusted friends from back home.

In London, Bowyark based himself at Darneth Road in Stamford Hill, though he also had addresses in Brixton and Stoke Newington. Describing himself as a musician/record producer, he set about making his name, first legitimately, cutting a record, 'Hey Fatty Boom Boom', which reached the top ten in 1980.

'I was famous. I had the Mercedes. I had flashy jewellery and clothes. I had it all. And there were always girls. Sometimes I had a different girl every night,' he said later.

But Bowyark's heart wasn't in the music business. From a base in Hackney, north London, he slowly started to build a new criminal empire. He opened a drinking club, ran a string of prostitutes, dabbled in counterfeit currency, and funded a series of cannabis shipments to both Britain and America through a number of armed robberies.

Along the way he also picked up two rape charges – later dropped when the victims refused to testify – and ten children from eight different women. But he never lost sight of his main goal – financing the JLP's struggle – and did so in single-minded fashion.

Considering that there were only around twenty men like Bowyark in the country, their activities had an astounding impact on the British drug scene. Between 1974 and 1978, the amount of herbal cannabis seized in the country averaged around 2500 kilos each year. In 1979, the amount more than doubled to 6445. In 1980 it increased threefold to 18,419.

Customs officials agree that most, if not all, of this growth can be attributed to Jamaican trafficking operations in London and Birmingham.

The drugs were brought into the country on the principle of little and often. Bowyark's couriers, for example, would regularly slip through customs with a bunch of coconuts, each of which had been sliced open and filled with a kilo of herb (about £1,500 worth) and then resealed. As a refinement, a small bottle of water would be placed in the middle so that when shaken the coconut still sounded as if it had milk in it.

Other consignments came in concealed inside bottles of rum or large shells taken from the island's numerous beaches. Blocks would also be wrapped in polythene and simply hidden in the bottom of suitcases.

But by far the most popular method of bringing the goods into the country was to use human couriers or 'mules'. Nurses, teachers and other white professionals unlikely to attract the attention of customs officers would wear girdles holding up to three kilos of prime ganja close to their bodies.

However, such methods were painfully slow when it came to moving bulk shipments, and as the scale of Bowyark's operations increased so did the scale of the smuggling.

One of his associates set up a restaurant business and began importing exotic foodstuffs and shellfish. Batches of deep-fried fishcakes could contain dozens of kilos at a time while the regular perishable deliveries of exotic fruit (less likely to be held up by customs) included some that had been hollowed out and filled with drugs.

In April 1980, £60,000 worth of herbal cannabis was found on the aptly named flagship freighter *Jamaica Producer* when it docked at Newport, Gwent. Some 30 kilos of the drug had been hidden among a cargo of bananas and other fruit stored in the hold.

By the time of that year's election in Jamaica, Bowyark and the other expatriate Dons had earned so much money through their drug trafficking that the island was literally awash with guns. In a bloody nine-month-long campaign, 889 people died, the vast majority from gunshot wounds.

News footage from the time shows police, soldiers and civilians crouching at street corners, blasting away with machineguns at unseen opponents; makeshift armoured cars full of pistol-packing youths canvassing support; the twisted bodies of men, women and children piled up against the walls of their tin-shack homes.

When the fighting was over, the JLP had been returned to power, though no one was quite sure how. Seaga had mysteriously won 51 of the 60 seats even though 47 per cent of the electorate had voted for the opposition. (Perhaps the fifteen CIA operatives identified as being in the country from the preceding summer night have been able to shed some light.)

Soon after the election, the PNP gunmen followed their JLP counterparts abroad and started getting involved in the drugs trade. By the end of 1980, the ganja trade was worth an estimated $1.5 billion a year − more than the value of all Jamaica's legitimate exports combined, and a badly needed source of foreign income. Despite increasing pressure from outside, the last thing the government wanted to do was clamp down.

As Edward Seaga told the *Washington Post* in December 1980: 'The ganja trade in the last month was virtually what was keeping the economy alive. It supplied black-market dollars . . . the question of legalising it so as to bring the flow of several hundred million dollars in this parallel market through the official channels would mean an extremely big boost to our foreign exchange earnings.

'Regardless of whether we want it or not, the industry as such is here to stay. It is just not possible for it to be wiped out.'

But under pressure from the new Reagan administration, Seaga agreed to try. It was a disaster. A mass eradication programme, aided by some US$500 million from the USA, destroyed the source (though by 1984 production had actually increased) but left the supply line and network of distributors intact. And nature abhors a vacuum.

It was around this time that the final aggravating factor which would push the ganja gangs into becoming the Yardies came into play. The Colombian drug cartels, who had been slowly expanding their operations in North America since the early seventies, suddenly began to experience problems moving their cocaine around.

Their favoured clearing house – the Bahamas – was the subject of yet another Reagan-backed clampdown. Private airstrips were being destroyed, frigates and war planes were milling about, attempting to intercept shipments, and increased activity by the Drug Enforcement Administration meant that more Colombian planes found themselves surrounded by armed agents as soon as they landed. An alternative route had to be found.

The Colombians had already crossed paths with the Jamaicans – the Bahamaian islands were also the main transshipment point for ganja entering the USA. And while there were serious reservations from many cartel members about how trustworthy and efficient the local Dons and their gangs of enforcers might be, a deal was soon struck.

The Colombians switched to moving their coke through Jamaica, using private planes, small boats and occasionally simply dumping waterproof bales of the stuff off the island's coast. From there, the gangsters would retrieve the bundles, break them down into manageable packages, and make use of the old ganja supply and distribution lines to get the drugs to America.

As with the influx of guns, the effect on Jamaica itself was disastrous. Cocaine prices fell through the floor and the drug that was once the reserve of the cognoscenti quickly found its way to Kingston's ghettos, where it pushed the already sky-high levels of violence even higher. Having a seventeen-year-old gun-toting enforcer standing on a street corner looking for trouble is bad enough. When he's out of his head on coke he becomes little more than a bomb waiting to go off.

One Interpol officer stationed in Jamaica at the time recalls the transformation. 'Nobody ever got dead of the herb. Kingston had always been violent but most of it had been tied up with politics, not the drugs. But then the cocaine came in and everybody started going crazy. People were getting shot for no reason. The homicide rate went up like a rocket.'

The effect on the British scene was equally dramatic. In the mid-eighties, little Colombian cocaine was finding its way to the UK, chiefly because, unlike America and Spain, Britain had no sizable Colombian community to form the first link in the distribution chain. What did exist, however, was the British end of the ganja-smuggling network. And for Dons like Bowyark, cocaine was both golden goose and golden egg all in one.

While a cigarette packet of ganja would hardly cover the cost of a courier's ticket, the same amount of cocaine could yield enough cash to buy a small plane. Overnight, drug smuggling went from being a way of making a good living to a way of living like a god.

And as the profit margins rose, so did the stakes the dealers were playing for.

By early 1986, Bowyark was concentrating so much on cocaine that he had to buy his ganja from others. On 1 March he and four friends, including Largie and Yankie Man, ventured to the eighth floor of Stanway Court, a tower-block flat in Islington, to purchase £150 worth of canna-bis from Innocent Egbulefu, a well-known Nigerian drugs dealer.

But Egbulefu wasn't so innocent. The batch of dope he sold Bowyark was made up of herbs and tea leaves. As soon as the posse discovered this they returned. Their power was based almost entirely on the fact that people were scared of them. If they allowed this to go unpunished, their reputations would be worthless.

Egbulefu tried to hide in the toilet, but they smashed the door down. What happened next is unclear, but the Nigerian was either pushed, thrown or jumped out of the window. He fell ninety feet and ended up, in the words of one detective who visited the scene, 'squashed like a flat-iron.' It had all happened

so quickly that Egbulefu was still holding the remote-control
unit for his television.

It was the shape of things to come. On 23 May 1986, Derek
Walters, who had strong links with a gang of coke dealers,
was standing in the doorway of the Old Queen's Head pub
in Stockwell when a plush blue Mercedes pulled up outside. A
man got out, walked calmly up to the thirty-one-year-old DJ and
blasted him in the head with a shotgun at point-blank range.

A few days later, a doorman at Cynthia's nightclub in Acre
Lane was shot through the head for trying to stop a gang of
Jamaicans entering the club and shooting their real target – a
rival coke dealer.

Police efforts to nip this sudden wave of violence – which
included an increase in assaults and rapes – in the bud were
immediately frustrated. Few witnesses agreed to provide any
information. The best the detectives could hope for would be a
meaningless street name and a nervous whisper that a 'Yardie'
had been responsible.

(Then, as now, the 'Yardie' tag was the cause of much
confusion. While it has now been accepted as shorthand for
the black mafia, its origins are far less sinister.

For a Jamaican in Britain, the Yard is the island of Jamaica
itself. Friends will talk about going 'yard' instead of going home.
Rather than describing themselves as Yardies, most gangsters
would say they are 'yard men' – Jamaicans as opposed to
any other Caribbean islanders. The Yardie tag is simply a
bastardisation of that.

In America, where Afro-Caribbeans have a history stretching
back three hundred years, Jamaica's status as a 'home' is less
pronounced. Hence in the US, the gangs are known as Posses.)

Police officers active at the time say that ideally they would
have liked to have launched a special team to investigate the
Yardies there and then, but Scotland Yard was, to say the least,
reluctant. The bloody inner-city riots of Handsworth (1980),
Brixton and Toxteth (1981) and Tottenham's Broadwater Farm
(1985) were still fresh in their minds.

A *de facto* criminalisation of the black community through the establishment of a special squad to police it was too hot a political potato even to consider. Instead, the brief for those at street level was to watch, take whatever action was possible, but not to devote specific resources to the project.

But the deaths continued. In May 1987, Michael 'Mickey' St George Williams was found slumped over the wheel of his blue Porsche which had crashed into a tree. He had died from shotgun wounds to the chest.

Williams ran a baby-clothes stall in Whitechapel, but the fact that he drove a prestige car, kept excessive amounts of cash in a string of safety deposit boxes and owned a number of spacious properties gave many the impression that he made his real money some other way.

They would have been right. On the night of his death, bystanders recall seeing him involved in an argument in the Bronx club in Stoke Newington about splitting the spoils of a £100,000 armed robbery. Williams apparently wanted to take the money and invest it in a cocaine shipment while Leroy 'Fitz' Hughes and Norman 'Bicycle' Campbell wanted to take their share and live it up.

When Williams left the club later that evening, Fitz and Bicycle were waiting for him. Bicycle, whose excessive cocaine use had left him suffering from acute paranoid psychosis to the extent that he believed there was a snake growing inside him, pulled the trigger. The fact that he had been blinded in one eye by an earlier axe attack made him easier to identify.

A few months later, a party at a council-funded club at the Priory Centre in Acton turned nasty. Trevor 'Sammy Dread' Miller, who was wanted for at least three ostensibly political murders in Jamaica, and Barron 'Danger Mouse' Campbell, a cousin of Bicycle Campbell, blew off the head of rival coke dealer Alwyn 'Shankie' Alfred.

As the gun went off, the terrified crowd sought cover on the floor. The subsequent court case heard that those who were

brave enough to look up at the pair as they strutted out could
see that they were smiling.

Even Bowyark himself didn't survive the year unscathed.
While drinking in a shebeen he was attacked by a machete-
wielding British-born black, keen to take over his business
interests. Bowyark was left with eighteen head wounds and
his left wrist was almost severed. True to his superhero status,
he was back on the streets within ten days.

The fact that a couple of the murders had been solved
relatively easily gave the top brass the impression that this
Yardie thing was under control, nothing to worry about, to the
extent that the first warning bells, again sounded in America,
were virtually ignored.

In July 1987, eighty-five representatives of United States and
Canadian law enforcement agencies attended a conference in
Miami to discuss how to combat the Posses.

Scotland Yard sent along two detectives, who heard how the
Posses now had several thousand members and associates, how
politics had taken a back seat, and how the gangs now had a
single, well-defined business plan: 'The accumulation of vast
amounts of wealth quickly and easily through the trafficking of
narcotics.'

Yet when the detectives returned to paint their grim picture
of Britain's future, their senior officers remained sceptical and
unwilling to commit resources. Even the dramatic increase in
cocaine seizures – from an average of 80 kilos a year between
1983 and 1986 to more than 400 kilos in 1987 – wasn't enough
to spur the top brass into action.

Nor was a report by the then National Drugs Intelligence
Unit which had identified more than twenty Jamaican criminals living in north and east London. The report gave their
descriptions and street names, their addresses in Kingston and
London, and details of their lifestyles and criminal records. One
suspect was credited with twenty murders. But the report was
dismissed as being too anecdotal to be relied upon.

In fact it wasn't until around 4 p.m. on the afternoon of 19

October 1987 that the British police realised something simply had to be done. It was then that 250 armed officers from the federal Drug Enforcement Administration surrounded a group of houses in the Jamaican quarter of Dallas, Texas.

Explosives charges were used to blow the reinforced doors off their hinges and the cops rushed in. Minutes later, fifty-four members of a gang known as the Shower Posse had been arrested on charges of murder, kidnap, extortion, drug dealing and firearms violations.

But what was of most interest to Scotland Yard were not the knives, machines-guns, shotguns and boxes of live hand grenades that were found, but the itemised phone bills showing dozens of calls to London, Birmingham, Bristol and Sheffield. And the fact that several of the most wanted, most violent offenders had themselves visited Britain in the preceding months.

Within weeks, Operation Lucy, staffed with twelve detectives gleaned from all parts of London, had been established with a brief to investigate the links between illegal Jamaican immigrants and violent drug crime. The tabloids lost little time in dubbing them the Yardie Squad.

In an attempt to divert the critics, who claimed the operation was merely an attempt to stereotype blacks as criminals, the first major Lucy outing was turned into something of a media circus with journalists almost outnumbering police officers – a public demonstration that fair play was the order of the day.

Clad all in black, wearing riot helmets, shin guards and body armour, though (bizarrely in retrospect) unarmed, the thirty officers of the newly formed PT18 assault squad entered a semi-detached house in Clapton at 5.38 a.m. on a dreary April morning with the aid of steel mallets and crowbars.

Despite the early hour, there were sixty-seven people in the near-derelict house, drinking, chatting, smoking joints and snorting lines of cocaine. Taken totally by surprise and dazzled by powerful searchlights, they were forced to the ground and their hands tied behind their backs with plastic cuffs before they could even think of resisting. 'They hit us like an express train,' gasped one stunned woman as she was led away.

Among the twenty people eventually arrested, there were two prize specimens. Top of the list was Bowyark himself, who was soon deported, but Devon 'Foodhead' Plunkett, who was wanted for a number of murders in Miami, was intially missed.

He had been deported from Britain two years earlier but had returned with a fake passport in the name of Frederick Gordon. So convincing was this cover that Foodhead was released after the Clapton raid, though he was recaptured in October after being found in possession of a half-kilo of cocaine.

By the latter half of 1989, the Lucy team had made more than four hundred arrests and obtained dozens of convictions. A database of more than two hundred names and some three thousand incidents had been built up, and almost fifty illegal immigrants had been deported.

Then the unthinkable happened. Operation Lucy was shut down.

Officially, it was announced that the Yardie problem had been brought 'under control' and that the vast expense could no longer be justified. Privately, other reasons were put forward. There was the fact that only three of the eight London police divisions – those with sizable black communities – actually had a Yardie problem. The others resented having to donate money from their precious budgets for something that had little bearing on them.

There was also steadily increasing criticism from civil rights and black groups to the effect that the operation was racially divisive. It was seen as counter-productive to the shift towards 'community policing' that was taking place. Whatever the reason, the end result was the same.

It couldn't have come at a worse time. Although it had succeeded in putting dozens of top men out of the picture, one good reason for keeping the operation alive was that the team had totally underestimated the ability of the gang to diversify and heal itself.

But there was another, more pressing, reason for keeping Lucy – the emergence of a new product line which made being a Yardie even more profitable and ensured that, no matter how many were killed or wounded or imprisoned or deported, there would always be others looking for a way in.

Five years before I met Digga, in early February 1989, a monthly youth magazine asked me to investigate a new, supposedly instantly addictive drug which had just begun to appear in significant quantities around certain run-down areas of London and the South-East, Crack.

At the time, there was far more hype than hard evidence. Most of the drug users and drug agencies I contacted had heard of it, but had not yet seen it. A few hadn't even heard of it.

It was two months before the tabloids went crack-crazy, an event triggered when the head of the New York office of the Drug Enforcement Administration, Robert Stutman, came to Britain and delivered to startled police and customs officials the following ominous warning:

'I personally guarantee you that two years from now, you will have a serious crack problem – we are so saturated with cocaine in the United States, there ain't enough noses left to use the cocaine that's coming in.'

The prediction was accompanied by grim accounts of what the drug had done to America's inner-city ghettoes. There were tales of teenage crack-head mothers selling their own babies to get the money for their next hit, stories of twelve-year-old dealers involved in gun battles with the police, and countless tales of acts of violence committed by those under the influence of the drug – in 1988, 73 per cent of all the children battered to death by their parents in New York were the offspring of crack users.

This time, the sound of the alarm bells from across the Atlantic was taken seriously – there was no way crack was going to be allowed to take hold here. An official from the British Embassy in New York summed up the general reaction most eloquently: 'We have been shown the ghost of Christmas future, and Tiny Tim doesn't have to die.'

No one quite knows who invented crack. There are reports of it appearing in Amsterdam in 1978 but, probably because it was a little too harsh for mellow Dutch tastes, it soon faded away. Two years later, it surfaced in the Bahamas and quickly took hold to the extent that, by the end of 1982, there had been a massive increase in the number of psychiatric admissions to hospitals on the islands.

By 1983 the drug had begun to filter across the water to Miami, then to New York and beyond, particularly Los Angeles, where the black street gangs began pushing it like there was no tomorrow. By the end of 1984, American law enforcement officials were warning that within three years, crack would have swept across the entire country like a firestorm, a prediction that turned out to be a ghastly underestimate.

In August 1985, not one of the tens of thousands of telephone calls to America's national cocaine hotline concerned crack. By February 1986, every other call was from a user of·the new drug.

The speed at which crack spread surprised everyone, with the exception of the mostly Jamaican dealers. They knew only too well that by pricing the new product well within reach of society's lowest common denominators, there would be no end of takers. At $100 a line, cocaine was still having trouble leaving its jet-set roots behind. At $10 a hit, crack wasn't just cheap, it was a miracle of modern marketing.

The effect of the drug alone was enough to guarantee its success. The instant euphoria that a rock crack produces usually lasts forty or fifty seconds, a few minutes at the most, and a mere flash in the pan compared to the thirty-minute cocaine high or the three-to-four-hour trip from a dose of heroin.

But with crack, the high has no parallel; there simply isn't anything else like it. 'If you'd never touched drugs before,' says Pete, a white middle-class user/dealer, 'taking crack would do to your mind what lying in bed for a year and then running a marathon would do to your body.

'With coke, it's all quite subtle – not so much a high, more a feeling of super-awareness. With crack there's no mistake, no way,' he smiles. 'It's a heavy-duty rush.'

Some 80 per cent of crack users go on to develop an addiction, usually within two weeks of their first smoke. With cocaine, just 7 per cent of users become addicted and even then the process can take up to eighteen months.

For those destined to get hooked, the $10 hit at first seems like a bargain, but within minutes of their first puff, most abusers are begging for another hit. With each new intake, the body's resistance rises so that more and more is needed to produce the same effect.

For its consumers, the ultimate curse of crack is that, because the high is so short-lived, it's almost impossible to overdose. If you could afford it, you could smoke your way through $2000 worth in a day and still end up smiling. And even if you couldn't afford it, you'd still want to, and you'd happily rob, steal or kill by way of trying.

For dealers, crack is an equally intense experience. An ounce of cocaine will produce just sixteen decent snorting lines but some 370 rocks of crack. For the dealer, selling the cheaper product will on average quadruple your profit margin.

And when your customers get hooked after a few days, want more of your product each time they see you and are prepared to do anything to get you the money, how can you lose?

Crack officially arrived in Britain in May 1988 when a few rocks were found in a council block in Handsworth, Birmingham. The following month, traces of the drug were found in a Liverpool squat. In September of the same year, a reinforced flat on the Milton Court estate in Deptford, south London, was raided and turned up the country's first crack factory.

(The 'factory' tag is something of a misnomer. Crack is made by mixing cocaine powder and baking soda in water or ammonia and then heating the mixture until the liquid boils off – a frying pan and small cooker are all the equipment you need.)

In November 1988 Paul Matheson, a £15-per-week van driver from Kingston, became the first man in the country to be convicted of selling (as opposed to simply possessing) crack.

Touring the maze of walkways that made up the North Peckham Estate in south London, an area once described as the most deprived housing development in the EEC, Matheson and his minders would make at least one hundred deals a day. In less than six weeks, he sold more than £105,000 worth of crack until worried residents tipped off the police and he was arrested.

At his trial Matheson explained how, despite earning thousands of pounds for his bosses, he himself earned only £450 per week. The court also heard how, since his arrest, Matheson's family back in Jamaica had received death threats. Not surprisingly, he refused to name his backers.

By the time I started the research for my article, the North Peckham Estate's dealers had gone to ground, but I'd heard that crack was being offered for sale in a couple of pubs close to Ladbroke Grove, west London, and, in retrospect somewhat naively, I set off there one Thursday evening to see what I could find.

It was dark when I arrived in the area and, on my way to the first pub, I bumped into a dreadlocked Rastafarian shouting and swearing at the barman who had just thrown him out.

Rudy, as his name turned out to be, was steaming drunk. Well over six feet tall and in his late thirties, he walked slowly with the aid of a stick – the result of a recent car accident. He was about to fall over when I caught him and listened patiently as he thanked me and then explained how he was desperate for another drink but the landlord had refused to serve him.

With no other leads to follow up, I offered to buy him a drink in the next pub in the hope that he might know something about the local drug scene. It turned out to be an inspired move.

Rudy was celebrating that night because he'd just got out of prison for poncing – living off immoral earnings. Everywhere he went, local prostitutes would come out and hug him and silver BMWs with tinted windows would slow down and salute him with their horns.

Rudy, I rapidly discovered, was an old-style ganja-trading Yardie who commanded great respect around the Grove, even from the younger generation. And in his thoroughly inebriated state, I was his best mate.

We found another pub and I bought the drinks as we sat in a quiet corner, chatting about nothing in particular. Periodically, young hoods would pass by and stop to say hello. Almost all of them had some item of 'business' to discuss and eyed me anxiously. 'Who's your friend?' they would ask. 'He's safe,' Rudy would reply.

Suddenly, I was one of them. Any friend of Rudy's was a friend of theirs. About two months' worth of undercover work had been accomplished in less than an hour.

Over the next week, I spent every evening at the pub under some farcical pretext of having been offered a job, claiming that I was planning on moving to the area later that month and wanted to get to know my local. Thankfully, no one ever sought to question this further.

I soon became friendly with Desmond, a forty-two-year-old Jamaican fond of drinking brandy and port mixed together, who had lived in the capital for some fifteen years. As the evenings passed, he slowly began to open up to me.

He told me how he'd spent six years in prison for manslaughter in his twenties after getting carried away trying to persuade a floating voter which way to turn; how he ran a cocaine distribution ring across the south of England, packing the drug into tins of white Dulux paint and sending young couriers in overalls ('about your age') by bus, train and taxi to deliver to his small band of customers.

'You pour out half the paint and put air-tight packs of Charlie in the bottom. Even if you get stopped, no cop's gonna stick his hand into a paint tin. And if he wants to pour it out, where's he gonna put it? Down the gutter? Down the sink? Not likely.'

He explained how crack hadn't taken off big-time yet – the only people who seemed to be interested were the long-term heroin addicts who no longer got any buzz out of their addiction. He also told me about Ladbroke Grove's main crack den, and the 'secret' code for gaining access.

'It's based above the newsagent's,' he said. 'You go in and ask for George, then tell him you want some din dins. He'll tell you the meals are served upstairs.'

When I put this to the test, George, a fiftysomething pot-bellied specimen with a wicked twinkle in his eye, pointed to a curtained stairwell at the back of the shop. A short hallway led to a dingy staircase down which was rolling a faintly sickly-sweet smell. Crack.

The door of the first room was missing. It was totally unfurnished and poorly lit with painted-out windows. Four or five young men sat against three of the four walls, two smoking, one staring into space in a kind of waking sleep. The conversations stopped as soon as I appeared.

There was a door in the centre of the empty wall which, despite being in the middle of the house, had been fitted with a letter-box. This was the entrance to the 'factory' itself where, for security's sake, deals were done through the slot. As all the glassy eyes in the room began to focus on me, I made a bullshit excuse about looking for someone and left.

Desmond was also right about heroin addicts and other long-term abusers forming the bulk of the initial crack market, a factor that wrong-footed many observers of the scene who mistakenly believed that Stutman's apocalyptic prediction had been wide of the mark.

The scare stories had given the impression that crack would sweep into otherwise crime- and drug-free communities and turn them into Armageddon whereas, as Matheson's success had shown, all the early growth was restricted to the 'problem' estates.

A new generation of drug users was certainly at risk, but it was the older generation turning to dealing to support their habits, not the drug itself, which would corrupt them. While in early 1991 senior police officers were explaining how crack could not take hold because Britain's slums were not as poverty- and violence-ridden as their American counterparts, unpublished government-backed research showed that it was fast becoming a serious problem.

The study by researchers at the Charing Cross and Westminster medical school uncovered a number of disturbing findings, most notably that the crack market was worth an estimated £450 million and doubling each year; that drug agencies were not equipped to help addicts; that despite media images to the contrary, the drug was used equally among the black and white communities; and that typical users had habits costing £20,000 per year, money they acquired chiefly through crime and prostitution.

But it took a particularly vicious robbery in April 1991 before the Yardies finally received the recognition they truly deserved from law enforcement officials.

The near-fatal shooting of Charlie Fisher, owner of a Brixton jeweller's shop, resulted in a Flying Squad inquiry which by August had developed into Operation Dalehouse, a major anti-crack initiative.

The shooting, it emerged, had been carried out by a Jamaican gang who had been linked to dozens of other incidents in south London, including the gun-point robbery of three hundred youths at a disco. None of the incidents had been reported to the police, such was the fear the gang inspired.

As the thirty-five-strong team began to investigate, they discovered a whole spate of unsolved shootings, murders, robberies and assaults stretching back to 1988. They found that most of the incidents were linked not only to each other but also to the activities of a handful of Jamaican gangsters operating chiefly between London, Kingston and New York. Gunmen and crack dealers had been flying into and out of the country almost at will, battling over territory, bumping off rivals and making millions of pounds from selling crack.

Over the same period, the two other Yardie strongholds – Birmingham and Manchester – also reported a sharp increase in shootings and incidents of violence. In Manchester in particular, police logged thirty shootings during 1990 alone, and noted that at least a further hundred had gone unreported.

One of the more grisly hits involved the murder of a dealer in a notorious drug pub. When police arrived, the victim, who had been shot in the head at point-blank range with a shotgun, was slumped in a corner while the barman pulled pints and other customers continued to play pool and darts. 'It was an awful mess, blood dripping off the walls,' says the first detective on the scene. 'Yet judging by their reaction, you'd think nothing had happened.'

The growth of the new drug radically changed the black crime scene, as one Birmingham community worker notes: 'In the mid-eighties, a lot of people were into illegal gambling and drinking clubs, but that scene has virtually died out now.

'It's partly because of the increase in violence. It's no good having ten or fifteen thousand pounds on a gambling table if some geezer's gonna walk in with a double-barrelled shotgun and take it away. The only clubs these days have security cameras and all that.

'But the crack has been the real change. People just don't have the time to gamble any more. If you're selling crack, you're out there 24/7 [twenty-four hours a day, seven days a week]. When the guys were robbing or poncing, they had time. If you're kiting [cheque fraud], there's a time when you finish and you want to relax, but not with crack.

'A lot of people used to run women as well, but men can make more money out of drugs. They'd rather work the streets themselves. There are only two ponces left and their names are Charlie and Henry – cocaine and heroin.'

In just over a year, the Dalehouse squad seized more than £1 million worth of crack, made 274 arrests, and investigated fifteen Yardie-related murders. Despite this success and the widely voiced protests of serving officers, in November 1992 it too was disbanded,

Officially, the problem was once more seen to be under control: 'The unit has reduced the number of offences in south London to a level where it is no longer justifiable to employ a full-scale squad,' said a spokesman.

When, a year later, the shooting of PC Dunne showed that perhaps this hadn't been the case, Scotland Yard attempted to defend the move, claiming that the unit's experience and role had been absorbed into divisional drug squads operating across London.

But the decision to close Dalehouse demonstrated a complete underestimation of how the Yardies work. According to the hypothetical textbook on British organised crime, traditional police work involves taking out the main man – the Mr Big. If, for example, you have a problem with the Kray gang, you take out the Kray brothers and, hey presto, the problem ends.

However, the Yardies, along with every other international organised crime syndicate, structure themselves like a pyramid with a rolling hierarchy. Take away the top man and up pop dozens of wannabes, eager to take his place. So eager in fact that it is often they who provide the information to help put their former leaders away. Ask Tuffy's friends how they saw his death and, while some will mourn, there will be a few who describe it as 'a good opportunity'.

'It's like dealing with a plague of ants,' says one drugs squad officer. 'You can't limit it just to dealing with the ones who are causing the immediate problem. You have to find out where the nest is and take that out.'

To most Westerners, Jamaica is nothing more than a tropical paradise – the ultimate travel brochure come to life. Montego Bay, Negril and Ocho Rios are the gems of the island's tourist crown, each specialising in all-inclusive resort 'clubs' where holidaymakers are subtly persuaded to spend all their time (and money) in the hotel or on the private beach, rather then venturing out into the real Jamaica.

Tourists are not generally encouraged to travel into areas like downtown Montego Bay unless accompanied, though if they do they are unlikely to face anything worse than the prospect of being fleeced by some wide-boy con-man or besieged by hawkers.

Kingston, however, is a very different matter. Such is the level of risk to outsiders that the most notorious and unstable parts of the city don't even feature on the official tourist maps – the area occupied by the extensive Tivoli Gardens development, for example, is simply a large white space.

But it's not just the danger. Once you've seen the ghettoes of downtown Kingston, it's easy to see why the government conspires to keep them hidden – the sight of such abject poverty might affect foreigners' willingness to spend so freely.

Of course, Britain has its ghettoes – hundreds of them spread throughout the inner-city housing estates. But the difference between, say, a Birmingham ghetto and a Kingston ghetto is almost immeasurable.

In Birmingham, virtually every flat, no matter how run-down, will have a fridge, a cooker, running water and electricity. There will be doors and windows, many of which close and lock, and each leading to individual rooms.

In Trenchtown, Kingston, the streets are made of houses knocked up from sheets of corrugated steel or zinc. Most have just one room to serve as everything from bedroom and bathroom to kitchen, and they have no lights, water or toilets, let alone labour-saving appliances.

All around, the gutters overflow with raw sewage. Rubble, decay and debris are everywhere; the roads are patterned with treacherously deep craters and every visible window has been smashed. The only cars to be seen are the burnt-out shells of those that have been stolen and dumped here – if you can afford a car, you can afford not to live in Trenchtown.

The whole scene is strongly reminiscent of the photographs

of a devastated Hiroshima after the atom bomb was dropped. Only in Trenchtown, the people are still there.

Survival is a constant battle in the ghetto. Shootings occur almost daily, and some 90 per cent of all Jamaican crime takes place within these districts.

Violence is an accepted part of life. The young men sport guns and knives in the waistbands of their trousers like fashion accessories, while the women routinely carry vials of acid to disfigure opponents. The evidence of their work is all around.

Young and old alike loiter in the street to escape the oppressive heat of their poorly ventilated homes. Stand and watch for a while and you'll see the children playing in the water from the standpipes and middle-aged women using empty buildings as public toilets. You may even see some enterprising young hood secure an electricity supply by tapping into a nearby pylon or street light.

Stay a little longer and you may see a gleaming new Mercedes or BMW cruising down the otherwise deserted streets. All the loiterers will stop and stare, straining to get a look at the occupant who invariably turns out to be a well-dressed young man, dripping with gold, come to 'chill out'.

For the Jamaican gangster, wealth is meaningless if people don't know what you've got, so the most successful dealers travel back to the Yard, rent flashy cars and visit the ghetto haunts of their youth. They will take cases of beer, suitcases packed with clothes, and hand out jewellery like sweets.

Often, the real motive is to recruit new muscle from a pool of trusted friends back home in order to expand their operations and build their own posses which, as is the case with the Dunkirk Boys, the Rema Rats and the (Concrete) Junglers, are inevitably named after the area where the members grew up.

According to 'Tiffany', an undercover FBI agent who has infiltrated the Yardies both in England and America, admission by invitation is usually the only way in.

'You have to start by doing your own thing. You start up your own little gang and go out and rob some banks or hold up a few soda trucks. The Dons will come and see what you have been doing and, if they like you, they'll help you out with some guns and a few extra men – in return for a share of the profits, of course.'

As with many organised crime syndicates, true membership is granted only after a serious crime – almost always murder – has been committed, in order to ensure that the potential recruit isn't an undercover cop.

In Tivoli Gardens, it is said that victims would be held in a makeshift jail in the basement of a shop and that newcomers would be sent along with a pistol to prove their mettle before being admitted to the organisation proper.

'There's no ceremony, nothing formal,' says Tiffany. 'But in some posses there is a kind of blood vow, not unlike the Mafia. You vow to kill or be killed. The only way out is in a box.'

There are as many different posses as there are individual districts in Kingston, but the two best known – the Shower and the Spanglers – don't actually exist in the formal sense. While many believe them to be the largest and most notorious Yardie gangs, they are in fact simply umbrella organisations for all the JLP and PNP posses respectively.

The story that the Shower posse is so called because they love to shower their victims with bullets is also something of a myth. Any analysis of Yardie killings shows that all the gangs use excessive firepower as a matter of course.

In fact, the name came about in the early eighties when a group of PNP and JLP supporters met at a football match. A temporary truce had been called to allow the game to proceed unhindered, but that didn't stop the insults. Soon the PNP side were making gun shapes out of their hands and pretending to shoot their opposite numbers while shouting 'be-pow, be-pow'.

One JLP wag retorted with a comment something along the lines of: 'Our guns don't shoot one bullet at a time, they fire a shower of shots!' Since then, 'shower, shower' became the mantra of any large JLP meeting. Their rivals were initially known as the Bibo posse, but this later changed to the Spanglers, a reference to their love of gold jewellery.

In Britain they call them Yardies, in America they call them Posses. But in Jamaica there is yet another name for the gangsters who have become the scourge of society. Deportees.

Since June 1988, much to the chagrin of the island's politicians, America, Britain and Canada have had a policy of deporting Yardies back to Jamaica to save on the cost of expensive trials, except in cases where there is direct evidence of criminal activity.

According to figures compiled by the Jamaican police, on average three deportees arrive back on the island every single day. By the end of 1994, more than 5,500 will have been sent back. The majority come from the US and Canada but at least one in ten is deported from Britain, a figure that appears to be slowly rising.

Most of the deportees are convicts. A survey of the 3,962 who had been sent back up until May 1993 found that 3,734 had been convicted of some crime: 2,202 had drugs convictions, 155 had committed firearms offences, while a further 1,377 came under other categories.

Many Jamaicans believed that the influx of deportees would lead to a growth in the island's internal crime problem, but only sixteen of the thousands sent back before May 1993 had subsequently been linked to any criminal activity in their own country.

In reality, most of those who are deported only wait around as long as it takes for them to get hold of the money they need for a new false passport and then return.

But because the Yardie philosophy deems that those who have wealth must flaunt it, the assets of even the most successful dealers tend to be tied up mostly in cars and jewellery – just the kind of items they have to forfeit on departure. Hence, back in Jamaica, almost all the deportees are penniless, living shadows of their former lives.

The phenomenon has even been immortalised in song by controversial Jamaican gangsta rapper Buju Banton, best known for his track 'Boom Bye Bye', which advocates the murder of homosexuals. 'Deportee', with its snide references to the riches-to-rags story of the returning villains, proved no less controversial, prompting death threats from those who took the chorus a little too personally:

> Now you see how life hard
> why you never send no money come-a-yard
> you wretch you, you spend the whole-a-it abroad
> squander your money, now ya living like dog

Yet the 'spend, spend, spend' doctrine persists, a hangover from life in the ghetto where there is no point in saving for a rainy day because every day is a rainy day.

'The problem', says Michael Andrews, deported from Britain after three years of stealing and dealing in Bristol and London, 'is that we grow up with nothing and when we get something, we don't know how long it will last so we use it THEN!, straight.

'When a man migrates, especially when he comes from a certain section of Jamaica, the life he sees – it's like heaven. I know many people who didn't even know a toilet until they came to England. One man who visit me said on day one: "Boy, that toilet is nice, for when it flush it bring you back clean water to wash your hand."'

When I met Michael he'd been back in Jamaica for five weeks and had just celebrated his twenty-sixth birthday. In England, he was feared and respected as a ruthless operator. He had money, a nice car, fine clothes and plenty of women. In Jamaica, he had nothing.

In a quiet roadside bar in uptown Kingston, his tongue eased by a near-endless supply of Red Stripe and Swiss-style pork chops, Michael told me his story.

'My experience', he says softly, 'is just an unlucky one. I have some family in England and my dad used to live there so my gran

said she'd pay for my ticket so I could have a holiday. That was
how it started. Just a holiday.

'I got there and saw it was a very different kind of living. Life
was nice and easy. I'd met a nice girl but after two months she
got pregnant. I thought to myself, okay, you've got responsibility
now – it was my first child – so I thought, why not stay? My visa
was about to run out but I wasn't thinking of marrying, I wasn't
even thinking positive. If I was everything would be okay.

'You've got to live, your family isn't going to support you for
ever. I was doing a bit of plastering for a guy, mixing the muck
for him, doing some skimming. I was learning quite a bit but
after a little while, the recession hit and the building trade was
doing nothing much.

'I was an alien. I didn't have a social security number so I
couldn't get any other kind of job. But I had to do something
to survive. One portion of chicken and chips is less than two
pounds, but when you can't even buy that, you feel bad,
especially when you've got a kid coming.

'The baby was only a few weeks away and I was suffering.
The girl was on the social but that money, that can't do nothing.
People knew I was desperate.

'I was living in Bristol and I used to hang around the
Grosvenor Road and the Black and White Café with a few
guys that I knew from Jamaica. Some of them used to sell
stuff on the front line. They knew I had nothing and one of
them said to me: "Come on and sell some weed, it's easy."

'I'm gonna be honest with you. The first time I went on the
line, I bought just an ounce of black hash. I didn't want to get
in too deep. But within the space of an hour, that was sold out
and I bought two more ounces and went back on the line. I just
double my money in an hour! At the end of that first night, I
went home with about two ounces of black, an ounce of weed
and three hundred pounds in my pocket.

'So I say to myself, YEAH! A few hours and I get this!
Come on, I going to do this full time. So I start waking up in the afternoon, going on the line, coming back at

six in the morning, sleep until midday then hit the streets
again.

'After about a month, life started to get nice. I start making
money, wearing pretty clothes and ting. The girl was all right,
we was ready for the baby. Everything was sweet.

'Then a friend of mine, his name was Squitty, he used to
deal coke on the same line as me, he approach me. And now a
bit of greed got caught up in me. I said to myself: "Why not sell
some cocaine?" The first time I bought a sixteeth of an ounce,
the smallest portion, for a hundred and fifty quid. I got on the
line at 5 p.m. and the first man that came up to me five minutes
later bought four grams. In the space of ten minutes, that was
sold out and I had made one-fifty on my one-fifty.

'I started dealing coke big time. Then I start cooking crack
and selling that too. I was making money, making money –
four, five thousand a week – but I still wasn't thinking. I had a
flash car, flash clothes, flash girls all over the place. I was living
up in Bristol but I would drive up to London to go clubbing.
I went to Maxim's or Nations, Night Grooves – I was all over
the place because I had money.

'And ting was cheap. A lot of people who smoke crack would
go out and shoplift and give you ting in exchange for drugs. I
got a Rolex for less than a hundred quid's worth of coke, then
I just sold it on for five hundred quid to a man that wanted one.
Other man would go ram-raiding and bring television, video and
hi-fi to swap.

'I got a piece, a Magnum three fifty-seven Python, and
I didn't even had to pay for it. I was driving with my
brother-in-law and some friends one day and the gun was
brandished. But as a rougher man than them, more ragamuffin,
I held on to it and say, "Hey, lend me dis."

'Then I'd be out there selling drugs and one of the guys
would come up to me and say, "I'm skint, man, give me a
bit of change", so I'd give them fifty quid. I was paying for it,
but on hire purchase, giving them a little money now and again,
now and again until they stopped asking and it was mine.

'Gun was a priority but guns with us was for niceness, not to kill or such. We'd be at a dance and a nice Jamaican sound like Stone Love would come up and we would take out our guns and salute and ting like that.

'But gun was for other ting too. I remember one time there was no coke in Bristol. None at all. I drove up to London. I had my piece on me. When I got there I went to see my friend Clive [a clothing-shop owner and associate of tailor Emma Grant, Tuffy's executioner] in Brixton. I said: "There's nothing in the country, man, I need some coke."

'So he sent me to a restaurant on the Atlantic Road, a black restaurant. I went up to the counter and said I looking for some stuff. The guy was a Jamaican, but he'd been in the country a long time. He went around the back and five minutes later he came back and told me to wait. I said okay, but then I saw a man come in and lean on a table to one side of me. I watch him and he watch me. But still nothing.

'So I took out my money and said: "Don't worry, I'm serious, man. I want some stuff, there's none in Bristol", and I see the guy's eyes light up when he saw the money. He was thinking Bristol is the country, so I'm a fool and because London is the city, he's a Don.'

(This is another hangover from Jamaica where any place outside of Kingston is known as 'country'. City boy/country boy jokes follow the same vein as Englishman/Irishman or Essex Girl jokes.)

'Fifteen minutes later, still nothing. I went up to the guy and said: "What you dealing with?" Then a second man come in and lean on a table on the other side of me. I was there for an hour and nothing had turned up.

'Then I realised the man was calling down his friends, trying to get a team together. He had sent word – come, there is money and a fool. But they were scattered and taking time to get there.

'So I just pop out my piece, point it at the man head and start talking raw: "You can't rob me. None of your friend can rob me. Man will die if you wanna rob me. You're a pussy, I'm a cold-blooded yard man . . ."

'Then they start to realise who I was and they start to respect me. They were saying, "Cool, everyting criss." I got my stuff. That is the closest I have ever been. I know in my heart they wanted to rob me. I would have been killed.

'But you see I had a bad rep[utation]. I have dealt with men they are afraid to deal with and they knew it. I was introduced to some of the Dons, Irish man. One man took me to his home and on the table in the living room was just pure coke. He say anything you want, just ask. If man mess with you, just come tell us and we'll eliminate them.

'People knew not to mess with me. I was in the Black and White Café one time when a lot of man was robbed. These people came in with balaclavas and shotguns and start taking people tings. I stood up and wait but no man touch me. At first I wondered why but later I found that because of the man I was dealing with, I had been branded. The robbers didn't want to get involved because they knew that somewhere down the line they'd get it back.'

Seemingly safe from other dealers, it was the police who finally brought the curtain down on Michael's world as he returned to a girlfriend's house one morning.

'I had a lot of women as well as my baby mother – I lived all over the place. I was at one of my woman's yard and I had just come back from the laundry – I like to wash my own clothes. I threw them on the bed and told her she should iron some. Then I heard a knock at the door.

'Now a lot of cops in the area knew me but didn't know exactly what I was up to, or I didn't think they did. Whenever they passed me by, I'd just say: "Look, it's the Bill", and laugh because of the television programme.

'The girl called out: "Who is it?" They called back: "It's the Bill." I thought Gaaawd! I was thinking what's this. I went to make my way out the back but when I looked out the window

I could see some men waiting for me. I knew I could never make it.

'The girl look at me, a bit confused like, then she opened the door. These men come in and held on to me and said, "You're under arrest, suspected of being an illegal immigrant and of being involved in drug trafficking."

'But these men were fools. They didn't bother to search the flat. I had an excess amount of cash, about five grand in fifties, twenties and tens under the pillow along with a large amount of drugs. But they never found them. My girl took the money and threw the drugs out once I had left. I was caught on the Tuesday and I was thrown out on the Thursday.'

Michael considers himself lucky. Although he lost much of his money, he got away without a jail term. He is now awaiting delivery of a fake British passport and plans to return.

Rather than arousing suspicion by trying to fly in directly from Jamaica, he will fly to Frankfurt, posing as a businessman, and then travel to Amsterdam where he will hitch a lift with a truck driver and come into the country via Dover. If everything goes to plan, he will be back around the time this book is printed.

His friend Squitty, who introduced him to the joys of cocaine trading, was less fortunate. Squitty was deported to Jamaica a few weeks before Michael. Two months earlier, he had stolen a considerable amount of money from a major London dealer. Squitty had little to fear in England and once he was back in Jamaica, he thought he'd be even safer.

He planned to smuggle himself to America and was confident that his enemies wouldn't track him down, but his friends knew the end was inevitable. They gave him a brand-new street name – Walking Death – and while Squitty prepared for his trip, they made plans for his forthcoming funeral. They didn't have long to wait.

On 18 February 1993, Squitty was gunned down on a street corner in Brown's Town. His friends chased after one of the two gunmen, a Yardie known as Dumb Dumb, cut his throat and left him for dead. The second gunman, a former army officer whose street name is Soldier, paid an impromptu visit to Squitty's funeral a week later, shooting dead Vincent 'Kevin' Maxwell, before hopping on a plane back to England.

Soldier is far from being the only international Yardie assassin in the country. When twenty-year-old student Richard Higgs was found shot dead in south London on New Year's Day 1993, the police at first thought he had been the unfortunate victim of some drug-crazed killer who had got the wrong man.

Higgs had arrived from Jamaica the previous June, had no known underworld connections or convictions, and had just applied for an extension to his visa to enable him to continue his studies. To all intents and purposes, the eager young student appeared to represent the flipside of the Jamaican underworld, a glimmer of hope for a new generation.

However, as the police began their investigation, a very different picture of Higgs emerged. It turned out that his move from Jamaica to London was not so much about broadening his mind as broadening his career as a hitman.

Following the suggestion of his Don, Higgs based himself in London and flew back to Kingston regularly to carry out murders of rival drugs barons. His name was also strongly linked to two killings in London the previous year.

Then there is Leon Virgo, believed to have killed at least seventeen people, travelling back and forth from his quiet council flat in south London to both New York and Jamaica.

When he was arrested, he had two genuine British passports in the names of Kenneth Smith and Kenneth Barnard which he had used to facilitate his work. Having been extradited back to New York early in 1992, he was tried for the 1987 murder of James Fernandez, shot nine times, and the killing a week later of drugs courier Tanya Lang. A further fifteen cases were left on file.

The trade in hired killers works both ways. In February 1991, Prince Morgan, Peter Griffiths and Owen Wiggin, all in their early twenties, were ambushed by armed police on their way to execute a north London dealer. They had flown in from Kingston the previous morning.

The ease with which members of the Yardies can obtain genuine passports can be partly explained by the actions of desperate crack addicts who happily hand them over in return for their next fix.

But the ease with which they had been obtaining indefinite visas for the USA only made sense shortly after the murder of Jamaican Marie Burke in her central London flat in May 1989. The sixty-three-year-old widow had been stabbed several times in the shoulder and neck with a six-inch knife while lying in her bed. At first, she was thought to have been the victim of a burglary gone wrong, but it soon emerged that there were no signs of forced entry or theft.

However, when it was learned that she worked in the passport division of the US Embassy, the investigation took a more sinister turn. Checks through the records showed that senior members of the Yardies had been paying £6000 a time to embassy officials to get visas stamped into their passports.

Burke was working in the department where six hundred signatures were checked, cross-referenced and processed every day – hers was the last counter-signature needed before the final document was issued.

What is not known is whether Burke herself was in on the racket. She may have noticed that something was wrong and been about to blow the whistle or she may have been the scapegoat when a visa for a top Yardie was not issued.

All that is known is that she herself was the victim of a hitman who made good use of the passports and visas she once issued. Glen Abdul had first surfaced in the UK in November 1988 when he attempted to murder Clifton Scott in a north London nightclub. Abdul himself was shot dead in Maxim's nightclub in July 1990 by another hired killer, employed to ensure that details of Burke's murder (which incidentally was organised by the same Mr A whose exploits are detailed earlier) didn't leak.

They needn't have worried. Two years later, visa restrictions for British nationals travelling to the USA were abolished, but in the light of such corruption of high-level public officials the 'disorganised' crime tag begins to look less and less appropriate.

Early in 1994, Scotland Yard announced a new thirty-three-point action plan based on a new intelligence-driven strategy which is intended to improve the success rate against crack gangs.

The undercover techniques, used for years to great success in America, include the use of fake pubs, clubs and brothels staffed by plain-clothes detectives in order to entice gang members into committing crimes under controlled circumstances.

One early example of these techniques being used successfully was Operation Motion, launched against crack dealers in west London. Undercover female officers posed as prostitutes and, at first, carried out small deals in the streets in order to gain the trust of the suppliers and their mobile telephone numbers.

A luxury flat at Heatherley Court in Westbourne Grove was then taken over and fitted with video cameras. The three women would then call the dealers and ask them to 'come and sort me out'. As soon as the deal was concluded, a back-up team would pounce. By July 1994 thirty-five dealers had been arrested. When confronted with the video evidence, all pleaded guilty.

Similar operations have been carried out in King's Cross and Stoke Newington and, with video evidence being seen as the way forward, chiefly because it eliminates the need to compromise informants, a special Scotland Yard unit has been set up to co-ordinate drug-dealing stings.

The use of such techniques makes perfect sense as, so far, the British experience of the Yardies has more or less mirrored that of America. While they are highly unlikely to reach the dizzy criminal heights of the Mafia or Triads, the indications are that the gangs are becoming ever-more sophisticated and growing fast.

A confidential 1993 report by the Bureau of Alcohol, Tobacco and Firearms (ATF), which estimates that the gangs gross more than a billion dollars each year from their operations, states: 'As the posses have become an established worldwide drug trafficking network and expanded their territories, they have increasingly recruited workers who are not Jamaican nationals but American blacks.'

The FBI has also identified the Jamaican Posse expanding their criminal horizons with increased involvement in extortion, loan sharking and kidnapping. There are also indications of increasing refinement on both sides of the Atlantic.

Wendell Daniels, for example, Britain's first crack millionaire, has so far paid only a fraction of the £662,000 of drug profits he was ordered to hand over after being sentenced to ten years in December 1992. He has boasted to fellow inmates that his investments and property interests are so well hidden that the authorities will never get hold of them.

Similarly, Alvin Appleton, who made at least £800,000 supplying crack to north London from his fortified Cricklewood flat, has yet to hand over a £400,000 forfeit after being sentenced to eighteen years in April 1994.

Appleton, who regularly deposited shopping bags stuffed with £20,000 in small bills in his local banks and building society, is believed to have laundered the money into offshore bank accounts in countries where no reciprocal policing agreement with Britain exists. Customs may know exactly where the funds are, but they are powerless to touch them.

There are also increasing signs of co-operation with other criminal syndicates. Ghanian drug gangs, with their access to thousands of expendable drug 'mules' and cheap cocaine (see chapter Ten) are becoming ever stronger.

In March 1995, Southwark Crown Court heard that, manufacturing crack using microwave ovens in their plush Park Lane apartment, Ghanians Chanda and Mariame Keita had made more than five million pounds in little over a year. When Mariame was arrested she was found with 5.5 kilos of high-grade crack – the biggest haul ever, worldwide. Chanda, aged forty, managed to flee, possibly back to his homeland, and is still at large. 'There is no doubt he is a Mr Big in the international drugs world,' said one officer on the case.

For many, such incidents are the inevitable consequence of Yardie involvement with other criminal syndicates and the mutual exchange of information and ideas which follows.

'They have reached the stage of their Mafia counterparts. They are operating in neckties and carrying attaché cases and seem to be holding high positions in legal and lucrative businesses which makes them difficult to link to the drug trade,' says Jim Moody of the FBI's Organised Crime Division.

And with the price of cocaine still two or three times higher in the UK, with prison sentences remaining shorter, and with no nationwide body tackling the Yardie threat, there can be little doubt that the British end of the operation will follow suit.

Chapter Three

As My Brother Does

The Asian Mafia

'Money is our god'

Former member of the Holy Smokes gang

It was in the early hours of 17 January 1993, outside an inconspicuous Tandoori restaurant on the Whitechapel Road in London's East End, that, following a boisterous but profitable Monday evening, the nightmare began.

Just after 4 a.m. the head waiter, who was outside the Mughal Brasserie retrieving a window box, felt something grab at his shoulder. But before Abdul Mirza could cry out, a rough hand was clasped round his mouth, he was dragged backwards and viciously punched and kicked into unconsciousness.

The three attackers dragged Mirza's senseless body into the restaurant, now deserted but for the two remaining staff. As they entered, waiter Azizur Rahman rushed to the aid of his colleague, but was felled with a single blow from a table lamp. The third waiter, Amirul Islam, was hit repeatedly with the handle of a mop until it broke in two.

The attackers ushered the battered trio into a corner and made them stare at the floor while they searched for the previous night's takings. One thug stood guard, brandishing a ten-inch carving knife he had liberated from the Mughal's kitchen. Each time one of the waiters moved, he slashed, repeatedly cutting first their heads, then their fingers and the backs of their hands as they tried to protect themselves.

The cashbox was proving elusive, so when Mirza regained consciousness the attackers turned on him. 'Where's the money?' they demanded. Mirza, a slight, timorous man, made the mistake of making eye contact with the knifeman. 'This bastard has seen me. He will tell the police. I'll finish him,' he screamed, slashing at the back of Mirza's head.

A three-inch-long chunk of scalp fell to the floor. The knifeman prepared to slash again and Mirza covered his bleeding head with his bleeding hands. This time it was a section of Mirza's ring finger, complete with nail, that fell to the floor.

Rahman looked on in disbelief. How could one human being do this to another? he thought. The attacker met his stare. 'You want to see us? I'll take your fucking eye out,' he spat, pushing the end of the blade into one of Rahman's sockets. The waiter is now blind in his right eye.

While the torture was being carried out, the two remaining attackers had finally found the takings which, combined with money stolen from the waiters' wallets, meant a haul of £1100 in all. The knifeman and another celebrated with lager from the Mughal's bar while the third thug sadistically lit a strip of tablecloth and waved it in front of Islam's face, threatening to burn him.

Eventually, after nearly two hours, the raiders tired of their game. They shoved and dragged the waiters – Mirza was by now unable to walk and was lapsing into and out of consciousness – into the tiny ladies' toilet at the back of the restaurant, jamming the door shut with an iron bar.

Barely able to use their hands, Islam and Rahman took more than two hours to force the toilet door open. The main restaurant door had been locked and neither had the strength to smash the glass. Instead, they crawled upstairs and slapped their bloody palms against the window until eventually a passer-by spotted them and raised the alarm.

Technically speaking, Rahman, who had lost nearly a third of his blood, died in the ambulance on the way to hospital. The crew managed to resuscitate him, but he died once more on the operating table, only to be brought back once again. Mirza's severed finger was found and taken to the hospital, preserved in a bag of frozen peas, but it had been left too long. Surgeons were unable to reattach it but replaced his missing chunk of scalp with a plastic plate.

It was four days before the three waiters were physically and mentally strong enough to be able to give interviews to the police and make statements. Each patiently explained how the three black men had attacked, robbed and mutilated them with such horrific brutality, choking back tears as they relived each and every awful moment.

As they listened, the detectives assigned to the case knew that they had to tread carefully. Tension within the area's well-established ethnic community was – and still is – high, with many, especially the young Asians, believing that the police do little to protect their people from the white racists and black thugs who prey on them.

Previous, seemingly similar attacks had led to emotional marches, protests, mini-riots and calls for government action to force the police to do something. In the weeks after the incident at the Mughal, familiar questions again began buzzing around the streets of Bethnal Green. How could such a crime happen? Why hadn't the police caught the bastards? How many others had to suffer before something was done?

The inextricable link between London's East End and racial violence dates back long before the arrival of the forty thousand Bengalis who now call the area home. Almost a century ago, tens of thousands of East European Jews settled there and suffered many of the same problems then as their Asian counterparts are now experiencing.

The situation was exacerbated in 1932 when, following his expulsion from the Labour Party, a certain Sir Oswald Ernald Mosley founded the British Union of Fascists – an ill-fated attempt to mirror the success of Hitler's Nazi Party in Germany. Along with his Blackshirts, Mosley embarked on a series of provocative marches, many of them focusing on the East End, where he and his followers openly incited and preached anti-Semitism.

One such march, on 4 October 1936, was intended to scare Jewish traders along Cable Street into moving out, but was abandoned after twenty-four-year-old Jack Comer led a gang of vigilantes against the fascists. Comer, who is better remembered by his post-war nickname of Jack Spot, felled Mosley's bodyguard with a lead-filled chair leg and became an instant local hero.

Over the next few years, there were many similar marches and confrontations, and the local Jewish traders fell happily into the habit of paying Spot and his many associates in order to ensure that their properties were not damaged. Handing over a weekly £10 to Spot and Co. was, by all accounts, the best insurance policy money could buy.

Support for the British Union of Fascists evaporated during the Second World War, but support for Spot grew. By the war's end, he was receiving hundreds of pounds in payment from traders each week. But the Blackshirts had gone and the traders were no longer paying to be protected; they were simply paying protection. Spot had made the smooth transition from good fellow to Goodfella.

A few decades later, the spectre of racial violence raised its ugly head once more. The protests, marches and attacks returned in the seventies as the National Front gained support on the back of what it saw as an invasion of job-stealing, benefit-claiming immigrants from the Indian sub-continent. 'Paki-bashing' first entered the nation's vocabulary in the summer of 1969 as gangs of white hooligans went in search of victims. For the most part, they found them easy targets, the first-generation Bengalis and Pakistanis in particular being mostly small and wiry individuals with little or no propensity for violence. But the worst of the problem seemed to be nipped in the bud by public outrage and extra police patrols in the area.

By the mid-seventies, the East End's Bengali community was just five thousand strong, a fraction of its current size but still large enough to inspire continued hatred from the far right.

As police interest in the area waned, so the number of attacks steadily grew, escalating early in 1977.

In June that year, after six weeks of sustained race attacks which had left several Bengali teenagers seriously injured, gangs of vigilantes took to the streets, providing unofficial escorts for Bengalis walking home alone late at night. 'The police are failing in their duty to protect us. Indeed, we believe they are discriminating against us,' said one resident, setting the tone for police/community relations for the next generation.

Over the next two years, the risk of casual racial attack failed to evaporate. Any Asian-occupied house left empty was likely to attract a brick through the window and a pile of dog-shit through the letter-box. But such was the antipathy towards local law enforcement, few victims even bothered to report such incidents.

Then, in the late summer of 1979, a gang of National Front supporters chased Altab Ali, a young Bengali worker, down the pavements of Brick Lane, eventually catching him and kicking him to death in the long-abandoned churchyard of St Mary's.

The spark had finally hit the tinder and the phenomenal anger the incident triggered throughout the whole community, and beyond, helped to drive the worst of the inciters out of the area. Support for the National Front floundered shortly afterwards, chiefly because their strong policies on immigration control and law and order were hijacked by Thatcher's Conservative Party, and, with the exception of isolated incidents, the area enjoyed a kind of uneasy peace.

But as the eighties progressed, the rise of the extreme right in Europe again sparked a revival in the UK, with the British National Party picking up considerable popular support, not just in the East End but also in Scotland, the Midlands and West Yorkshire, where other Asian communities had begun to make an impression.

This time, however, the anger of the racists was matched by that of the third generation of disaffected Bengali youth who rapidly formed themselves into a second wave of vigilantes in order to fight their oppressors. Tall, stronger and sassier than those who had gone before, this generation had seen their parents suffer at the hands of the thugs and were determined not to follow suit.

'One of my earliest memories', says Ranu, a Bengali living on the East End's Ocean Estate, 'is of seeing my father come home one Friday night covered in blood. A bunch of skinheads had spotted him coming out of Whitechapel station and started chanting "NF, NF". When he ignored them, they got mad and chased after him. He tried to run but they caught up and kicked him down to the ground.

'By the time they'd finished he needed eighteen stitches in his head and had two cracked ribs. I was only four, but I knew I didn't want to end up like that. Once I got older, I thought, If I don't fight them back, they're going to step over my little brother and his generation and then my children and it's going to go on. It won't stop.'

The new youngsters were nothing like their parents. They eschewed the traditional religious beliefs, indulged freely in alcohol and tobacco. They grew up strong and proud, studied self-defence and built up their confidence by fighting among themselves whenever no common enemy could be found.

'Ten, fifteen years ago, nobody used to bother, they just used to take it,' says Ranu. 'It's not that way any more. We are prepared to defend ourselves now.'

At first, support for the new vigilante gangs was widespread with traders, shopkeepers and factory owners happy to pay the youngsters in order to ensure that their properties were not damaged during marches and demonstrations. After each new attack, the vigilantes enjoyed a massive wave of popular support and were seen as the guardian angels of the community.

The threat did not fade. Incidents like the near-fatal attack on Muktar Ahmed, pounced upon by between twenty and thirty white men in February 1994 and beaten so badly that his head swelled up to twice its normal size, were all too common.

As the years went by, Asian youths were being ferried to

hospital and stitched up for stab wounds on an almost daily basis. Some felt it was the beginning of some long-awaited war. The truth, sadly, was that history was simply repeating itself.

A few days after making his statement and leaving hospital, Azizur Rahman, the waiter who had been half blinded in the attack on the Mughal, contacted the police once more.

'That first statement I made, I was lying,' he explained hesitantly. 'Now I want to tell the truth.' Slowly, Rahman recounted how, during the attack, the men had rifled through the waiters' wallets, picking out their home addresses, then forcing them at knifepoint to give their telephone numbers. 'We know where you live so when the police ask,' the attackers said as they left, 'tell them we were black.'

They added that if the waiters dared to tell the truth, they and the seventy other members of their gang would come to their homes during the night and beat up both the waiters and their families. The threats were far from idle. While Rahman was in hospital swinging between life and death, his brother-in-law, Hussain, had received several telephone calls: 'We have killed your brother-in-law. Now we are going to kill you,' they told him.

Rahman's second statement explained how the attackers and the callers – the men who had aroused such strong emotions in the community – all spoke perfect English, albeit with youthful estuary accents. It also explained how, like Rahman, Mirza, Islam and some forty thousand others living in the East End, they were not black, but Bengali.

The investigation rapidly changed tack and detectives discovered that the attack on the Mughal was far from an isolated incident. In the preceding months, there had been a wave of similar violent robberies at restaurants across the home counties in Sevenoaks, Hitchin and Tunbridge Wells.

Also, the previous September, four Bengali gangsters wearing balaclavas smashed their way into the home of a local travel agent and held his wife and children captive while they demanded money. The travel agent was slashed in the hand, buttocks and legs, the wife was assaulted, while one of the sons was knocked out from a blow to the forehead with a hammer.

Second-hand reports of dozens of similar incidents began to come in from all across London, but local police were unable to take action as the injured parties invariably refused to make statements or press charges. For a community traditionally seen as law-abiding, quiet in the extreme, even repressed, the exposure of this violent underbelly naturally came as something of a shock.

It also became a cause of great concern among those campaigning for greater protection from the racist attacks that remain a very real, very frightening menace. In Tower Hamlets, race-motivated assaults are being reported at the rate of one every day, while in other areas, such as Hounslow, attacks have increased by up to 110 per cent on some estates.

But for some, the threat from the gangs is now equal, if not greater, to that from elsewhere.

'Since the attack, we have received almost constant threats from the gangs,' says Abdul Malik, manager of the Mughal. 'They call up the staff at home, threaten their families and tell them not to come to work. They smash up their cars, vandalise their houses and most of them have been viciously attacked on their way to the restaurant. One of my waiters lives right in the middle of a gang stronghold. Twice, he has been beaten up on his front doorstep.

'Several times now, members of the gang have turned up mob-handed. They demand money, usually a couple of hundred pounds. They say: "You need protection, the police cannot protect you but we can." But all they are doing is offering protection from the other gangs, and even then if you pay one, you have to pay them all.

'They say if you don't pay, your windows will be smashed – which has happened three times now. My car, which I park right outside, has also been smashed. Other times they come in and eat and drink then refuse to pay or try to use a stolen credit card. I can't afford to let that happen. At least once, one of the gang had a handgun. My staff are all terrified.

'The truth is that most of the restaurants around here are in the same situation but nobody wants to talk [delicate enquiries reveal that local Asian-owned businesses certainly do seem to get through an alarming number of windows]. I'm the first person to speak out and tell everyone what is going on.'

So far, Malik has refused to pay, hence the repeated attacks on his staff and his premises. 'I have lost three other businesses, this is all I have left. My partner [one of the attacked waiters, Abdul Rahman] is not fit for work. His face has been smashed, his hand has been smashed. I have lost a lot of money on this place and I am still losing. No one wants to buy it because of the problems with the gangs. I'm here until my last drop of blood.'

On 17 September 1993, three Asian youths appeared at the Old Bailey charged with grievous bodily harm, robbery and kidnapping (reduced from attempted murder) in connection with the attack on the Mughal.

Detectives based at Bethnal Green police station had spent weeks staking out the makeshift headquarters of one of the gangs – an abandoned flat just off Brick Lane – yet despite the cost of such an operation, there was little evidence to support the case.

There was no forensic evidence, no fingerprints, nothing. And while the waiters identified the charged men on identity parades, the defence submitted that they had been shown photographs of the men by the police beforehand, making much of the fact that the waiters had changed their statements and descriptions of their assailants. All three were cleared.

For the most part, the East End Asian gangs are fair-weather concerns – *ad hoc* collectives of schoolkids and unemployed teenagers who come together on cool summer nights to bemoan the lack of recreational facilities in the area.

As one local solicitor puts it: 'There simply isn't anything else for the youngsters to do. There is no work around other than what's on offer from within the community – the rag trade or restaurants. If they can't get anything in these two areas, or if they have set their sights on something else, they often don't work at all. Even then, few of them move out of the area.'

(It is this same lack of recreational facilities, combined with insensitive policing, that has been blamed for sparking the riots in Bradford and which has led the Home Office to warn of an Asian crime timebomb about to explode in the UK.)

There are four main gangs. The largest and most notorious is known as the BLM or Brick Lane Massif. It is the members of this gang who are believed to have been responsible for the attack on the Mughal and the other restaurants, as well as a number of seemingly unprovoked attacks on white and black youths in the area.

The BLM, along with other gangs including the Stepney Street Posse, the Bengal Tigers and the Cannon Street Posse, passionately defend their territory, marked out with graffiti, both from one another and from visiting Asian gangs from other parts of the country.

When such fracas occur, they are generally played down by community leaders. For example, following two weeks of running street battles between rival gangs in September 1991 which led to fifteen arrests, a spokesman from the Brick Lane mosque insisted to the local press that the fights were simply kids mucking around rather than anything to do with organised gangs.

Similarly in May 1990, when community leaders in Birmingham were forced to call off the final day of a four-day festival to mark the end of Ramadan because of fights between rival gangs, they claimed it was merely high spirits.

Indeed, to most people reports of a few teenagers having a mass punch-up on a Saturday night is about as far removed from the notion of organised crime as can be. Even the attack on the Mughal and other restaurants, as vicious and cold-blooded as they were, can hardly be said to have heralded the dawn of an Asian mafia.

But to understand the significance of such events, one has to understand how Asian organised crime works and the specific role that the street battles fulfil within the overall hierarchy. For the shape of things to come in the East End, one has to look west, to Southall, where the mostly Indian and Pakistani community pre-dates east London's Bengali one by almost a decade and where the Asian mafia operates in its purest and deadliest form.

It was in Southall that the first serious racial problems were encountered by Asian immigrants, reaching a tragic climax in June 1976 with the stabbing of student Gurdip Chaggar by a white gang, leading to weeks of mass demonstrations, rioting and vicious, random attacks on whites.

But the first tentative clues that something untoward might be happening didn't emerge until May 1983 when local police received reports of a massive street battle close to a Sikh temple in the heart of the Asian community. Eyewitnesses reported dozens of youths battling it out in the streets, armed with axes, machetes and ceremonial maces, but by the time the police arrived, all had scattered.

Bar a few bloodstains and the odd discarded weapon, the detectives were left with precious little information about what had been going on or the reasons behind it. In fact, it would take another five years for the truth to come to light. As was the case in the East End, it all started with the best of intentions.

After the 1976 riots, a sizable vigilante group had formed and begun patrolling the streets to protect the community from the white racists. Most of the members belonged to a higher Sikh caste of Jats, a warrior race from the Punjab, and dubbed themselves the 'Holy Smokes', a reference to the connections their parents had with local temples. The vigilantes proved successful and, despite the threat of violence fading, continued to grow in numbers, taking new members from all parts of the community.

In the early eighties, a dispute broke out over the leadership of the group. Those from lower castes felt their interests were not being best served by the Jat leaders who tended to look down on them. Taking this ideology to its fullest conclusion, the lower caste broke away and formed their own gang – the Tooti Nungs – which roughly translates as The Worthless Ones.

Thus where once there was harmony and a common cause, there was now bitterness and rivalry. The 1983 battle was the debut confrontation, and from there the level of violence escalated over the next few years to incorporate fire bombings, kidnappings, shootings and stabbings, all of which took place with alarming regularity.

One series of battles was sparked off after an attack on a boy of fifteen who had ties to the Holy Smokes. He was cornered by a group of Tooti Nungs one afternoon; they slashed his face with Stanley knives and beat him about the head and body with hammers.

In a revenge attack, the Holy Smokes ambushed and assaulted a man who was believed to be a senior member of the rival gang and pierced his lungs with a *khanda*, a ceremonial pike. They followed this with petrol bomb attacks on the homes of two other suspected gang leaders.

The police were confused and frustrated. Firstly, they had no idea what these fights were about. So far as they could ascertain, there was no territory that was being defended; no drugs market that was being controlled; not even any religious differences.

Secondly, whenever they tried to elicit information, they came up against that stalwart of the organised crime game – the wall of silence. Nobody in the community would say anything about the gangs. Some of those approached feared reprisals, others had received direct threats.

By 1988, the situation was going from bad to worse. During one ten-day period in February, there were sixteen separate incidents, including several serious assaults. The street battles too were growing in scale, arranged for Saturday nights weeks in advance with forty or fifty combatants on each side.

At one such encounter in August 1988 which left several gang members crippled for life, fifty-three arrests were made, leading to fifty-three separate charges ranging from affray to attempted murder. However, none of those who had been injured would talk and none of the others could be persuaded to make statements. The police were forced to withdraw all charges and release the lot of them.

But slowly, as many in the community realised that the police were trying to do something about the rising tide of violence, information began to filter through.

'There was nothing concrete,' says Roy Herridge, a former Southall detective superintendent, 'just a few hints that we should be directing our enquiries away from the fights and towards a few of the wealthy, prominent businessmen in the area and asking where they got all their money from.'

Those initial enquiries led to the launch of Operation Shampoo which, in just over a year, uncovered something Herridge and his men would never have dared at the outset suggest might have existed: a crime network with a level of organisation and range of activity exceeding even that of far better-known gangs such as the Yardies and the Triads: a highly sophisticated organisation with more than two thousand 'soldiers' and dozens of others at higher ranks; with criminal connections not just all over the UK but also in West Germany, Belgium, North America, Canada, France and, of course, the Indian sub-continent; with interests in armed robberies, illegal immigration, violence, extortion and fraud. And all controlled from Southall.

Despite links with a strong cultural tradition and the deeply religious background of most of its associates, the Asian mafia has no formal joining procedure or initiation ceremony. Instead, membership is simply 'earned' by proving oneself worthy to one's peers and, once attained, can be passed on or down from brother to brother or cousin.

The structure is most akin to a series of concentric circles that provide three distinct levels of membership. The outermost ring – the lowest level – is composed of teenagers and sometimes children as young as ten, recruited by brothers and friends who are encouraged to gain status by committing petty crimes ranging from the theft of car radios to house burglaries.

Invariably it is the members at this level who become involved in the street battles which, despite the risk of serious injury or even death, are over nothing more than the honour of the gang.

According to Nasir, a twenty-two-year-old former police informer and associate of the Holy Smokes, there is no shortage of willing recruits. 'In Southall, everyone wants to prove themselves,' he says. 'But if they are not good academically or have a talent for some sport, the only way they can become a bigger man is to join one of the gangs.

'The older kids go up to the little ones in the school playgrounds and pat them on the back. They tell them they are big men and that they respect them. The kids love to hear that. Once you've told them, they will do whatever you want. Rob someone, stab someone, burgle a house, steal a car or get involved in a big ruck.'

(According to former members of both gangs, those higher up in the organisation started out encouraging the fights as they felt they helped to distract police attention away from the real activities of the gangs. But with the launch of Operation Shampoo, this approach was seen to have backfired. While the gangs still exist, the fights – in Southall, not the East End – are now few and far between.)

The next circle contains the gang members who do the bulk of the day-to-day work and earn the bulk of the money. Typically aged between eighteen and twenty-five, they range from unemployed strong-arm types, used to enforce protection rackets and collect debts, to educated business types who indulge in sophisticated frauds.

According to Nasir, as well as joining for respect, many find themselves in the gangs simply by association. 'If you live in Southall, you simply have to get involved with the gangs. You have no choice. If you have a friend who is in one gang and you're seen walking with him or talking to him, you're immediately put into a pigeon-hole.

'People will assume you're on one side or another and then the next time there's any trouble, you become a target. So you have to join in order to prevent yourself from becoming a victim.'

And once inside, the new recruit will be expected to contribute towards gang funds by indulging in a wide range of criminal activity.

The nature of these schemes and scams is constantly changing, largely owing to a desire to keep one step ahead of the police. But a detailed picture of the breathtaking range of criminal activity the gangs indulge in emerged out of Operation Shampoo.

For example, Detective Superintendent Herridge and his men found that some gang associates, using false names, had taken jobs with the Post Office where they could keep a look out for the distinctive envelopes in which cash and credit cards arrived. These would be kept aside until, a few days later, the even more distinctive letters containing PIN numbers arrived.

The cards and numbers would then be passed on to other gang members who would have at least two weeks of 'free' credit before anyone became suspicious. Most commonly, the credit cards would be used to put a small deposit on an expensive item such as a video camera, secured on hire purchase, which could then be sold for cash. This could be repeated dozens of times before the card's limit was exceeded.

Other gang members were found to have set themselves up as bogus insurance agents, raking off considerable commissions by arranging endowment mortgages for their bogus associates who would meet the repayments for three months (long enough for the agent to collect the commission) and then default, leaving the property to be repossessed.

This particular problem grew so widespread in the late eighties that the major insurance companies were forced to form a special department to deal with it. Around £2 million was believed to have been stolen in this way.

Then there were the gang members specialising in blatant rip-offs. A wide-boy would be approached in a pub and asked if he wanted to buy some cheap gold. A single genuine bar would be provided at a bargain price and the buyer enticed to a meeting where dozens more bars would be made available.

The meeting would invariably take place in a pub car park where the gangsters would arrive and first collect a sizable deposit, often running into several thousand pounds. They would then leave – telling the buyer they were off to collect the gold – but instead call the police.

A few days later, they would call the buyer and insist that he must have called the police and that, as a result, they would be keeping the deposit and did not wish to have any further dealings as the buyer clearly couldn't be trusted.

Gang members with the strongest family ties in India and Pakistan were drafted in to assist in a massive trade in human cargo, bringing truck- and plane-loads of illegal immigrants into the country. Typically, a 'client' would be unable to pay all the 'fare' and would have to pay off the debt by carrying out numerous illegal tasks for the gang once in the country.

The development of the illegal immigration division led to a need to provide numerous false identities which in turn led to the gangs developing a highly sophisticated forgery operation, capable of producing fake passports, driving licences and visas, as well as birth and death certificates, all of which only an expert eye could distinguish from the real thing.

Car theft was yet another fertile field, particularly among the young boy-racer types. As well as running networks to give stolen cars new identities and transport them around the country or abroad in a few hours, the more enterprising gangsters also took the opportunity to launch another insurance scam.

Gang members would take their cars to 'friendly' garages which would strip them down and dump the empty shell in a side street. The car would be reported stolen allowing the member to claim the insurance money. The car would then be reassembled and returned to the owner.

Operating on a less sophisticated but equally profitable level were the protection rackets. These were, and continue to be, widespread, targeting virtually all Asian-run businesses in Southall and far beyond. The best bandits in this field stuck to the golden rule of making sure that their threats were always very subtle, ensuring that in the unlikely event of someone calling the police, they could claim it was all a misunderstanding.

Often it was simply a case of two thugs walking into a shop one at a time, buying some low-value item and then giving the owner a long, hard stare. A third thug would then walk in and make a comment such as: 'Must make plenty of money in a shop like this. You wouldn't miss a few thousand pounds.'

This would be repeated every few days until a payment was made. Of those who failed to comply, some were badly beaten, others had their shops burned down or found that delivery drivers suddenly excluded them from their routes. The police suspected some small-scale rackets were taking place but the frightened shopkeepers refused to make statements.

The true extent of the enterprise only emerged when it tried to embrace Greenford off-licence owner Mohinder Parmar. A few weeks after the genial forty-five-year-old and his wife Jashan had deposited their £20,000 life savings in a local building society, two young Asian men walked into his shop and invited him outside to discuss a 'business proposition'.

Outside, in a scene reminiscent of some American fifties gangster epic, the back door of a large BMW opened and Mohinder was encouraged to climb in. As he sat down the subtle approach was consigned to history as a gun was pointed at his head.

'We are from Tooti Nung,' one of the men told him. 'You know how powerful we are. We want twenty grand. It is a simple choice. You pay us the money or we shoot you and feed you to our dog. We will be back next week. Consider yourself a dead man if you don't pay.'

Mohinder was terrified and drew out the money the same

day. When the men returned the following week he went to hand it over but was first forced to speak into a tape recorder, 'confessing' that the money was being given willingly in order to buy stolen gold.

It was soon after the men left that Mohinder decided to go to the police. He realised that if he did not, the gang would simply wait until his savings had grown once more then return. He was also worried because they had asked for the exact amount in his account. The gang must have had spies in the banks. He felt there was no one in his own community he could trust.

Three weeks later, acting on Mohinder's lead, police swooped on the homes of twenty-nine-year-old Jhamal Dhillon and twenty-eight-year-old Armarjit Sandhu. Between them, the pair had more than £95,000 in cash stashed around their homes. Both were later jailed for four years.

Occasionally, victims of the protection rackets would be used as outlets for stolen credit cards with the owners 'persuaded' to allow goods to be bought with bogus plastic. Sometimes this reached ridiculous proportions – an internal investigation by Barclaycard early in 1990 discovered that 86 per cent of all the transactions made at Roop Electronics, an electrical shop in Hanwell, were being made with stolen cards.

On occasions the shopkeepers themselves would receive some benefit. In one case, police began investigating a vicious armed robbery in Brixton where an Asian postmaster and his family had been raided by a three-man black gang who poured petrol over the wife and demanded that the safe be opened. More than £117,000 was taken.

Frustrated by a lack of clues, the investigation was quickly wound down. But six months later, the postmaster was seen driving about in a flashy new car. The case was quickly reopened and fresh enquiries soon revealed that there had never been a robbery at all. Instead the bulk of the money had simply been passed on to the gang with the owner keeping the balance as a bonus for himself.

But whatever the scam, venture or endeavour, the final

destination of the bulk of the money earned by those at the two lower levels of membership was always the same – the inner circle. Few gang members outside this élite earned anything more than pocket money for their efforts, yet the promise that one day they too might rise above the rest proved strong enough to ensure the utmost loyalty.

Operation Shampoo discovered that, within the Asian mafia, there is no single boss or overall godfather. Instead, the inner circle contains dozens of leaders, many of them highly respected businessmen, each running their own parts of the conspiracy.

Somewhat ironically, while at street level the gangs exist as rivals, within the inner circle there is total co-operation. Leaders from different gang factions would regularly hold meetings in cities such as London, Birmingham, Cardiff and Glasgow to agree on the scope of each other's operations.

But there are no twopenny scams or schemes being debated at this level in the organisation. Instead, all the money generated by those below is invested into the one area guaranteed to provide the best return of all. Heroin.

One typical, if somewhat inept, member of the inner circle was Barkat Kahn, a wealthy businessman and prominent member of the local community who contributed regularly to police charities and counted several senior officers among his personal friends. He even appeared in the Asian version of *Who's Who*.

Kahn came to notice when, during Operation Shampoo, a property developer was arrested for attempting to bribe a witness not to appear in court. Kahn was loosely implicated and as a result became the target of a sophisticated surveillance campaign comprising methods including video, telephone taps and long-range microphones.

Unlike his peers, Kahn hadn't mastered the art of delegation and getting the lower-ranking gang members to do his dirty work for him. Instead he trusted no one and preferred to do business himself. This proved to be his downfall.

Within a few weeks, the police had gathered tapes, film and video showing beyond any doubt that Kahn was attempting to arrange the import of £500,000 worth of heroin. Kahn had even gone so far as to meet the London-based agents of the Pakistani suppliers face to face. He was jailed for four and a half years.

The Kahn case also provided an insight into the methods employed by the gangs to bring heroin into the country. Much of the distribution was run by gang-owned restaurants. These are ideal because they have legitimate reasons to import large quantities of goods from India and Pakistan on a regular basis, have a high cash turnover enabling money to be easily laundered, and have extensive storage space where illicit items can be concealed. Best of all, nobody needs an excuse to go into a restaurant.

As for getting the drugs into the country in the first place, one particularly novel method came to light through the Shampoo enquiry as a result of telephone taps on the home of a member of the inner circle.

Female gang associates would travel to Pakistan for a 'holiday' and then return to Heathrow a few weeks later with a couple of kilos of heroin in their hand luggage. Once inside the baggage reclaim hall, they would go to the toilet and, using a key that had been provided to them, open the tampon dispensing machine and insert the drugs in the space at the top.

A few minutes later, other gang associates who had taken jobs as cleaners would go into the toilets and, using their own keys, remove the heroin from the tampon machines, hiding it among the bagfuls of tampons they carried with them.

The loophole was immediately closed, but up until then it is believed that around 10 kilos of heroin a day were being brought into the country by this route. It may have been running for ten years before discovery.

Kahn's conviction was one of the highlights of Operation Shampoo's climax which was reached during the second half of 1989. More than 150 arrests were made in Southall, Birmingham and West Germany which in turn led to nearly 130 convictions. Police also recovered close to a million pounds' worth of heroin, numerous forged papers, a variety of weapons including pistols and shotguns, and discovered twenty illegal immigrants.

Detective Superintendent Roy Herridge estimated that, between them, the two gangs were raking in more than £30 million each year. After the arrests, figures for violent crime in the area dropped by 50 per cent. 'But we still had a long way to go. There were dozens more leads to follow up and dozens more arrests to be made,' says Herridge.

Yet shortly after Kahn was sentenced, Shampoo was unceremoniously shut down for reasons that have never been fully explained. Widely circulated rumours of police corruption came to nothing and the reality probably has more to do with the bizarre internal politics of the Metropolitan Police which has developed something of a reputation for suddenly pulling out of operations aimed at a single ethnic group.

Since then, however, the gangs have returned. With a vengeance. In addition to the Holy Smokes and Tooti Nungs, there is a growing, mostly Muslim gang from Hounslow called the Apache who have recently appeared on the scene, while in Birmingham there are two newcomers: the Shera Punjab and the Panthers.

Nasir recalls how, in January 1994, an argument broke out at Thames Valley University between a bunch of guys from Southall and another bunch from Hounslow, all of whom were drinking in a corner of the student bar.

'One of the guys had some connections,' says Nasir. 'He took out his mobile phone, went to one side of the room and made a call. Within minutes, two transit vans had arrived and out of the back piled a load of guys waving guns and knives.

'The security guards at the university called the police and the whole lot of them vanished at the sound of the sirens, but it was frightening how quickly they got there and the weapons they were brandishing. It scared a lot of people but also sent out a message that the gangs are still around, still powerful, still a threat.'

As the gangs grow stronger elsewhere in the country, so other problems are starting to come to the surface. In Bradford, for example, there is a fast-growing petty crime problem among the Asian youth, something Detective Chief Inspector Brian Steele of the West Yorkshire police believes can be directly linked to gang activity higher up the scale.

'If you go back a few years, the number of Pakistani people involved in the drug scene was very small. The people didn't for the most part actually take the drugs themselves, it was just a business for them.

'They had the contacts in the producer countries and arranged for the stuff to be brought into the country. But now the situation is different. Slowly but surely the drug has begun to permeate into the community itself and there is an increasing number of street-level Asian dealers, and also an increasing number of addicts.'

A recent Home Office report, 'Drugs Usage and Drugs Prevention,' was hopelessly inaccurate. It found only one person in Bradford who had ever used heroin and no one who was a current user. But the director of the Bridge Project, a local drugs counselling centre, says his own internal studies have exploded the myth of Asians not using drugs themselves. And with the Asians now dealing, the future threat of rival gangs becoming involved in violent battles for the best pitches and sites, as well as turning to more serious crime in order to fund habits and buy into shipments, is something the local police are only too well aware of.

Twenty-year-old Javed, a gang member from Walthamstow, east London, has already spent three years behind bars after a string of robberies and attacks.

'I never wanted to get into this game. When I was fifteen, me and my mates would go to this snooker hall where the hard-boys hung out. Sometimes they'd offer us a spliff and make us all feel part of their gang, but eventually they got us hooked on heroin.'

From that point, Javed effectively became a slave to those above him who would order him to steal car radios, jewellery and electrical goods.

'If I said no, they would beat me up and stop my supply of heroin. But there were some good times. Being part of a big gang gave me respect. No one messed with me, not even the blacks because they knew I had back-up.'

But Javed's back-up vanished after another gang member grassed on him after a row over money. He was locked up in 1992 for a violent armed robbery on a petrol station.

There is also evidence that some of the more established gang members are now moving into other drugs. In Birmingham and parts of Bradford in particular, Asian gangs are even challenging the Yardies for control of the super-lucrative crack trade.

In April 1994, Azim Ahmed was sentenced to life imprisonment, with a recommendation that he serve a minimum of twenty years, for the murder of a rival dealer.

Ahmed, twenty-four, spent so much time hanging about with Yardie crack dealers he even acquired his own street name – Indian. In February 1993, he had been approached by small-time hoodlum Paul Baker who, along with a friend, had decided to open a crack house on Carrera Walk in Brixton.

But Baker had no cash and offered Indian the chance to put up the stake money in return for a share of the profits. Indian eagerly handed over £1300 but was less pleased a few days later when one of Baker's associates called to tell him the money had been lost in a mugging.

Indian, quite rightly, suspected Baker and Co. of having deliberately ripped him off. He and four friends went to Carrera Walk where a fierce argument erupted, culminating in Indian producing a handgun and shooting Baker in the upper chest.

But while men like Indian will continue to be caught and replaced by others, those in the inner circle of the Asian mafia, and therefore the driving force behind much of the criminal activity, seem destined to be left largely unscathed.

'We would love to have taken out the upper echelons but they had protected themselves by being distanced from the crimes,' said one detective who worked on Operation Shampoo. Today, many of the men are multi-millionaires, owning vast amounts of property and commanding the absolute respect of much of the community. Yet even they are merely pawns in a far larger game in which the stakes and the profits are much, much higher.

According to local law enforcement officials, the area is 'inaccessible' and nothing much happens there anyway, so they never go. In reality, while the thirty-three-mile-long road is often uncertain and at times just a few metres wide, the steady stream of camels, trucks and traders demonstrates that this definition is far from the truth.

The Khyber Pass is the most famous mountain road in the world, a sun-bleached gateway between Pakistan and Afghanistan and the main transit route through central Asia. This too is the source of around 30 per cent of the heroin on Britain's streets. At times the nearby growing regions, known collectively as the Golden Crescent, have been responsible for as much as 90 per cent.

The 'inaccessible' tag refers not to the quality of the road itself but to the quality of the laws governing it. While the area is undoubtedly part of Pakistan, it does not abide by its laws. In fact there is no law. Neither is there any police force or station or courthouse.

This seemingly ridiculous situation comes about because Pakistan is divided into settled areas which are under full police control and tribal areas in which virtual anarchy exists. Consequently, virtually everyone in the area carries a gun with ex-Soviet Army AK47s being the most popular choice.

Whereas criminals from the settled areas who flee thousands of miles abroad can be extradited, those who take refuge a few miles away in the tribal areas can live without fear for the rest of their lives.

Each morning groaning, overloaded buses take the heroin addicts and traders from the nearest town, Peshawar (also the provincial capital of Pakistan's north-west frontier), to the Landi Kotal market ten miles away on the edge of the pass, an area well outside government control.

At the daily bazaar, the trade, from smuggled soap and razor blades to East European guns and video recorders, is said to be 100 per cent illegal, all brought on mules over the mountains. It is prohibited to take any such goods from the tribal land to the settled area, but no one seems to care and the markets are constantly busy.

In the shacks and stalls, you can also find without difficulty cellophane-wrapped packages of opium and hashish. Heroin is a little more difficult to track down but is a bargain at 30,000 rupees per kilogram, roughly 5 per cent of the street price in London.

The Pakistani authorities lay virtually all the blame for the burgeoning heroin trade on the Pathan tribesmen who inhabit the lawless areas, but while many are doubtless involved to some degree, in reality it is those from the settled areas who control the business, often with compliance from the highest levels.

Men like Ayub Khan Afridi, a prominent MP, a close friend of the former prime minister and president, Nawaz Sharif, and a paragon of virtue, donating money to charity, building schools and medical centres.

Afridi's vast fortress-like home overlooks the Khyber Pass. While the surrounding mountains are dry and featureless, his home has exotic fountains and sumptuous gardens. Inside there are marble rooms lit by French chandeliers.

There is an underground bunker with enough food, water and ammunition to sustain a month-long siege. There are also anti-aircraft gun emplacements on the roof and firing positions for heavy machine-guns at regular intervals along the twenty-five-foot high, three-foot thick outer walls.

But the house is now empty. According to a confidential CIA report, Afridi is the 'biggest drug baron in Pakistan'. He is also one of sixteen people named by the Drug Enforcement Administration in extradition proceedings launched in September 1993 as ringleaders of Pakistan's heroin mafias. He is still on the run, believed to be hiding in Afghanistan.

In a chain of events similar to those that eventually led to the downfall of Panama's General Noriega, the authorities are turning on those once considered allies.

Many of the drug barons now being pursued were first hired by the CIA and Pakistani military intelligence to transport arms to the Afghan mujaheddin. They started bringing back heroin.

American anti-narcotics officials who were based in the area at the time, although they knew who was involved in drugs, say that they were told to keep quiet by the CIA who wanted no hiccough in the arms pipeline.

A blind eye continued to be cast over the growing drugs trade in 1979 when the Shah of Iran fell. That same year, the Soviet Army began its occupation of Afghanistan while a year later Iraq declared war on Iran. Thus, the two countries that for years had been the chief source of heroin for the West suddenly had most of their outlets cut off. The only possible way to get drugs out was through the Khyber Pass.

As a result Pakistan quickly became the main centre for the production and processing of heroin from the 'Golden Crescent', which comprises Pakistan, Iran and Afghanistan. This new regime also had a new range of contacts who decided to expand the market to incorporate Pakistanis living elsewhere in the world.

In the summer of 1979, a young Pakistani was arrested at Heathrow with a kilo of an unidentified substance concealed in his suitcase. The customs officers had never seen anything quite like it before. Neither had the government chemist who analysed it, who, having ascertained that the substance was a new brand of heroin, asked where it came from.

The smuggler had flown to London from Karachi so it seemed natural to assume that the heroin had come from Pakistan. But when customs officers sent a telex to the American Drug Enforcement Administration officer in Rawalpindi, a town in the foothills of the Himalayas, his reply was stark: there is no heroin problem in Pakistan. He could not have been more wrong.

In fairness, the trade was just beginning, but it grew rapidly.

In the first half of the eighties, the street price of heroin in London fell from £140 to £40 per gram while purity rose as output from the Golden Crescent rose rapidly and the links between the two countries grew stronger.

In February 1985, customs officers intercepted £20 million worth of heroin. When the courier and associates were arrested, the trail led directly back to Pakistan and a man called Mustaq Malik who had become a billionaire during a ten-year smuggling career. Prior to the seizure, Malik's palatial mansion in Karachi had been visited many times by a number of Southall's top traffickers, several of whom have yet to be apprehended.

(India too is now a major transit country for heroin, as is Sri Lanka. British-based members of the Tamil Tiger guerrilla movement have been heavily implicated in heroin trafficking. According to customs officials, the scale of their activities is 'similar to other groups who operate from India and Pakistan'.)

Under President Zia, who took charge of Pakistan after a military coup in 1977, the drug barons achieved a degree of influence in the society comparable to that of the Mafia in Italy and the cartels in Colombia.

Zia took international aid, often totalling more than $3 billion a year, to assist in eradicating poppy cultivation, but the most profitable fields were always those based in the 'inaccessible' regions which had the habit of surviving each new crackdown virtually unscathed.

Zia died in a plane crash in 1988 but the regimes that have followed have had equally little success in cracking down on the barons. Much of the reason for this is that many of the best-known smugglers, like Afridi, were MPs. According to the CIA, the two main contending parties – Benazir Bhutto's Pakistan People's Party and Sharif's Muslim League – are still infected with heroin money.

Pakistan produced 250 tonnes of raw opium in 1993 but also helped refine more than 2,000 tonnes from Afghanistan. The expected total for 1994 from Afghanistan is 3,000 tonnes, about

30 per cent of which will end up in Britain. With the heroin trade worth around $25 billion (ten times more than all Pakistan's total legal exports), the CIA has warned that drugs are 'becoming the lifeblood of Pakistan's economy and political system'.

The trade also threatens to destroy the country from the inside. Not a single heroin addict was reported anywhere in Pakistan before 1979. Today there are more than two million.

Operation Shampoo was a great success – while it lasted. Five years on, the situation is, bar a few refinements, mostly unchanged. Not only have the protection rackets returned, they have expanded across the country to other Asian strongholds like Bradford and Birmingham. Many of the original schemes and scams have also made a comeback.

'It's all still there but it's just more hidden,' says Nasir, the former police informant. 'Before the crackdown, the guys were a lot more arrogant. They would sell drugs openly; I even saw one guy selling them at a wedding. But now they are a lot more careful. They want the money but they don't like the idea of doing time.'

Most of all, the fear remains. In mid-1990, just a few months after Shampoo had been shut down, the spectre of the gangs returned with front-page headlines in the local papers following the bizarre death of Hounslow off-licence owner Mohinder Singh Cheema.

In August a young Asian man had walked into Cheema's shop on the Cromwell Road and, without a word, shot him in the stomach with a sawn-off shotgun, the pellets narrowly missing his kidney. As the fifty-four-year-old recovered in hospital, his sons told police how he had received death threats and demands for money for several weeks. But curiously, when police interviewed other nearby shopkeepers, they insisted that they had not been threatened themselves.

Cheema was released from hospital on 3 October and returned home. That same afternoon, another Asian man ran into the back of the shop where Cheema sat watching television and shot him in the neck. This time, death was instantaneous.

Talk of the gangs continued right up until late October when Cheema's wife Julie, her nineteen-year-old lover Neil, his friend and Cheema's son Kismet were charged with setting up the murder. However, the gangs weren't entirely innocent. The Holy Smokes were said to have provided the weapon and the gunman had definite gang connections.

Since Shampoo shut down, there have been at least five murders in London alone, all still unsolved and all linked to the gangs – for example, the death of Southall financial consultant Surinder Gill, found hacked to death in the back of his customised Mercedes in a field just outside Hounslow in January 1990.

The officer in charge of the case, Detective Superintendent Stewart Hull, said shortly after the murder: 'It was an execution. A ritual-type killing meant both to punish him and to tell others what happens if you do what he did – whatever that was.'

Despite being a supposedly happily married father of two, Gill was known to have been involved in numerous sexual indiscretions, some with married women. But a more likely theory is that his death was related to his work selling insurance and arranging mortgages. It seems a fair bet that someone would have tried to use his financial skills for money laundering, and he had either crossed those he was working for or somehow let them down.

The deaths of two other Asian businessmen, Raojibhai Patel and Baldev Hoondle, have also been linked to gang activity, which in recent years has become far more visible and even more violent.

In June 1994, sub-postmaster Bharat Mehta was stabbed to death at his Highgate premises during a raid. Three Asian youths were seen running away and were thought to have been captured on film. But the nearby traffic cameras which they would have passed turned out to be decoys.

A few weeks later, the gangs had expanded their remit and

were carrying out unprovoked attacks on whites across London. The 20 July edition of the east London local paper, the *Docklands Recorder*, carries four separate accounts of gang attacks on its front page alone, including one where restaurant manager Zahir Ahmed suffered a fractured skull after being robbed of £1000 by a gang.

At the begining of August, a seventeen-year-old white boy was kidnapped by an Asian gang while visiting Spitalfields Market. He was punched and kicked, threatened with a knife and made to telephone his parents to make a £250 ransom demand.

On the evening of 13 August fifteen-year-old Richard Everitt was stabbed to death by a gang behind King's Cross Station. It later emerged that the same gang had been looking for victims for some time and had wounded another white youth earlier in the day.

In a community used to holding on to its secrets, nothing can be taken at face value. Looking back, other incidents and murders initially dismissed as race-motivated may not stand up to closer inspection.

The attack on the quiet, well-kept council house at 28 Flower Dean Walk, Stepney, took place with all the speed and ruthless violence of a commando raid. If such an inconspicuous side street seemed an unlikely target for such ferocity, then the family who lived there were even more so.

Fifty-two-year-old clothing factory worker Waris Ali shared the three-storey house with his wife, their three daughters and his uncle, fifty-two-year-old Esmoth Ali, who worked as a carpenter – an extended Asian version of Mr and Mrs Joe Average.

Just after 9.30 p.m. on Sunday, 9 July 1989 there was a knock at the door. Family friend Muktar Ali Pir, who was visiting the Alis at the time, opened it and was immediately rushed by three men.

A gun was pushed against his temple and he was told in

no uncertain terms that, unless he did exactly as he was told, he would be killed instantly. The first attacker forced Pir into the sitting room and made him lie on the floor face down while his two colleagues raced upstairs in search of their true target, Waris.

As the knife-wielding intruders reached the first landing, they were spotted by the two eldest daughters, Ambia and Nazia, who were playing. Their screams as they rushed to hide under their bed brought Waris, who had been on the telephone in another room, out to meet his assailants face to face.

One man grabbed him from behind while the other held a knife to his throat. 'Where's the money?' they hissed. Waris thought he saw a chance and tried to grab the knifeman's arm but he misjudged it and the blade pierced his chest three times.

Waris fought on. 'For God's sake, won't somebody help me?' he yelled as the struggle became ever-more violent. Esmoth, who was on the top floor of the house, came rushing down the stairs to his aid but was immediately impaled on the ten-inch blade of one of the attackers. He collapsed and fell down the stairs, the knife having pierced his heart and one of his lungs.

Meanwhile the third attacker, who was still downstairs, had come across Waris's wife, Asia, and youngest daughter, Sajia. The gunman began shouting at her, demanding to know where the money was hidden, but it was no use. Asia spoke no English and could only stare back at him in blank horror. In frustration, he began beating her repeatedly with the handle of his pistol, then kicked the two-year-old child out of her pushchair and across the room.

Having collected what money they could find – around £1000 – the gang met up at the base of the stairs and decided to flee, leaving Esmoth dead on the landing and Waris collapsed on the stairs with a total of five stab wounds to his chest and back.

The father of three was rushed to hospital and had a kidney removed to save his life. However, he had suffered brain damage and immediately fell into a deep coma, unable to move or give police any clue about the nature of the attack.

Five days short of a year after the attack, he died without ever regaining consciousness.

The survivors told police that two of the attackers were black and one was white. This time it was true. A passing driver almost ran over one as they made their escape from the house and independently confirmed it.

The protests were immediate. The following Saturday, hundreds of local Bengalis staged a march in Altab Ali park, calling for police action to protect the community. 'Law and order is for all,' Aodul Gaffur, vice-chairman of the Bengali Welfare Association, told the crowd. 'We have paid for the police with our money, we have as much right to aid as anyone else.'

The atmosphere quickly turned sour, with some of the more youthful elements of the crowd becoming involved in running battles with the police. Riot teams were called in and there were twenty-five arrests.

A week later, with no significant progress having been made in the case, feelings were running as high as ever. The local paper reported the march with the headline 'The Day Anger Hit the Streets', while local businessmen announced that they had put together a reward of £5000 for information leading to the arrest of the attackers.

But there was far more to the lives of Esmoth and Waris Ali than met the eye. Despite their conventional appearance, the pair were heavily enmeshed in the underworld. A hint of their double life came shortly after the attack when, looking for motives for such an organised, brutal robbery, the police were told time and time again of the high esteem in which both men were held.

As one detective put it in a throwaway remark to a local journalist, such was the level of respect for the pair that 'they acted as a kind of bank to local friends, collecting money from families in this country and sending it back to loved ones abroad.'

In fact, the Alis were the heads of a sophisticated underground banking and money laundering system known as *hawala*, from which they earned at least £100,000 per year in commission.

Hawala, which means 'reference' in Urdu, is a system dating back at least a thousand years which relies totally on trust between banker and client. Originally, a merchant travelling overseas took with him a letter of credit issued by a *hawala* banker in his own country which would be honoured by a *hawala* banker in the other country. In its modern incarnation, a depositor hands over a sum for which he receives some token: half a banknote, a playing card or a picture. The banker then instructs his foreign counterpart to pay the sum deposited, less some agreed adjustment for currency exchange rates, on receipt of the token. Sometimes, bankers in different countries simply send a fax.

(A broadly similar and equally ancient system known as *chipchop*, *chopshop* or *chitti* banking is operated by the Chinese. *Chops* are personal seals while a *chitti* is a colonial expression meaning promissory note.)

The first generation of Asian immigrants to come to Britain brought the *hawala* tradition with them, using it to transfer a proportion of their salaries back to their relatives in Pakistan, Bangladesh or India.

Use of the system declined with the ending of foreign exchange controls in 1979 but made a significant comeback after laws on financial transactions were tightened up with the introduction of the 1986 Drug Trafficking Offences Act.

While *hawala* is still chiefly used for its traditional purpose, the system is increasingly being employed for the repatriation of drug profits to the Golden Crescent which currently provides some 30 per cent of the heroin and around a fifth of the cannabis on Britain's streets.

The system is ideal for money laundering: law enforcement experts readily admit that *hawala* transactions are virtually impossible to trace as they leave no physical record, a factor that has made the system increasingly popular. At an Interpol conference devoted to underground banking in November 1991,

Indian delegates estimated that the system processed between $10 and $20 billion each year.

The best estimates suggest that there are just over 1,000 *hawala* bankers in the UK with around two dozen thought to be involved in moving drug money. Most of the participants are based in outlets such as gold dealers, travel agencies, sub-post offices or import/export agencies, though some, like the Alis, have little or no connection with money.

Little can be done to curb such activities. *Hawala* does not constitute 'deposit taking' under the terms of the 1987 Banking Act and therefore cannot be regulated by the Bank of England. To date, no *hawala* bankers have been prosecuted as it has been impossible to prove that they handled money 'knowing or suspecting' it to be the proceeds of drug trafficking, though recent changes in the law may alter this situation.

The massively disgraced Bank of Credit and Commerce International operated a refined version of the *hawala* system. At its simplest, the bank arranged for a deposit in the local currency at one end and a withdrawal in a different currency at the other without audit trail or paperwork. More sophisticated versions were applied to the needs of the money launderer and the international arms trader.

In 1989, detectives arrested a consortium of six *hawala* bankers who admitted to having laundered more than £80 million each year. Another, caught after a long-term surveillance operation in which police watched as sacks of cash were brought into his house, was found to be dealing with around £8 million each week.

No charges were brought in either case as the police could not prove that any of the money was connected to drug- or terrorist-related activity.

Esmoth and Waris Ali were relatively small fry in the *hawala* world, dealing with around £20,000 a week. Still, like all those involved in the business, they tended to keep this side of their lives fairly secret, partly for tax purposes, partly for legal reasons, and partly for security.

Few people outside a circle of close friends and clients would have known what they were involved in, and even fewer would have known that most of the money was collected at weekends and therefore that Sunday evening was the ideal time to strike.

So while the men who attacked the Ali household were both black and white, the men who hired them and who, had they been more successful, would have taken a share of the spoils were almost undoubtedly local Asian gangsters.

The most persistent theory is that the Alis took a considerable deposit for some heavy characters and that the money never made it to Bangladesh. The robbery was their punishment.

Two months before the raid at Flower Dean Walk took place, another East End *hawala* banker and moneylender, Sao Miah, was kidnapped from his home. He was found a few days later bound and burned to death (such a fate is the ultimate disgrace for a Muslim, leaving little doubt that this murder too was Asian on Asian). His killers have never been caught.

Chapter Four

The 1% Crew

Hells Angels and the Motorcycle Mafia

'Three can keep a secret
if two are dead'

Motto of the Hells Angels Motorcycle Club

The dark-haired man in the scruffy leather jacket was calm but insistent. 'I'm really terribly sorry, officer,' he said softly, 'but I just can't say anything about that. I'll happily talk to you about something else, but not that.'

For Detective Sergeant John Snow, it was one polite refusal too many. He turned off the tape and allowed Andrew Trevis to go free. The pair had been 'talking' for nearly forty minutes and, with the exception of a new insight into the technicalities of motorcycle chain lubrication, the policeman had learned absolutely nothing.

It wasn't as if Trevis couldn't have been helpful. On the afternoon of Tuesday, 10 October 1992, two days before his abortive interview, the twenty-two-year-old biker had been sitting in the passenger seat of a battered C-reg XR3i outside Liverpool's Molyneux Way shopping centre with fellow Hells Angels Michael 'Long Mick' Rowledge and Stephen Pollock.

Trevis had been right there when, oblivious to the crowds of horrified shoppers, a young black man had run over to the car, thrust his hand in through the open window and, at point-blank range, pumped four bullets from a handgun into Rowledge's chest.

The assassin had worn no mask and made his escape in an open-topped car driven by an auburn-haired woman. Trevis, along with Pollock, had undoubtedly seen both killer and accomplice clearly and might even have remembered part or all of the getaway car's registration number.

Having witnessed the brutal execution of a close friend, any

normal person would have been beating a path to the nearest
police station to tell everything he knew. But then in situations
like this, members of the Hells Angels are about as far from
normal as it is possible to be.

Snow's interview with Pollock a little earlier that day was
equally barren, and it had been the same story when Detective
Superintendent Geoff McDonald made a visit to 'The Fort' –
the headquarters of the Wolverhampton chapter of the Hells
Angels where Rowledge had lived.

It started well enough. After the detective announced himself
on the intercom, a young biker emerged from the half-timbered
detached bungalow and unlocked the external steel gates. Then,
as surveillance cameras monitored his progress past the ranks
of parked motorbikes and empty beer kegs, McDonald was
led towards the main building where the steel-reinforced
double front door swung open welcomingly. Once inside
and settled into a corner of the makeshift bar area, he was
offered tea, biscuits and every hospitality. In fact it was only
when McDonald mooted the possibility of some of the Angels
accompanying him down to the station to make statements that
the bikers suddenly discovered the word 'No'. 'I'm sorry, but
we won't be making any statements. Out of the question. More
tea, Officer?'

It wasn't that Trevis, Pollock and the others were scared of
reprisals; it wasn't even that they had received threats or were
under pressure to keep quiet. Their reasons for silence were
far more profound – they didn't want to break the law. Angel
law, that is.

While biker gangs like to revel in a maverick image – hence
the 'outlaw' tag – and brag about their freedom from the
constraints of mainstream society, they enforce merciless rules
and regulations within their ranks and dish out fines, beatings
and expulsions for those who step out of line.

Nowhere are these byelaws more binding than within the
ranks of the Hells Angels. They may not be the largest outlaw
motorcycle gang in the country, but few argue that they are the

best organised and best disciplined – a factor that has made them the most formidable and most notorious.

Their exact code of conduct varies widely from chapter to chapter though some elements are common to all: Angels are forbidden to make any statements to the police, must abstain from using needle drugs, must not wear their colours – the distinctive back-patch logos – on public transport, and have to make weekly contributions to the club purse.

There are other, mostly unwritten rules that deal with the day-to-day business of the club: prospects – probationary members – must do whatever fully made-up members tell them to do; Angels must fight back when attacked; members who are out of town for some reason must make regular phone contact.

Insiders say that the regulations are designed to help keep order, maintain standards, and prevent information about the club's business activities being leaked. But for outsiders, they beg the question: just what exactly is it that the Hells Angels do?

According to its press spokesman, Ian 'Maz' Harris, PhD, the Hells Angels Motorcycle Club is: 'A loosely based organisation for motorcycle enthusiasts who own bikes of 750cc or more.'

The Memorandum of Association for Hells Angels Limited, registered at Companies House in October 1976, adds the following objectives: 'To foster, encourage and advance the sport and recreation of motor-cycling and to promote the acceptance of the ethical code of morality of the Hells Angels Club; to encourage, promote and hold race meetings, happenings, rallies, reliability trials, exhibitions and shows and give entertainments of all kinds related to motor-cycling.'

Indeed, each year the club's two hundred-odd members, along with hundreds more associates, attend a number of exclusive rallies and conventions, stage huge, highly profitable shows where customised bikes are displayed, and donate thousands of pounds to various charities. 'We are primarily and exclusively a motorcycle club,' says Harris. 'That is all.'

However, according to the police, the Hells Angels are a major international criminal organisation, a 'pure form of organised crime' who 'have accomplished in 25 years what it took the Mafia over 200 years to do.'

Each year, according to detectives at the National Criminal Intelligence Service, the club's members, along with hundreds more associates, manufacture, smuggle and distribute millions of pounds' worth of drugs, particularly amphetamines. They run huge theft rings which target high-performance motorcycles, extort money from dozens of businesses, and launder the profits through scores of seemingly legitimate enterprises.

At a conference on organised crime at the Police Staff College in Bramshill, Hampshire in May 1993, delegates heard that the Angels were a 'small but lethal' force and that when their activities are combined with those of other biker gangs 'there are indications that they could be involved in more killings and woundings than all other organised crime gangs in Britain put together.'

Interpol describes outlaw motorcycle gangs as 'one of Europe's fastest-growing criminal networks' and closely monitors their activities which were said to be extending into prostitution, armed robbery, and firearms smuggling.

Worldwide the two main US law enforcement agencies, the FBI and Bureau of Alcohol, Tobacco and Firearms (ATF), believe that the Angels and the other outlaw gangs collectively earn up to $1 billion a year from drug dealing, prostitution, gun-running, theft, extortion and murder.

In 1986 the US President's Commission on Organised Crime stated: 'Outlaw motorcycle gangs engage in almost every conceivable crime . . . They have been known to co-operate with La Cosa Nostra figures in their ambitious criminal undertakings.'

Not surprisingly the bikers disagree. They insist that the police are paranoid and that, because they live an alternative lifestyle yet remain highly visible, they are the ideal soft target.

'We're so prominent it's untrue,' says Dr Harris. 'We ride about on big bikes and wear patches on our backs to say who we are and where we're from – I mean, if you're hell bent on collective criminality, it's hardly the way to go about it. We'd all have been arrested years ago.'

Writing in *Back Street Heroes*, a magazine devoted to motorcycle subculture, Malcolm 'Taff' Evans, a long-standing Angel from the Tyne and Wear chapter, took the argument a stage further, blaming a desire on the part of certain enforcement agencies to justify their existence:

'The rather sudden removal of the [Eastern Bloc] threat to our national security has left 007 and Co without any specific targets upon which to train their skills . . . enter the Outlaw Motorcyclist, a ready-made public enemy number one with an unhealthy behaviour image.'

Harris agrees. 'We're not trying to claim that we're all perfect. Nobody ever is, but to suggest that we represent a significant threat to the peace and prosperity of Britain is taking things too far.'

So when, as happens periodically, Angels are arrested, charged and convicted of crimes ranging from murder and mortgage fraud to drug dealing and assault, the usual excuse is that the fact that their ranks contain a few bad apples doesn't make them a new Mafia. 'The club,' says Harris firmly, 'cannot be held responsible for the actions of individual members.'

'Michael was a smashing lad and we all got on really well,' Alf Rowledge told a local newspaper the day after his son's death. 'He kept in touch, but we had not seen him for a couple of months. I knew he was in with the biker crowd, but from what I could tell they were a good bunch of lads. I was never worried about his safety.'

But then even Michael himself had vastly underestimated the threat. Knives and coshes were found in the back of the car (Trevis and Pollock fled the scene and weren't tracked down until a couple of days later), so it seemed a fair assumption that the trio had been out to cause trouble, but had bitten off more than they could chew.

The obvious motive seemed to be a feud between rival gangs of bikers, but the theory didn't stand up. For one thing, there haven't been any bike gangs in Liverpool for decades and such battles rarely take place on neutral turf. Also, while Rowledge and Trevis lived at the Fort in Wolverhampton, Pollock was a member of the Windsor chapter and had travelled over from High Wycombe – even further afield.

The second problem was that the gunman was black. The Angels, along with most other biker gangs, are a stone's throw from being white supremacists.

In fact the chain of events that led to Rowledge's murder had begun some months earlier with the latest money-making venture by one of Liverpool's top family firms.

The criminal quintet, all brothers, are not only all heavily involved in the drug trade but are also immensely successful at their work, and hence, at the time, still at liberty. In the autumn of 1992, for example, the youngest member of the clan, twenty-three-year-old Thomas, drove a K-reg Mercedes and lived in a £60,000 detached house on the outskirts of the city.

The small house was, of course, just a temporary measure while he was waiting for building work to be completed on the £250,000 detached bungalow he had commissioned. Not a massively impressive lifestyle, perhaps, but not bad for someone who was ostensibly unemployed and claiming dole.

Earlier that same year, Thomas, along with two of his brothers, had made a substantial down-payment on a large shipment of cannabis from Amsterdam which was to be supplied by a veteran Dutch trafficker by the name of Lars who has a long track record of such deals.

Transportation and delivery dates had been agreed but then disaster struck – the entire shipment was seized by British customs officers during a routine check of a Dutch-registered ship docking at Manchester. Under the terms of the agreement Lars insisted that, once the drugs had left Dutch waters, they were no longer his responsibility, so the balance of the payment was still due. Not surprisingly, Thomas and Co., out of pocket as well as luck, refused to hand over a single penny.

With some traffickers, it wouldn't have mattered too much, but Lars was different. Before adopting his new identity, 'Lars' had lived in Britain (he is still known as 'English Bill'). He had been a Hells Angel. He had been used to getting his own way. And now he had moved abroad to help supervise the gang's drug interests, nothing had changed. With £140,000 outstanding, he turned to his former colleagues to collect.

The Wolverhampton mob were the nearest but had problems accepting the contract. Despite having one of the most impressive clubhouses in the country, the chapter has for some time been severely under strength – at the time when Lars called there were just six full-time members, the minimum needed under Angel law to prevent the chapter being 'suspended'.

Of the six, not all were available for any such 'extra-curricular activity' – one was on bail on a multiple attempted murder charge while another had been injured after a motorcycle accident.

For this reason, the Wolvos decided to cut the Windsor chapter into the deal with Lars. The precise terms have never been revealed but almost certainly involved 10 per cent of the total monies collected plus a preferential rate on a future drug shipment.

The bikers set to work. Threatening phone calls, leaning on associates, unannounced visits to offices – the standard debt collectors' fare was meted out, but all to no avail. It became clear that there was going to be a confrontation.

Further threats and warnings had passed between the two groups for a few days before the Angels arranged to drive up for a 'surprise' visit and show that they meant business. Thomas and his brothers were caught off guard, only learning at the last minute that the Angels had arrived.

Witnesses report seeing a car-load of 'biker types' on one

side of the street having an animated argument with a group of men parked on the other side of the road before both cars drove off.

Thanks to Pollock and Trevis keeping their vow of silence, assessing exactly what happened next involves some speculation. It seems that the brothers finally agreed to pay up. 'We'll meet you outside the shopping centre in Old Roan in twenty minutes,' they told the bikers. The Angels got there early. Rowledge was dead on arrival.

Long Mick was vice-president of the Wolverhampton chapter. He was also a family man, leaving a wife, Denise, and two young children. But after his death, the Angels had more pressing considerations. The carefully nurtured image of invincibility generated from years of outrageous violence – the hard-won philosophy of 'don't fuck with us, we're the Hells Angels' – had all been destroyed.

The legend had been born on 17 March 1948 when World War II veteran Otto Friedli formed a new bike gang out of the remnants of two notorious fighting and drinking clubs – the Boozefighters and the Pissed Off Bastards of Bloomington. Both had disbanded after a riot the previous summer in which they took over the small town of Hollister, California during a drag racing meeting organised by the American Motorcycling Association. The AMA later pronounced that only 1 per cent of bikers were troublemakers. Outlaw gangs have worn '1%' patches ever since.

Basing himself in San Bernadino, Friedli adopted a name favoured by fighter pilots – Hell's Angels – structured the gang along military lines and continued the theme on the gang's crest: a grinning winged death's head wearing a pilot's helmet. (Friedli's seamstress forgot to include the apostrophe and it has been officially omitted ever since.)

The drinking and fighting tradition was maintained, hyped up by the 1953 release of *The Wild One* (based loosely on the Hollister incident), but it wasn't until 1964 when four US

Angels were falsely accused of rape that the club first made headlines state to state.

The first British chapter of the Hells Angels was formed in London in mid-1969, a few months before Angels who had been hired to guard the Rolling Stones concert at Altamont stabbed to death a black spectator who had allegedly pulled a gun on one of their number. For years the Angels reportedly had a contract out on the life of Mick Jagger, who they say failed to support them after the killing. Dubious FBI intelligence suggests that the contract was terminated after the Stones paid the Angels $50,000.

The British Angels themselves became the ultimate tabloid enemies of the people in late 1972 when eighteen-year-old Ian Everest, along with two others, abducted a fourteen-year-old Girl Guide off the streets of Winchester and dragged her along to an Angel party where he raped her in front of cheering clubmates. The girl told the court that Everest had laughed throughout the assault.

Sentencing him to nine years, Mr Justice Waller launched a thousand tabloid shock-horror headlines, telling him: 'We have heard of Hells Angels as an utterly evil organisation, evil and corrosive of young people. I do not sentence you for being Hells Angels, but no doubt the evil nature of that organisation has led you into this situation.'

Every few years, something new happened to keep the image alive, often helped by the media's inability to tell the Hells Angels apart from other gangs. In 1980 a group of Angels ambushed members of the 'bootleg' Windsor chapter and shot its leader, Richard Sharman, in the head three times. He survived.

(The Windsor chapter was originally started by local rockers and had never applied for an official charter. They were finally accepted into the fold in 1985 shortly after one of their members, John Mikklesen, died in police custody. The fact that Mikklesen was black – an Angel taboo – had played a part in the club failing to be sanctioned earlier.)

In 1983 a Hells Angels party in Cookham ended in violence after a fight broke out in a queue where bikers were lining up to gang-rape a woman who had been staked out in a corner of a tent. The ensuing battle, chiefly between six members of the Road Rats and twenty-four members of the Satan Slaves, involved axes, knives, guns and chains.

Two Rats were killed but the remaining four fought on, stabbing and beating the Slaves and eventually herding around twenty into an old barn. They had just managed to set the building alight when the Angels intervened, wanting to know what was being done for the dead and injured.

Two years later, the Angels made headlines again after terrorising a family living next door to the Windsor clubhouse. The bikers famously held axe-throwing competitions and, after complaints, first offered to buy the family out, then changed their minds. 'They had a meeting and we could hear them deciding it would be easier to kill us. They were shouting "kill them, kill them",' said Pat McSorley. The family decided to move.

But with Rowledge's death, the notion that the Angels were the ultimate hell-raisers was open to question. It was part of a downward spiral that had begun two years earlier when a group of Angels from Lea Valley chapter, who at the time were chaperoning the visiting president of a German chapter, got into an argument with a group of Luton Town's designer football hooligans – the Men In Gear.

The battle took place in the Blockers Arms public house on Hightown Road in Luton in May 1990. Other drinkers ran for cover as both sides made vicious use of chairs and broken glasses, but it was the MIGs who quickly gained the upper hand and forced the Angels, many of them badly injured, in particular their German guest who had suffered a fractured skull, to make a hasty retreat.

Retribution seemed inevitable and Luton's police prepared themselves. Undercover officers were assigned to stalk the key players on both sides and the next eight weekends were spent on red alert with riot teams and firearms units on twenty-four-hour stand-by. The Angels duly put on an impressive show of strength, wearing their colours and riding their bikes in ominous formation up and down the streets where the MIGs lived. But the bloodbath never came.

'We were certain that the Angels would try to get back at the MIGs,' says Superintendent Ralph Miller, 'but the whole thing just seemed to fizzle out. It wasn't what we expected to happen at all.'

In fact, what had happened was that the MIGs had clubbed together and paid the Angels £2,000 'compensation' for having beaten them, rather than face the continued threat of ultra-violent reprisals. Business had been allowed to take the place of 'pleasure'.

For this reason, and the fact that the Angels lost in the first place, the battle of the Blockers Arms was seen by many as the first sign of change. The Hells Angels, once the most notorious and anarchistic of biker gangs, had come of age. The carefree biker boys of the sixties and seventies had grown into astute businessmen and taken their club with them.

The Hells Angels of the nineties sit at the top of a sizable commercial enterprise comprising four limited companies, property holdings, and fiercely defended copyright interests. Worldwide, the Angels have more than six million pounds spread throughout numerous bank accounts and a plethora of business interests. When today's Angels ride out, they make loot, not war.

But rival bike gangs aren't at all impressed. They saw the battle with the MIGs as proof that the Angels were getting soft, and concluded that, if ever there was an ideal time to take them out, this was it.

A sizable chunk of the lucrative outlaw biker criminal enterprise was ripe for the picking, but even the best established rival gangs were no match for the Angels. Yet something had to be done, something had to give.

Albert Road is a quiet street of tall Edwardian terraced houses in a well-to-do Birmingham suburb. Talk to the residents about the wild young men who live at number 156 and you'll hear nothing but praise. 'Lovely chaps,' says the grey-haired woman who runs the grocer's a few doors along. 'Never any trouble, always polite. Very nice boys.'

But the hospitality goes only so far. Casual visitors are not welcome and the denim-clad figure who opened the heavy steel-reinforced front door to me could only manage a terse 'No comment, so fuck off.'

Yet for the first few hours after Rowledge's death, before common sense had seen off the 'biker feud' theory, it was here that the finger of blame was pointed.

The men at number 156 are members of the Cycle Tramps, the only remaining representatives of Birmingham's outlaw biker scene which fifteen years earlier had supported six or seven others, including the Outcasts, the 69s, and the Satans Slaves.

Despite dwindling numbers, the Cycle Tramps had still managed to get themselves barred from most of Birmingham's pubs and had put fear into the hearts of most landlords. The fact that there were no real (legitimate) bikers' pubs in the city centre was widely put down to the fact that the Tramps had wrecked them all.

The now-defunct *Second City Biker* magazine also clashed with the gang when the editor put an ad in one issue asking for someone to do a column on the outlaw gangs. He received threatening telephone calls and promptly dropped the idea.

While the majority of recent rows around Albert Road have taken place between fellow gang members, the Cycle Tramps have, for as long as anyone can remember, also been involved in a vicious feud with the Wolverhampton chapter of the Angels which, over the years, has seen dozens of assaults, a couple of stabbings, and a handful of rumbles.

For a short while, it all fitted neatly into place. In the early evening of 23 March 1992, five months before Rowledge was killed, there had been a drive-by shooting outside the Cycle

Tramps' HQ as two members and their girlfriends emerged and climbed into a waiting car.

At least twelve shots were fired from a passing stolen BMW, wounding one of the men and both women. Just two weeks before Rowledge's last stand, a prospective member of the Wolvos had been arrested and charged with four counts of attempted murder.

It was a convenient theory, but completely wrong. The events were totally unconnected. The Cycle Tramps were certainly planning to take their revenge on the Angels (whom they still blamed for the shooting, despite the prospect later being acquitted) but in a very different way.

Shortly after the March shooting, intelligence officers with the West Midlands police noticed that the Tramps were spending less time at their own clubhouse and more time on the road visiting other, supposedly rival gangs. These were not the usual inter-club fracas but sedate, social engagements. More puzzling still was the choice of company.

The Tramps were tracked as they travelled to Leicester to visit the Ratae and then to Leamington Spa to visit the Pagans. This made no sense at all as, six years earlier, these last two gangs had fought a bitter six-day war which had driven a wedge between them even greater than that between the Tramps and the Angels.

It began early in May 1986 with a series of raids by Pagans on members of the Ratae deemed to be 'living on their territory' – two in north Warwickshire and one in Leicestershire.

Two days later, more than thirty members of the Ratae and reinforcements from Humberside and Norfolk drove in twelve vans to the Pagans' headquarters in Leamington Spa, Warwickshire and laid siege.

After a brief stand-off, the quiet street was engulfed in flames as both sides threw petrol bombs and the clubhouse began to burn. Shotgun blasts rang out and a team of Ratae 'commandos' made a frontal assault, firing a gun through the front door before storming the building.

The first two to enter made it only as far as the hall before they were beaten back by knife- and sword-wielding Pagans. One was scalped Red Indian-style while the other was stabbed in the neck, but both survived and the Ratae withdrew. By the time the police arrived they met an all-too-familiar response: no one had heard or seen anything.

Three days later the Pagans visited Brackley, Northampton-shire and attacked the home of the then vice-president of the Ratae, who kept his attackers at bay using repeated blasts of a .410 shotgun. One of his attackers fired back with a weapon of his own but accidentally hit fellow Pagan Stephen 'the Rabbi' Brookes, killing him.

The death resulted in a major police initiative, Operation Biker, which reached an apex a few months later when 150 officers from three forces carried out a series of dawn raids. Nine Pagans were eventually convicted of manslaughter, eight Ratae were convicted of conspiracy to cause grievous bodily harm.

Yet in 1992, when the Cycle Tramps visited the two gangs, the rifts of the past were quickly forgotten and representatives of all three clubs travelled to Derby to visit another gang.

The Road Tramps run the Rock and Blues Custom Show held each June, the largest event of its kind in the north of England. The show has been going since 1985 and has become well respected and a solid money-spinner.

The Road Tramps, like their cycling namesakes, had been in dispute with the Wolverhampton Angels who, ever anxious to boost their income, had expressed an interest in taking over the Rock and Blues show, with or without the Road Tramp's blessing.

A few weeks before the opening of the show on 31 July 1992, the Derby police received a tip-off that the Hells Angels would mount an attack at some point during the proceedings. The police promptly forbade the Road Tramps to allow any Angels on site and unwittingly cleared the way for the most crucial development in the biker war to proceed unhindered.

A few hours after the show had opened, members of the Road

Tramps, Cycle Tramps, Pagans, Ratae and several other gangs, including the Stafford Eagles and the Road Runners, appeared and slipped on new jackets.

Emblazoned on the back were new colours never before seen. The logo was a skull with a kind of Indian headdress made up of different coloured feathers. One was blue and white – the colours of the Pagans. Another was red and blue – the Road Tramps – and yet another red and yellow – the Cycle Tramps. There were seven feathers in all, each representing a different gang.

Photographers were kept at a discreet distance but other observers quickly appreciated that the supposed rivals had come together and formed a new gang – the Midland Outlaws.

The Wolvos felt rightly threatened. The Outlaws have around 150 members with dozens more associates – virtually the same as the number of Hells Angels in the UK, let alone in the north-west.

On 8 August, one week after the show, there was a bungled attempt to nip the new alliance in the bud. A former member of the Cycle Tramps narrowly avoided death after answering a knock on his door.

As he walked down the hall, someone pushed the barrel of a sawn-off shotgun through the letter-box and fired. He survived and has since been rehoused for his own safety.

Two weeks later, at the Bulldog Bash, the largest biker show in the country and the jewel in the Hells Angels' commercial crown, two Angels kidnapped a member of a neutral outlaw gang who was known to be friendly with members of the Midland Outlaws. He was tortured until he told everything he knew about their reasons for forming and their plans for the future. Members of the Outlaws smiled when they heard. They had achieved their aim – the Angels were already running scared – and they had yet to play their trump card.

At first it was believed that the new gang had formed simply to protect themselves and had no interest in challenging the Angels. But during that August, Interpol tracked several members of the Texas-based Bandidos entering Britain and visiting the new gang.

The Bandidos are one of the world's fastest-growing outlaw clubs whose battles abroad have been characterised by extreme violence. Sometimes referred to as the Bandido Nation, they currently 'own' southern France – their battles with French Hells Angels regularly involve machine-guns and bombs – and are expanding across the rest of Europe.

While other outlaw bikers persist in describing themselves as clubs, the Bandidos make no bones about it. Their colours, which depict a gun- and machete-toting Mexican cartoon character, clearly state they are an MG – motorcycle gang. Their motto is equally brash – 'We're the people our parents warned us about'.

Internationally, the only other gang that causes the Hells Angels real concern is, somewhat confusingly, called the Outlaws and currently has upwards of forty chapters, mostly in America and Australia. They too have a no-nonsense motto – 'God forgives, Outlaws don't' – and their colours are a close copy of those worn by Marlon Brando in *The Wild One*, depicting a skull sitting above a pair of crossed pistons.

In 1974, three Hells Angels were brutally murdered by two Outlaws in Chicago, starting a feud that continues to this day. However, the Outlaws and the Bandidos have a non-aggression pact stretching back to 1980. Members often tattoo themselves with the other club's colours and refer to themselves as 'sister' organisations. In August 1994, a delegation of the Midland Outlaws travelled over to Daytona, Florida to attend a biker convention hosted by the Outlaws.

Now the Angels really had something to worry about. Not only had a new and powerful gang formed right under their noses, but the Midland Outlaws also appeared to be 'prospecting' to join the ranks of one or both of the Angels' worst enemies.

This kind of *en masse* membership is usually granted after a gang proves itself 'worthy' of wearing the desired colours.

Exactly what this proof entails is not known, though a major attack or act of violence will often suffice. The Rowdies Motorcycle Club in Trondheim, for example, spent ten years hoping to be granted a charter to enable them to become the first Hells Angels in Norway. Then, in July 1989, they launched a vicious knife and chain attack on a rival club. Two weeks later, they received their charter from the Angels' American headquarters.

But the Angels aren't just concerned about a potential wave of violence. The Bandidos and Outlaws are just as heavily involved in the same criminal activities that members of the Angels use to line their pockets. For twenty-five years Britain has been a virtual monopoly. Now for the first time there is serious competition. And as far as the Angels are concerned, that just has to be bad for business.

A criminal record is a lousy indicator of criminality. Al Capone may have shot a man dead at point-blank range in a crowded bar, but he was only ever sent down for tax evasion; John 'Teflon Don' Gotti walked three times before the Feds made the charges stick; Rodriguez Orejuela, of the Cali cocaine cartel, didn't even have a parking conviction; while the late Jim Brown, founder of the Shower Posse, had been acquitted of fourteen separate murder charges.

The key is to put as much distance as possible between the crime and the criminal. As Canadian author and biker expert Yves Lavinge puts it, the outlaw gangs may have learned the finer points of raising hell by watching Marlon Brando in *The Wild One*, but they learned the finer points of running an organised crime empire by watching Brando in *The Godfather*.

The best students have undoubtedly been the Angels. 'They practice anti-surveillance as a matter of course,' notes one detective assigned to keeping tabs on their activities. 'When they leave the clubhouse, they do it in pairs. The first two go to the left; the second two to the right; the third pair do a complete lap.'

Many chapters appoint security/intelligence officers but scoff at law enforcement suggestions that they use women to infiltrate telephone companies and government offices in order to access privileged information. Nonetheless, the quality of their internal intelligence service is without question.

When, in February 1991, Interpol launched Project Rockers, a major intelligence operation looking into the activities of biker gangs, the Lyon-based secretary general sent a confidential communiqué to the heads of the European area offices along with those in Australia, Canada and New Zealand explaining how the information would be gathered.

The bureaus were also sent a number of Organised Crime Bulletins, outlining relevant cases and recent developments in the outlaw biker field along with a calendar of events in order to help identify new clubs and associates.

Senior Interpol officials were stunned, to say the least, when the supposedly secret documents were plastered over three pages of the Angel-run monthly magazine *Heavy Duty*. But for many who had worked the biker gang field for some years, it came as no surprise.

When Hampshire police raided the Southampton chapter of the Angels, they found copies of their own confidential reports on the gang tucked away in a corner of the clubhouse. Elsewhere in the country, local detectives specialising in keeping tabs on the gangs have come across long-range surveillance pictures of themselves tacked up on clubhouse walls.

In Berkshire, a local gang hoping to impress the Angels attempted to bribe a traffic warden (who had access to police headquarters) into obtaining the home address of a local detective who had been deemed to be paying too much attention to the biker scene.

When it comes to dealing drugs, the gangs are super-cautious, rarely carrying the product themselves and preferring to bury it then tell customers where to go to find it.

One speed dealer/addict supplied by the Angels complained to police how they regularly drove him half mad with his weekly delivery. Having deposited the money earlier in the day at a 'safe' drop zone, they would call him in the early hours of the following morning and simply tell him: 'It's in your garden.' The dealer's neighbours reported how he could regularly be seen in his underpants at 4 a.m. with a torch and spade, digging frantically.

One police surveillance team recently followed a pair of Angels (who, naturally, were not wearing their colours) to a local park where they sat about for two hours feeding the ducks and exchanging pleasantries with passers-by before leaving.

It was only later that it emerged that the two had been supervising the pick-up of a kilo of amphetamine. The drugs had been concealed in a rubbish bin earlier in the day and the Angels were there to ensure that no one but their customer picked it up.

Similarly, when Angel James Lyon was stopped on his bike during a routine check, he was found to have half an ounce of speed in his glove. He later admitted that the only reason he had been caught was because he had been to make a sale which had fallen through and he couldn't be bothered to take the gear back to the club stash site.

The biker gangs protect themselves from police 'buy and bust'-style sting operations by restricting themselves to selling to those on a list of 'approved' customers. Particular deals are generally co-ordinated and run by individual bikers using a few associates. That way, if they are caught, the whole club isn't implicated.

(As well as being highly refined and careful, the drug-dealing Angels are also innovative. During the mid-eighties a batch of speed appeared from the Netherlands which was at least twice normal strength but, owing to a mistake in the production process, had a distinctive pink tinge.

Dubbed 'Pink Champagne', the stuff sold like hot cakes at a premium price and the Angels were quick to cash in, mixing their own poor-quality speed with strawberry-flavoured Nesquik powder in order to pass it off as the top brand!)

The drugs themselves are either smuggled in from abroad or manufactured in 'franchised' clandestine laboratories like the one discovered in July 1993, in a secluded cottage in Kent, along with sufficient chemicals to produce a ton of the pure form of the drug with an estimated street value exceeding £70 million.

Speed is now the second most popular drug in the UK, behind cannabis. Its sharp increase in popularity is due to its low cost (about £15 a gram), the fact that it lasts longer than cocaine, and that it is more reliable that Ecstasy. Business is booming to the point where the Angels can hardly keep up. In many areas, as well as selling speed themselves, they also make money by collecting 'protection money' from other dealers.

A powerful example of just how sophisticated the biker gangs can be in their criminal dealings came with the conviction of the St Austell-based club, the Scorpios. In less than a year, the gang managed to corner the entire market for cannabis, amphetamines and LSD in the West Country, particularly Plymouth, using strong-arm tactics to drive other suppliers out of business, and earning more than £1 million.

The gang made casual use of extreme violence both to 'persuade' those who failed to pay their drug debts and also on those who dared to purchase their supplies from elsewhere. Potential witnesses were intimidated into keeping quiet.

Under the guidance of president Mark 'Snoopy' Dyce and vice-president Gary Mills, gang associates purchased large quantities of amphetamine powder and cannabis resin in Amsterdam, paying for them using money orders from Thomas Cook. Packets of the drug were then concealed in false compartments in a fleet of specially adapted Ford cars and driven through customs.

Then, from a safe house in Rainham, Essex (far away from the gang's home territory), the drugs were parcelled in brown paper, labelled 'motorcycle parts', and shipped around the country using British Rail's Red Star service. Although the entire scheme was being run by the Scorpios, the gang 'employed' a number of non-members to run the safe house and courier the drugs about – thus distancing themselves from potential prosecution.

The network had been operating successfully for more than eighteen months and would have carried on had it not been for a single incident which finally brought it to the attention of the police.

Shortly before Christmas 1985, Snoopy, former Royal Marine Commando Michael Harley, who was the club's sergeant-at-arms, and club associate William Burgess smashed their way into a flat in Stonehouse, Plymouth in order to carry out a vicious assault on a certain Stephen Graddon who they believed had attempted to rip them off.

All three were dressed in full combat gear and wore masks but they had failed to do their homework properly – Graddon was out. More to the point, the man they found, Andrew Rotton, knew nothing of their drugs empire. When what he described as 'three masked Hells Angels' broke into his home and threatened to blow him in half with a sawn-off shotgun, he did what any normal person would do. 'I ran straight to the phone and called the police.'

The news was something of a shock. So far as local detectives were concerned, Plymouth's drug problem had largely ended with the conviction of Eddie Zauluk, a big-time operator who sold millions of pounds' worth of drugs from a fortified council flat a year or so earlier.

But as they began to investigate, they received increasing (but always veiled) complaints that another mob had taken over. One addict/dealer told how he had been ordered to leave town or face certain death after it was found that he had been buying from a rival source.

Once the scale of the enterprise became apparent, the officer in charge, Detective Superintendent Malcolm Quick, realised that attempting to get any of the victims of the violence into court would be a waste of time. The chances were that, under pressure from Scorpio associates, they would retract and the case would fall apart. Instead, he selected twenty-four officers, fifteen of them experts in surveillance, and launched Operation Enmesh to try to infiltrate the gang.

It was an uphill struggle. In line with the 'good practice' code of biker crime, the Scorpios only ever dealt with those on an approved list of customers. New business was by introduction only and gaining the confidence of the gang's associates would be a slow, expensive and dangerous process.

Had it not been for a string of lucky breaks, the job might never have been completed. The first came when a few of the gangs members found themselves arrested after clashing with some Hells Angels in Falmouth. The remaining Scorpios stepped up dealing to establish a 'fighting fund' and began to relax a few of their rules. The major breakthrough, however, came from a completely unexpected source.

Helen White was the least likely member of the Scorpio entourage. Stunningly attractive, well educated, and the daughter of a highly successful businessman, she had trained as a ballet dancer and was expecting to have a glittering career before her. But the break-up of her marriage sent her into a spin.

She became fascinated with the biker scene and began modelling for numerous motorbike magazines. She picked up a minor drugs conviction, allowed her blonde hair to become matted and tousled, and finally had an eagle and F.T.W. – Fuck The World – tattooed on her left shoulder. Then she fell in love with Snoopy.

Beauty and the beast were not destined to live happily ever after. Helen rapidly developed a cocaine habit which Dyce agreed to support, provided she started working as a courier. The pair began living together and she was slowly taken more and more into the gang's confidence, being entrusted with large sums of money and huge quantities of drugs which she hand-delivered around the country.

But as Helen became increasingly disturbed by the levels of violence being employed, and sickened by her own role, she moved out of Snoopy's flat to live on her own. Once the police heard, they quickly moved in and asked her to play a dangerous game.

In return for immunity from prosecution, the police wanted Helen to continue as a courier and feed them information about drug supply lines. She agreed and for the next six months lived a double life, always friendly to and sometimes sleeping with Dyce while, by providing times, dates and drop-off points for shipments, helping detectives to build up a picture of the international network.

During this time, the Scorpios became ever more successful. Having cornered the amphetamine market, they expanded, dealing in LSD, shipping in vast amounts of cannabis resin from North Africa, and liaising with Colombian cartel representatives to receive cocaine direct from South America. But in line with most biker gangs, they refused to deal heroin.

When it was time to strike, Detective Superintendent Quick opted for a softly-softly approach at first to avoid arousing suspicion. One courier was known to be carrying cannabis resin worth £50,000 in a hired car, so an 'accidental arrest' was staged.

As the man made his way along the motorway, a standard patrol car pulled him over on the pretext that he had been driving too close to the car in front. The driver apologised profusely and the officers were just about to wave him on when one, making use of all his amateur dramatics skills, remarked that there seemed to be a 'funny smell' coming from the vehicle which quickly led then to the stash.

Then, on 5 June 1986, Operation Enmesh reached its climax. Teams of heavily armed police from five forces carried out a series of co-ordinated dawn swoops arresting thirty-six in the West Country, fourteen in London, two in Manchester, and one in Humberside. Copious amounts of cash, numerous weapons, shotguns, bullet-proof vests and cocaine worth £100,000 were recovered.

Documents seized at the Scorpio clubhouse revealed that the gang had kept accurate records of their success and were as tough and uncompromising with members who stepped out of line as the Angels. Minutes of meetings showed that one member was physically punished for 'drinking too much' while others were fined for being absent or late without good excuse. Ever conscious of possible police surveillance, drug deals were never spoken about, but were rather negotiated on paper.

The gang kept many of its drug stocks in well-hidden stashes: £20,000 worth of amphetamines was known to have been buried in Southway Woods, but a team of police and army engineers using dogs and metal detectors failed to find it. Luckily a pair of schoolboys out walking stumbled across it by chance.

Security was tight at Plymouth Crown Court the following May but, initially at least, not tight enough. Soon after the trial started, several of the jurors were approached by a mystery woman who told them: 'You're going to find them guilty, aren't you? Well, we never forget a face.'

When the judge heard, he dismissed the existing jury and replaced them with others who were well guarded throughout the entire proceedings. The prosecution witnesses were equally spooked. Two retracted their statements in the witness box, while Helen White, who had received anonymous death threats and has since been relocated to the north of England, required a permanent police escort.

Eight members of the gang and two of their suppliers were eventually jailed, Dyce receiving nine years, the longest sentence of the lot. But the fear didn't end there. Three of the cops on the case, including Malcolm Quick, also received threats which were taken very seriously. Quick has since left the force and the two officers who remain still refuse to have their role in Operation Enmesh publicly disclosed because of the potential danger.

As for the Scorpios, they were recently asked to join forces with the Midland Outlaws but refused, feeling that they were too far away from the bulk of the gang to truly benefit from membership.

Instead, they carry on quietly. 'We have no problems with

them in St Austell,' says one local detective. 'But then, they never did shit on their own doorstep.'

The initiation ceremony into the Hells Angels is shrouded in myth and speculation. According to one version, the new recruit must rape a woman over sixty followed by another under sixteen, perform an act of necrophilia, and finally bite the head off a live chicken and drink its blood – all of which must be witnessed by other members.

In fact the reality is generally far more mundane.

'If you're stupid enough to fuck a chicken, eat a dog or whatever, they'll let you do it,' says Craig, a former member of the Kent chapter of the Angels. 'But there are no hard and fast rules. There's nothing cast in stone. All you really need to do is show you can fight [or bring some other benefit to the club] and hang around long enough.

'You don't exactly have to run the gauntlet any more, but your mettle is certainly tested. Basically, one of the guys who is a bit tasty will do his best to wind you up to see if you'll defend yourself. Often, you are simply punched in the mouth to see how you react.

'Your face also has to fit, and exactly what that means has changed over the years. Now, you can get away with being a bit of a wimp if you're a good organiser or businessman,' adds Craig.

There are also associate and honorary members of the Angels who are lawyers and do much of their commercial/criminal work. Some are on permanent retainers. One definite non-biker member was raided and found to have the formula for amphetamine under his bed. He worked as a lab technician.

Most new members start out as 'prospects' and must show total dedication to the lifestyle as well as a willingness to do the dirty work, whether it is cleaning the bikes, guarding the clubhouse, or fighting the battles.

'A prospect is assigned to a full member,' says Craig. 'They have to do whatever you want them to. We used to wind a few of them up when we were out drinking by getting them to go and challenge some bloke who we knew was seriously hard. They'd have to do it and come back battered. It let them know who was in charge and makes sure they are genuine.'

When it comes to illegal activity, a prospect and his corresponding full member are usually the only ones who know all the details. This helps isolate the club from collective prosecution. The prospect stage continues until the club votes unanimously for the new member to be admitted.

As the club has become more sophisticated, so many of the more vulgar elements of Angel life have been discarded in a bizzare quest for respectability. In years gone by, new members were able to enhance their status by winning 'wings' for performing various sexual acts. While the wings are no longer worn, the sexual bravado continues.

Similarly, the wearing of ridges – ceremonial blue jeans on which all the other members of the club have urinated and vomited – is no longer required at special events. Few modern Angels even possess a pair, considering them to be a degrading anachronism.

One tradition that remains, however, is the taking of a group photograph of the entire chapter, along with the new recruit, which is then distributed to other chapters around the world, often in the form of a Christmas card. Whenever an Angel travels abroad, the photograph is produced and used to verify identity.

Full membership brings many benefits. There is a highly sophisticated loan system which can be hooked into for pretty much any purpose. 'You could get a house out of it if you wanted,' says Craig. 'But not many people took that one up. You'd have to open up to fellow Angels any time of day or night and ensure they were looked after. It wouldn't be your house, it would belong to the club.'

Then there is the support network for those imprisoned or injured. In some cases this works well, as in the example of the man who agreed to take a murder rap and was rewarded, at the end of his sentence, with a new £9,000 Harley and a half-share in a successful business. In other cases, the system falls apart and, despite having their details circulated to members worldwide, bikers fail to receive any letters of support.

Then there are the fringe benefits. Women aren't allowed to become full or associate members of the Angels, but they are pivotal to the lifestyle. They are divided into two categories – 'old ladies' are wives or steady girlfriends who are out of bounds to other club members. Mamas (from the expression 'Let's go make someone a mama'), on the other hand, put themselves at the sexual mercy of the chapter: agreeing to become a mama means agreeing to have sex with any member at any time.

('The mommas have to pull a train,' said an eighteen-year-old example in a rare press interview. 'Too bad if she can't last the time. Everyone has to sample the goods. I love being with the Angels. Before that I modelled for art classes and was once a secretary at a police station.')

In order to ensure that everyone knows the difference, old ladies wear special belts or cut-offs with the legend 'Property of [name] Hells Angels' stitched on. The more optimistic have a property tattoo. None of the women has to take any formal oaths of silence; they are generally kept in the dark about club activities. 'We don't talk about anything serious when women are around,' says Craig.

But the greatest reward of membership is the right, in return for £150, to wear the coveted colours. There are many stories, some undoubtedly apocryphal, of what happens to non-members who take a fancy to the fully copyright-protected winged death's head motif.

Some cases have been settled in the High Court, others have involved more direct action. When designer John Richmond produced a pinstripe suit with a leather back featuring the colours, teams of Angels turned up at his shops threatening staff. The clothing was quickly withdrawn from sale.

One nineteen-year-old Reading art student who had the design tattooed on his arm was less fortunate. He was kidnapped off the street, taken back to an Angel clubhouse, handed a bottle of vodka and a sharp knife, and told to remove the tattoo. Which he did.

The police caught up with him after being alerted by the local hospital where the boy went to have his wounds stitched up. But while the boy told his story off the record, he refused to make a statement or press charges. 'He thought he'd got off really lightly,' said one detective on the case. 'He was convinced they were going to kill him.'

This level of respect doesn't extend to the colours of other gangs, which are considered prized scalps, as Craig explains. 'My favourite thing used to be waiting at traffic lights with a couple of mates for a rival biker to pull up. We run up behind him, hold him and cut off his colours with a Stanley knife, cutting up all his back at the same time.

'Then there were times when we'd go off to 'visit' other clubs. We'd be in the back of some transit van and, as we got near the place, the sergeant-at-arms would throw open a sack full of pickaxe handles, baseball bats and rice flails, then shout "choose your weapons" and we'd all pile in. The idea wasn't just to kick shit out of the gang, we wanted their colours and then we'd burn or bury them.'

Common to all biker gangs is the rule that, if you lose your colours, it is almost impossible to get another set. When the Wolverhampton chapter of the Hells Angels was raided by police, their colours were seized. They faced a massive financial penalty from the governing All England chapter (which is composed of representatives of the thirteen chapters in the UK) and were forced to make a desperate plea to the authorities for their return.

In Craig's view, it is wrong to think of the Hells Angels or other bike gangs as criminal organisations in the mould of the Triads or the Mafia.

'I'd say that almost no one is joining the Angels specifically to be a criminal or get involved in drug dealing. Some just end up that way.'

'While I was there I got really heavily into bike theft. A few of us would club together and hire a decent-sized van then set off to where we knew a bike show was being held. There would always be long lines of unattended bikes parked up nearby and we'd just grab a few, chuck 'em in the back and drive off.

'Other guys were into selling drugs and stuff – they were the ones with the new cars. No one really gave a fuck what you got up to just so long as you paid your dues and didn't deal smack. Why not? It kills ya, don't it! Smack-heads don't care about the club, just where their next fix is coming from.'

Finding those who will speak out about life inside the Angels, even in the past tense, is rare. The club has many secrets and likes to keep it that way, so joining is generally considered to be something you do for life. Leaving means giving up everything – you have to hand in all your patches, get your tattoos covered up, have an 'outdate' inscribed instead and promise never to associate with the Angels again.

Most can't face it. The club becomes a kind of surrogate family and leaving would tear their world apart. But middle-aged men can't raise hell like they did when they were in their teens and with a dearth of fresh blood coming in, it's little wonder that many in the biking fraternity believe the British Angels are well past their best.

For the first twenty-one years, the commercial interests of the British Angels were covered by three companies: Hells Angels Ltd, Hells Angels (Kent) Ltd, and Hells Angels (London) Ltd. Then, in mid-1990, a new name was added: Hells Angels (Europe) Ltd.

The irony of such a move is inescapable: when it comes to the voices of dissent, the Europeans are among those shouting loudest. Ever since the president of the German chapter was injured in a brawl with Luton's football hooligans, the Dutch, German, Danish and French Angels have been complaining to the American parent organisation that the British are simply letting the side down.

Exactly how this situation could be improved is not known, but it is certainly the case that in Europe, the Angels' image is far closer to that of the American ideal.

In July 1991, for example, when a team of French narcotics officers 'disguised themselves' in leather jackets and biking helmets to raid the clubhouse of the Parisian chapter, they found a set of pump-action shotguns, strategically positioned so as to be within easy reach of the bar. There was also an elaborate system which could be used to evacuate several kilos of cocaine, via a compressed-air tube, to safety.

Searches of members' houses later that same day turned up 11 kilos of cannabis, 700 grams of cocaine, and 200,000 francs in cash. Other weapons included a machine-gun on a tripod, pistols, carbines, more shotguns and around a thousand rounds of ammunition. 'There is no doubt that we are dealing with a crime organisation of international dimensions,' said a police spokesman.

Yet despite the success of the raid, it did nothing to curb the Angels' firepower. On 22 August 1991, Michael 'Bubu' Burel, the founder of the French chapter of the Bandidos, was enjoying a few beers at the clubhouse in Marseille.

The steel-reinforced door had been left open for air so that when two motorcyclists rode by and fired a volley of shots from automatic pistols there was nothing to protect him. Burel was hit in the heart and died instantly. Two other Bandidos were wounded.

And it's not just France. In Zurich, the authorities are still searching for Angel Reinhard Lutz, wanted for trafficking 100 kilos of cocaine worth around £3.5 million. Police believe Lutz fled to Brazil and is holed up in an apartment owned by Angels in Rio.

Swiss Angels have also been convicted of murder, rape and producing explosives and have been strongly linked to prostitution and extortion rings. In Holland, they have been heavily implicated in drug smuggling, most recently acting as a conduit for Colombian cocaine moving into Europe, while the two chapters in Denmark are believed to extort money regularly from bars and engage in organised witness intimidation. Half of Copenhagen's amphetamine market is said to be in Angel hands.

Bikers are also heavily involved in trafficking drugs from the former Eastern Bloc. A large proportion of the high-quality amphetamine coming out of Poland (rapidly overtaking Holland as the major European source) via Sweden is believed to be moved by bikers.

The Angels are known in particular to want to open a chapter in Finland in order to take advantage of the increasing flood of drugs from Russia and Estonia.

'We are an official Hells Angel hangaround club and I'm fucking proud of it,' boasted Riko Roimu of the Helsinki-based Overkill MC to Finnish television in February 1993, the day after members of his club left several members of the rival Iron Hog MC badly injured in an attack said to have been carried out to prove the club's worthiness to wear the winged death's head.

If (or perhaps when) the Overkill MC are granted their charter, it will open up dozens of new smuggling routes into Europe and Britain, thanks to co-operation with the former Rowdies MC from Norway who received their charter in 1989 and the Dirty Draggels from southern Sweden who became fully accredited Hells Angels in 1993. All three clubs are 'controlled' by the Denmark chapter, rapidly becoming one of the most powerful in Europe.

This kind of international co-operation has always been one of the Angels' major strengths and helps bond chapters on opposite sides of the globe, often with breathtaking results. When David 'Goat' Rufus, a member of the Hells Angels Nomads chapter (so called because they have no set base), was killed in an accident near Tours in France during a 'run' in August 1993, more than a thousand Angels and associates from as far away as New Zealand and Holland, America and Canada attended his funeral and paid tribute.

(One British chapter arrived with all their heads shaved. It emerged that one had been accused of rape so all had turned slaphead in order to frustrate identification.)

Chapters in different countries stay in touch via monthly newsletters (though at the time of writing the Angels are moving into the techno age, setting up their own computer bulletin board) which detail changes in membership, imprisonments and hospitalisations. This information is sent first to a regional office and from there forwarded all over the world.

There are also regular intercontinental telephone calls which ensure that any major development anywhere in the world is known by most Angels within a few hours, all of which makes something of a nonsense of the claim that nobody knew exactly what was going on when Canadian Angel Robert 'Snake' Tremblay came to visit.

Canada has, for some unknown reason, been home to the most violent of all Angels. Between 1970 and 1985, one, Yves Apache Trudeau, admitted killing forty-three people during a spell as a professional hitman. So carefully had he covered his tracks that police had no evidence against him until he decided to confess.

The Royal Canadian Mounted Police hold their local bikers responsible for thirty murders between 1988 and 1991, while early in 1993 Angels were caught with more than £6 million worth of cocaine. Even at the time of writing Hells Angels in Montreal have become involved in a brutal war with an obscure rival gang which has so far seen dozens of street shootouts and left at least three bikers dead.

Tremblay's story was linked to one of the darkest episodes from biker history which began when a bloated body floated to the surface of Canada's St Lawrence River in June 1985. It had originally been placed in a sleeping bag and weighed down with chains and rocks, but the current had worked it free. Police frogmen looking for clues found four more ballasted bodies.

All were members of the Quebec-based North Chapter who had been accused of ripping off other chapters in drug deals and generally creating problems for all and sundry by talking indiscreetly about their illegal activities. The five had been lured to a meeting on the premise that the dispute would be sorted out. Instead, they were murdered one by one.

Most died in the Lennoxville clubhouse but Guy 'Chop' Adam made a run for it. Prospect Gerry Coulombe told police what he saw next. 'Tremblay had a gun in his hand and was running after Adam, firing as he went.' When Adam hit the grass, he had seven bullet wounds. Some of the bullets were 'exploding' dum-dums that shattered inside his head. Tremblay then dragged Adam into a nearby garage to join the other bodies.

A warrant was issued for Tremblay's arrest but he fled the country, first to Paris, where he was provided with a false passport and new identity papers by French Angels, and then on to England where members of the London chapter fixed him up with a council-flat squat on the Rockingham estate in Bermondsey.

During the three months he spent in hiding, Tremblay kept a close eye on events both back home and around the world. He sent £200 worth of flowers via Interflora when he discovered that one of the French Angels who had helped him had been killed in an accident, and received regular updates on police progress on the case back in Canada.

Tremblay also received a number of personal visits, including one from Anthony Tait, a former 'sergeant-at-arms' with the Angel chapter based in Anchorage, Alaska.

'He told me the purge was necessary because the five victims were extorting money, using the address book of a slain drug pusher,' said Tait later. 'This was acceptable but the group went wrong when they started putting the squeeze on fellow bikers.'

Tait was probably the worst person to tell. Ostensibly a highly respected member of the Angel brotherhood, he was in fact an undercover FBI agent who had managed to join the Angels after being sponsored by an informant who, in turn, had been offered the chance to join the club while in prison.

He travelled extensively, becoming a well-known face at chapters around the world. 'During my time with the club, I saw countless instances of narcotics use and sales, rape, felony, battery, petty theft, grant theft, weapons violations of all kinds, and extortion. I also heard murders being planned and descriptions of murders already committed,' he says.

Tait's testimony also provided the evidence for a major bust against American Angels in May 1985, and eventually led to the conviction of more than thirty senior members of the club. Membership procedures are said to have been considerably tightened up as a result.

But the international criminal links remain. In the summer of 1994, detectives swooped on London's Hilton Hotel and arrested two Canadian Angels, Pierre Rodrigue and David Rouleau, who had travelled to London to supervise a planned shipment of more than a tonne of cocaine, supplied by the Cali cartel.

Yet another cock-up on British soil has swelled the complaints from Europe that Angels in the UK simply aren't coming up to scratch. This has already had some effect – Windsor and Wessex have split from the All England chapter, having become dissatisfied with the direction they were taking – and there have been an increasing number of confrontations between Angels and vanloads of Outlaws and Bandidos.

With two, possibly three major gangs battling for survival, let alone control of the lucrative biker crime empire, it can only be a matter of time before there is a major confrontation, one which many predict will spell the end of at least one of the competitors.

The Angels are favourites to lose, but then the Angels have survived massive police busts, loss of leaders, huge financial drains and legal defeats only to come bouncing back. Having made it this far, they are unlikely to give up without a fight, particularly when they believe they still have a long way to go.

A selection of arms, including an Uzi sub-machine gun, pictured on the sofa of a south London underworld gun dealer. (© *Richard Reyes*)

Old style gangster Dave Courtney (centre) with his club act, the Courtney Twins, and a minder outside the East End's most famous public house.

The late Patrick Thomas, the quiet man responsible for the biggest robbery in the world.

Graffiti marks the limits of the territory of one of London's most notorious Asian gangs, the Brick Lane Massif.
(© *T Thompson*)

Christopher 'Tuffy' Bourne, the leading Yardie gangster gunned down in a Brixton crack house. (© *Observer Films*)

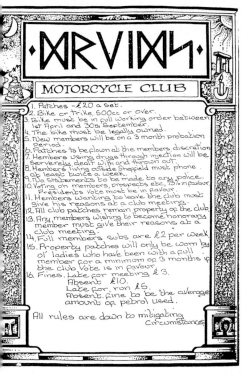

DRVIDS

MOTORCYCLE CLUB

1. Patches - £20 a set.
2. Bike or trike, 500cc or over.
3. Bike must be in full working order between 1st April and 30th September.
4. The bike must be legally owned.
5. New members will be on a 3 month probation period.
6. Patches to be flown at the members discretion
7. Patches using drugs through injection will be severely dealt with and thrown out.
8. Members living outside Sheffield must phone at least twice a week.
9. No statements to be made to any police.
10. Voting on members, prospects etc., 75% in favour. Presidents vote must be in favour.
11. Members wanting to leave the club must give his reasons at a club meeting.
12. All club patches remain property of the club.
13. Any members wishing to become honorary member must give their reasons at a club meeting.
14. Full members subs are £2 per week.
15. Property patches will only be worn by ol' ladies who have been with a full member for a minimum of 3 months if the club vote is in favour.
16. Fines. Late for meeting £3.
    Absent £10.
    Late for run £5.
    Absent fine to be the average amount of petrol used.

All rules are down to mitigating circumstances

Rules of the Druids motorcycle club, including the requirement that members do not speak to the police.

The reinforced clubhouse of the Reading chapter of the Hells Angels. Note the video cameras. (© T Thompson)

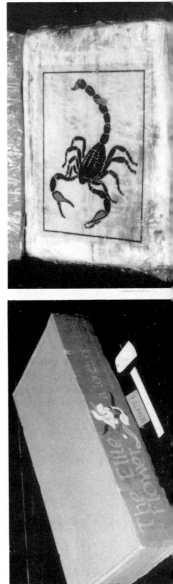

Numerous consignments of Colombian cocaine, disguised as chocolates, apricots (the ones in the left hand jar are genuine, the ones in the right are plastic) and flowers. The Scorpion logo is the trademark of the Cali Cartel. (© *HM Customs*)

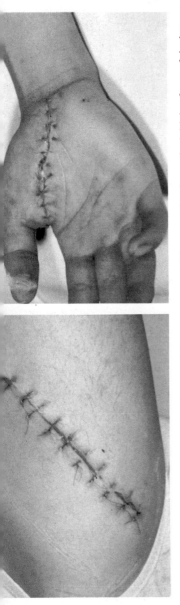

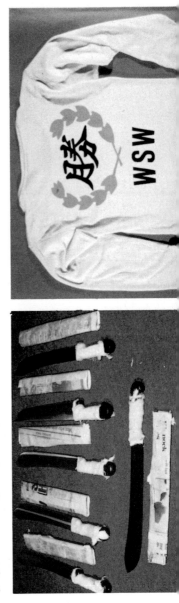

Injuries inflicted by Triad 'choppers' and some of the weapons used. The sweatshirt bears the initials of one of the largest gangs, the Wo Shing Wo. (© *NCIS*)

Khat, the natural amphetamine, which is at the centre of an illegal £50 million industry. (© *Charles Ommaney*)

Below left: Khat behind the counter of a Birmingham shop. (© *Charles Ommaney*)

Below right: Cannabis-filled condoms and a converted button, both used by Nigerian drug smugglers. (© *Barry J Holmes*)

A consignment of Turkish heroin hidden inside a long-distance lorry. (© *HM Customs*)

Illegal gambling at a Turkish cafe. (© *David Hoffman*)

As long ago as 1969, the controversial underground magazine *Oz* published a feature on Hells Angels including an interview with a certain Crazy Charlie, then president of the four-month-old London chapter and still a member today.

Desperate to shock, members talked about competitions where they had sex in front of the rest of the club as many times as possible without pulling out (eighteen was the record); they talked about shitting and pissing on their colours during initiation ceremonies; about performing oral sex on menstruating women to earn their red wings; and were pictured mooning at the camera and groping two naked mamas.

But when Crazy Charlie came into the frame towards the end, the interview took on a more serious tone. He looked beyond the folly of youth and talked about a dream which the Angels have been working towards ever since day one. 'So what's going to happen to the Angels?' *Oz* asks. 'They're going to get bigger and bigger,' he replies. 'There's no limit. One day it's not going to be Hells Angels London or Chapter California. It's going to be Hells Angels, Earth.'

Chapter Five

The Black Mist

The Yakuza and Sokaiya

'The time that a prisoner serves is colloquially
known as *otsutome*, "duty", especially
in Yakuza circles, where it is seen as
the "duty" of subordinates to do prison
terms in place of their bosses.'

From Japanese Street Slang *by Peter Constantine*

M asaru Takumi had barely set foot on French soil when he found himself surrounded by a posse of armed police and immigration officers. Oblivious to his protests, they frisked him then frogmarched him on to the return leg of the flight, sending him back to Tokyo with 'entry refused' stamped on his passport.

At first this enforced deportation at Charles de Gaulle airport in August 1992 set the antenna of local human rights campaigners twitching: the fifty-six-year-old businessman was clearly of substantial means and seemed unlikely to be planning to overstay his welcome.

His papers were fully in order, he was not drunk, carrying drugs or attempting to smuggle anything into the country. Moreover, Takumi claimed he was suffering from a severe liver ailment and diabetes – he pleaded to be allowed to stay if only to enable him to see a doctor. But to no avail.

There seemed no reason for such harsh treatment. Even the revelation that, up until the time he had left Japan, Takumi had been held in prison didn't seem to justify it. By Western standards, his alleged crime – buying a house in Canada without obtaining permission from the Finance Registry – seemed insignificant. And besides, the court had given him permission to make the trip.

But Takumi was no petty criminal. He wasn't even an ordinary member of the *yakuza*, Japan's 300-year-old criminal network. In fact, Takumi was the deputy head of the Yamaguchi-gumi – the largest of all the yakuza gangs – and thus one of the most powerful criminals in the country.

Furthermore, far from being some paltry act, his purchase of a $400,000 Canadian home was seen as further evidence of the yakuza doing that which European (and in particular British) law enforcement agencies dread most – reaching out overseas. It was a move that had been mooted since March of that year when Japan introduced its first-ever anti-gang law. Takumi's trip to Paris, it soon emerged, was proof that the predictions had been spot-on.

The liver ailment story was a lie – Takumi was simply desperate to meet up with his boss, Yoshinori Watanbe, and two other colleagues who had arrived in Paris a few days earlier. From there the quartet planned to travel across Europe, meeting with the heads of international crime syndicates to discuss collaboration in the era of the single market.

Venice, Milan and Geneva were all on the itinerary, but only as brief stopover points. The main arena was to be London, where a rendezvous with representatives of the Triads and Colombian drug cartels had been arranged. However, when Takumi was unable to join the others, the trip was called off.

The collective sigh of relief from senior officers at Scotland Yard, MI5 and the National Criminal Intelligence Service was almost audible: the yakuza are widely held to be the most formidable, loyal and motivated criminals in the world – not only will junior members happily go to prison in place of their bosses, but should they make some error of judgment, they will famously cut off a fingertip as a form of atonement.

Supposedly descended from the samurai (finger-cutting was used to weaken the sword-hand of errant warriors), the yakuza claim to be the last upholders of the twin virtues of *giri*, the obligation to repay favours, and *ninjo*, compassion for the weak – highly regarded traditional values which most of their fellow countrymen have allowed to fade.

Thus the yakuza have an image, reinforced by thousands of (yakuza-financed) films and novels, which in Britain would equate to a cross between Dick Turpin and Robin Hood. So convincing has this PR campaign been that since the end of the Second World War, the yakuza have been an accepted and tolerated part of Japanese life. Even for the police.

The official attitude was that crimes such as illegal gambling, prostitution, extortion, loan sharking and the sale of soft drugs were impossible to stamp out completely, so instead of trying, why not let the yakuza keep a tight rein? As the saying goes, better the devil you know ... And just so long as the gangs helped to keep hard drugs out of Japan and didn't involve the general public in their territorial disputes, the police were happy to leave them alone.

For decades, the arrangement worked beautifully. At the last count, the yakuza consisted of more than 90,000 members split into around 2,500 separate gangs – twenty times larger than the core head-count of the American Mafia which operates in a country with twice the population. Yet far from being over-run with crime, Japan is one of the safest countries in the industrialised world. The number of murders per capita is around four times lower than that of Europe and eight times lower than that of the USA. The typical householder is sixty-five times more likely to be burgled in London than in Tokyo.

And while some 600,000 Japanese are addicted to yakuza-supplied amphetamine, the country has no significant heroin problem and annual cocaine seizures amount to just one or two kilos each year.

Yet in 1992, according to admittedly conservative National Police Agency estimates, the yakuza made collective profits of £5.56 billion, eight times that of the country's second most successful organisation – the Toyota Motor Company. The true figure is believed to be between three and ten times that amount.

Such vast earnings became possible during the late eighties when the three largest yakuza gangs began to move away from their 'traditional' fields and cashed in on the fast-growing economy by investing in mainstream business – stock and property markets – and borrowing millions of yen to build hotel and golf course developments both in Japan and abroad.

But it was this very expansion which brought the gangs into conflict with the powers-that-be. When the recession hit, sending stock and property prices into freefall, bankers trying to call in huge yakuza debts faced a string of violent attacks including fire-bombings, stabbings and shootings. At the same time, a new law forcing anyone holding more than a 5 per cent stake in a company to declare their interest led to many of Japan's biggest companies suddenly discovering that their biggest shareholders were gangsters.

To top it all, between 1989 and 1991 cocaine seizures increased by 5,000 per cent and the Kobe-based Yamaguchi-gumi had begun to open satellite offices in Tokyo, leading to a spate of street shoot-outs including one in which a sixty-six-year-old bystander, mistaken for a gang leader, was shot dead.

For the police, who had taken to calling the gangs *boryokudan* (literally 'violence groups'), the three-century honeymoon was over. 'We are going to crush them,' Superintendent Shigeyuki Yamaguchi of the National Police Agency told a press conference in mid-1990, going on to propose a radical new law outlawing the yakuza.

But when the new measures finally came into force on 1 March 1992, many believed it was too little, too late. The yakuza, they said, had already diversified and the law would simply drive them underground.

Just five weeks later, they were proved right. London may have had a lucky escape with the Takumi incident, but a separate bust, also in Paris a few weeks earlier, showed just how well the yakuza were capable of operating abroad without law enforcement agencies realising.

The tip-off had come from an unlikely source'– shop assistants working in the most upmarket areas of the city. For some time, they had noticed increasing numbers of dourly dressed Chinese

and Vietnamese visiting their premises once or twice each week
and buying car-loads of luxury goods.

Considering their own poor state of dress, the mystery shoppers displayed excellent taste, buying only the most expensive,
exclusive designer items: Louis Vuitton suitcases, Hermès
handbags, Chanel scarves and the like. Payment was always
made with crisp 500-franc notes pulled from bulging wallets
and purses. And when staff checked, they found that the notes
always had consecutive numbers.

Suspecting a break-in at a bank vault or the work of
a highly sophisticated counterfeiting ring, the management
at Vuitton called in the police, who trailed the 'shoppers'
to a plush apartment near the Madeleine. Each and every
afternoon, several hundred of them could be seen lining the
surrounding streets, shopping bags in hand, waiting their turn
to enter.

One cold evening in April, when the last of the queues had
dispersed, the police made their move. Inside the apartment,
goods worth more than £700,000 had been packed up ready
for shipping overseas and a further £200,000 in cash sat idly in
a corner. Bank statements showed that the ringleaders had £1.5
million spread throughout numerous local accounts, while other
documents gave police enough information to piece together the
rest of the conspiracy.

It soon emerged that, since 1985, the yakuza had been
wiring vast amounts of cash into France, using foreign banks
and routing the money via Luxembourg, Switzerland and the
Channel Islands to frustrate attempts to trace the trail. Four
junior yakuza had been despatched to Paris where they rented
the apartment and set up the laundering system.

They placed classified advertisements for 300 'freelance
export assistants' in newspapers aimed at the French-Asian
community. For a small daily fee, these bogus customers were
supplied with money to purchase the luxury goods which they
then brought back to the apartment each afternoon. From there,
the items were shipped off to Japan to be resold (at a healthy

profit – designer goods are phenomenally expensive in Tokyo) by a string of yakuza-run retailers.

The exact amount of money that had passed through the operation was impossible to calculate, but conservative estimates suggested that, over the six years, £250 million might not be too wide of the mark.

Shortly after the bust, Takaji Kumnimatsu, head of the Criminal Investigation Bureau of Japan's National Police Association, wryly commented: 'Some people in foreign countries say that first we flooded their markets with Sony appliances and Toyota cars. Now we are exporting yakuza.'

According to embassy officials, there are some 57,000 Japanese living in England and Wales. Of these, around 14,000 are classified as businessmen and a further 6,500 as students, while the rest are simply classed as family. The numbers have grown rapidly – twenty years ago, the head-count would barely have reached triple figures.

For the most part the influx has been a welcome one: Japanese investment has been hailed as a great stabiliser for the British economy, bringing new life to the industrial heartlands and much-needed jobs to isolated new towns. There are currently more than 110 Japanese-owned factories across the country, the vast majority of which were built in the last ten years.

Most of the factories are in Wales or the Midlands, but they tend to have relatively few Japanese staff. At Hitachi's plant in Aberdare, for example, 590 of the 600 workers are British.

In fact, nearly half of Britain's Japanese community lives in London, working for banks, trading houses and stockbrokers, usually within the Square Mile. And to ensure they don't feel too homesick, hundreds of quick-thinking operators have sprung up to make their lives in the capital as familiar as possible.

London boasts at least twelve sizable stores selling nothing but authentic Japanese produce, many with prices marked in yen to avoid confusion. There are also three Japanese nightclubs and five specialist hairdressers, and of the seventy Japanese restaurants in the country, sixty-six are in London.

Japanese-language newspapers are widely available, transmitted by satellite and printed in London each morning to keep expats abreast of the latest developments back home. There is even a dedicated cable television channel with a non-stop diet of soaps, news and game shows.

When it comes to sporting pursuits, there are four wholly Japanese-owned golf courses around the capital with another out in Ayrshire. And in terms of health care, there are four specialist Japanese clinics. There are also dozens of social, business and games clubs and, to ensure that the right lessons get passed on to a new generation, there is a dedicated Japanese school in west London. Holland Park even has a Japanese garden.

The most concentrated area of settlement, between Golders Green and Colindale in north-west London, is locally known as J&J – Japanese and Jewish – Town, and it is here that the giant Yaohan Plaza can be found.

This, the country's first all-Japanese shopping centre, boasts an impressive range of authentic restaurants, a giant supermarket, arts and crafts outlets, a large bookshop selling imported titles, specialist travel agents, business services, a computer games emporium, and other elements to help the centre live up to its tag – 'all Japan under one roof'.

In fact, the life of the typical Japanese living and working in Britain is so wholly familiar that it would be preposterous if Japanese-organised crime had not become established here too.

Yet all conversations with members of the community contradict that view. Whether in the clubs, the restaurants, the clinics or on the golf courses, the reaction is the same: heads shake, fingers swing from side to side, shoulders shrug in exasperation. Some feign no knowledge of English, only to continue a perfectly fluent conversation the moment your back is turned.

And while staff at the embassy admit that, since 1992, a

Japanese police officer has been posted in London to monitor 'crime within the Japanese community', they claim to have no evidence of the yakuza being active in Britain.

But such denials have to be seen in the proper context. As recently as 1985, a Home Office investigation into Britain's well-established Chinese community concluded that the Triads were not in evidence because every interviewee told them so. It is only very recently that the Chinese have felt comfortable and safe enough to admit that they have been plagued by the gangs ever since they arrived in the country.

For the more recently arrived and less integrated Japanese, blanket denial of what is going on under their noses is still the favoured option. Of the many customs the Japanese have brought with them, that of the 'black mist' – the name given to the underworld dealings that everyone knows about but no one talks about – appears to be well established.

But then so are the yakuza.

It didn't take long for the shock-waves of the Paris bust to travel across the English Channel. In September 1992 the National Criminal Intelligence Service ditched the notion of Britain as an impenetrable fortress and announced that they had a 'suspicion' that the sokaiya – the white-collar branch of the yakuza – might be operating in the UK.

The sokaiya are gangs of professional shareholders who buy a nominal amount of stock in a company, attend the annual general meeting and threaten to disrupt the proceedings or disclose unsavoury details about the private lives of the directors – unless a fee is paid. Thanks to the Japanese obsession with 'saving face', such techniques are remarkably successful. In 1992, in a desperate attempt to minimise their effect, some 1,824 Japanese public companies organised their annual general meetings on the same day at the same time. As it emerged, there were more than enough sokaiya to go round.

The NCIS had no direct evidence of the sokaiya operating over here, but made it clear that they were anxious to head off the gangsters before they became entrenched in Britain. They were over ten years too late.

In 1981 a certain Seiji Hamamoto opened up a 'foreign correspondent' office in London from where he produced a wide range of business publications and in-house magazines. The quality of his work was appalling and the information contained less than useless, yet some five hundred blue-chip Japanese firms paid handsomely for the privilege of receiving his publications. Hamamoto was soon raking in nearly £100 million each year.

But while this particular sokaiya's front for blackmailing London-based Japanese firms shut down a year later when Hamamoto was arrested while visiting Tokyo, dozens of others continue to thrive.

Laws introduced back in 1982 which made it illegal to pay money to a known sokaiya (even for Japanese firms based abroad) have simply made the gangs more innovative. Often, instead of turning up in person at meetings, they threaten to circulate rumours of malpractice or publish false versions of company accounts.

Hence for the last decade, around a third of all Japanese finance houses and banks in London currently make regular donations to dubious 'charitable' institutes who research the effects of noise pollution at work, rent supposedly priceless paintings to decorate their offices at vast expense, or employ costly business consultancies to think up new strategies which are never implemented.

Then there are the pseudo market research organisations, the bogus travel and entertainment agencies, the property speculators and financial advisers who exist for no other reason than as a front to enable money to be extorted from businesses.

The yakuza are here too: well-known members from all ranks are regularly spotted in and around the capital and the home counties. The Kobe-based Yamaguchi-gumi aside, most of the 'visitors' tend to be from the next two largest gangs:

the Inagawa-kai and the Sumiyoshi-kai, both based in Tokyo with 10,000 members each and both anxious to spread their tentacles abroad.

Most are here temporarily, arriving on extravagant one- or two-week junkets during which they spend their days enjoying British golf courses and their nights sampling the delights of Malaysian or Thai prostitutes, either in restaurants-cum-hostess bars, illegal gambling dens or, increasingly, in elegant Triad-run brothels.

Others have settled more permanently and, in line with the unwritten rules of organised crime, find work that enables them to shelter among their own nationals. Two yakuza brothers run a karaoke bar in central London (funded of course with dirty money) from where they are ideally placed to report back home on the latest trends and developments, as well as finding opportunities for further investment.

Others hold innocuous jobs in souvenir shops, clubs and restaurants where they are notable only for their 'thuggish' behaviour. It is these gangsters who practise a less intellectual form of extortion which has resulted in dozens of Japanese restaurants paying way over the odds for their linen and cleaning services, though none think to complain or go elsewhere.

They are also notably active in London's stolen-art market, using indigenous underworld go-betweens (particularly members of the IRA's criminal wing) to purchase paintings purloined from across Europe, like those from the Corrot collection stolen from a provincial French museum in 1988 and later found decorating the Japanese home of a yakuza boss.

There are also fugitives like Kenichi Tanaka, head of the Tanaka-gumi, who was caught in the Philippines in 1989 with a massive cache of drugs and guns. Thoroughly fluent in English, he jumped bail, and has subsequently surfaced in London, Hawaii and New York. According to research submitted to the Home Office by Dr Barry Rider of Jesus College, Cambridge: 'Accounts have been identified in banks in London which have been used to facilitate Yakuza operations and associated enterprises. The involvement of the gangs with the entertainment, travel and holiday is well documented. Whilst the Yakuza has hesitated to directly impact on non-Japanese activities, there can be no doubt that it does have a very significant indirect effect.'

But while the numbers of yakuza present in Britain is undoubtedly increasing, at the end of the day their real aims don't involve the movement of men – just money.

'They are very co-operative, they really want to help,' says a yakuza-chasing FBI agent of Japanese law enforcement. 'The real frustration is with their legal system. You simply can't get on with the job.'

Japan's police have to work under some of the tightest privacy laws in the world: they are forbidden to use electronic surveillance such as telephone taps or concealed cameras and cannot work undercover or carry out sting operations. More poignantly, they cannot tell foreign investigators whether an individual has a criminal record unless that person is being charged with a specific crime.

Also, under current legislation, money-laundering in itself is not a crime. Dozens of FBI investigations into alleged yakuza activity overseas have hit a brick wall when agents attempt to track money movements back to Japan and find that the trail goes dead. Japanese banks offer their clients complete and total secrecy. There are no exceptions.

The FBI have good reason to worry. The yakuza have been present in North America, particularly Hawaii, since the early seventies and, while tracking their physical movement is simple – customs officers simply check passengers arriving from Japan for missing digits and all-over tattoos – Japan's lack of an anti-laundering law makes tracking their encroachment into legitimate business somewhat more problematic.

And encroachment there has certainly been. After hearing evidence from a number of 'confidential' Japanese informants, a Senate subcommittee investigation into Asian Organised Crime in 1992 concluded that half a billion dollars' worth of yakuza assets had been 'washed' through Hawaii, Nevada, Arizona and New York during the previous five years.

One such informant, known only as 'Mr Bully', revealed that he had personal knowledge of yakuza buying at least fifty properties in Hawaii including the Turtle Bay Hilton and that a considerable number of shares in the New York branch of Christie's auction house were in the hands of a Yamaguchi-gumi associate known as The Snake.

He also pointed to a number of American video game parlours, karaoke bars and casinos which were at least partly yakuza-backed, but the main target for the gangs seemed to be golf clubs.

Mr Bully told how the funding for the $841 million purchase of the famed Pebble Beach Country Club in Monterey, California two years earlier had been provided by the yakuza. Club memberships were being offered in Japan for up to $740,000 each but the executive acting as a gang go-between was eventually forced to sell the club at a loss when the FBI intervened and blocked development plans.

Though it may seem an unlikely route for organised crime to pursue, the golf club scam is a highly developed and efficient form of money laundering, peculiar to the Japanese.

Despite being famous for its lack of living space, Japan is host to an incredible 2,000 courses with a further 900 currently being planned. Around one in ten of the population are regular players and, such is the prestige attached to the game, the top clubs can get away with charging vast membership fees. To join Tokyo's top club, the Koganei, for example, costs nearly £2 million.

With fees a hundred times lower appearing to be a bargain, the criminal gangs who stump up dirty money to build new courses find it almost impossible to lose out. Tens of millions of pounds are funnelled into seemingly legitimate companies which then use the cash to establish a new club, often overseas.

The resort then collects huge fees – often well in excess of £20,000 to join plus annual subscriptions of £1,000 – which are funnelled back to the original investors as 'clean' money. These fees often afford a complete return on the original investment, an incredible achievement considering that most money-laundering schemes offer on average 80 per cent and often a lot less.

Moreover, the front company is left with a hugely valuable piece of real estate which, even if sold at a considerable loss, still provides even greater profits for the gangsters.

Other international criminal syndicates, struggling to launder their own profits, have recently begun to express an interest in finding out more about such schemes, ending a tradition that had prevented the yakuza forming an alliance with any other gang.

'We've seen the Japanese networking with the Cosa Nostra,' says the FBI's Head of Organised Crime, Jim Moody. He is not alone: his opposite number in Australia recently assisted in the deportation of three yakuza who had failed to reveal that they had previous convictions, while in July 1994 a leading member of the Sumiyoushi-kai was killed during a 'business' trip to Russia. Yakuza have also been apprehended buying guns in Milan and amphetamines in Germany (with the help of local Triads) and cocaine directly from Colombia.

In Britain, the same banking secrecy means that the National Criminal Intelligence Service is unable to say with any authority whether any of the £9 billion invested in the country from Japan in 1994 came from the yakuza, but that the Japanese believe they have a special affinity with Britain cannot be denied.

Both countries are offshore islands, both have royal families and, most importantly, both have long histories. It is said that if a Japanese author wants to sell a book on England, he should attempt to get the words Oxford or Cambridge into the title because those cities symbolise the tradition of which the Japanese are so fond.

They also represent the two great seats of learning which the Japanese so admire and so covet.

At a lavish ceremony held at Cambridge University in February 1994 to formalise a £9.25 million construction project for New

Hall College, the guest of honour was seventy-three-year-old millionaire Yasuto Kaetsu.

For many, the elderly benefactor was a godsend. The deal would provide the college with a new entrance court and accommodation block which would enable all its students to be accommodated on campus throughout the duration of their courses.

But for others, there were concerns. Students from an obscure women's university west of Tokyo which bears Kaetsu's name would also be entitled to use the new accommodation. But the Japanese university is so minor it does not figure on most lists of educational institutes and linking it to Cambridge was felt by some to be dragging down the good name of the latter.

St Catherine's College, Oxford had had a lucky escape a few years earlier when a link with a construction company led to the formation of a college in Japan claiming to be fully affiliated with the university.

But such concerns paled into insignificance when the media spotlight fell on the construction company – Kajima – that had introduced Cambridge to Kaetsu, and had been contracted to carry out the work.

Numbered ninety-second in the top one hundred Japanese firms, Kajima has a turnover in excess of £14 billion and in early 1994 was embroiled in a bid-rigging and bribery scandal where millions of yen were said to have changed hands to ensure that the company was awarded lucrative public works contracts. The chairman of Kajima resigned from his post as head of the Japan Chamber of Commerce and Industry and another senior executive was arrested. Links with the yakuza were strongly suspected, but never proved.

But the controversy didn't end there and the spotlight soon lit on Kaetsu himself. According to the Japanese *Who's Who*, Kaetsu is a benefactor of old people's homes and a former director of an organisation for encouraging the *Kidotai*.

A mobile task force of the Tokyo police department, used to control civil, particularly student, demonstrations during the sixties, the *Kidotai* is somewhat at odds with the ethos of Cambridge University. The group also had strong links with the yakuza who, as fanatical patriots, were often used to boost the *Kidotai*'s ranks. Kaetsu himself is believed to have associated with known gangsters in the past and almost certainly maintains some of these 'friendships' to this day.

And while there is no suggestion at all that any of the money which is being invested in Cambridge is anything other than wholly legitimate the fact of the matter is that, even if it was not, there would be no way of telling.

All of which leaves the National Criminal Intelligence Service, MI5, Customs and Scotland Yard certain of only one thing: if the yakuza don't already 'own' a significant chunk of Britain, it's only a matter of time before they do.

Chapter Six

Not Villains, but Gods

The Colombian Drug Cartels

'So you want to write a story about the cocaine trade.
Course you do. It's the only story in this place.
Any other story, you follow it hard enough, it
comes back round to *nosola*. They've got snow
in their blood here.'

From The Fruit Palace *by Charles Nicholl*

F rom the far end of the street you cannot quite see the house where the Goldsworthys used to live. Even standing directly opposite, the high hedges, overhanging trees and boarded-up gates ensure that the mini-mansion in Fulham, south-west London remains mostly hidden.

While in residence, the Goldsworthys themselves were equally shy. Near-neighbours with good memories recall an archetypal quiet family who 'kept themselves to themselves' and gave little away. Occasionally they'd have friends over for dinner and, during the summer, they'd sometimes lounge in the garden, but for the most part they were only barely noticeable.

Then it happened. In December 1988, a few months after her husband had taken a job in America, Claudia Goldsworthy and her young daughter suddenly disappeared. When the police came looking they found a domestic *Marie Celeste*: furnishings and clothes all in place, food in the fridge, schoolbooks on the kitchen table, and every creature comfort left behind as if the pair had just popped out to the shops.

Concern rapidly turned to astonishment when the neighbours learned they'd been fed a string of lies. Keith Goldsworthy hadn't gone to America for work, he'd been sentenced to twenty-two years for his part in running a multi-million-dollar cocaine ring. As for Colombian-born Claudia, she'd vanished six days before she was due to appear at Knightsbridge Crown Court on a charge of having laundered millions of pounds of her husband's drug profits.

So hasty was her departure that Claudia was forced to

abandon all work in progress: not only did she leave her £250,000 house completely intact but detectives found more than £200,000 spread throughout various bank and building society accounts.

The money was promptly frozen by the courts, but the real legacy of the Goldsworthy dynasty continues to evade the best that British law enforcement has to offer, providing the foundation upon which almost all modern-day organised crime is built.

In early 1985, when Claudia and Keith first arrived in England, the cocaine trade wasn't considered much of a threat. Average customs seizures for each year of the preceding decade were a mere 17 kilos while the haul for the whole of 1984 had been just 35 kilos.

Heroin, on the other hand, was being widely proclaimed the scourge of society: that same year a massive 312 kilos were seized while government statistics pointed to an estimated 50,000 addicts, leading to a flurry of magazine and newspaper stories on the 'heroin crisis'.

But then the Goldsworthys arrived and almost immediately the balance started to shift. By the end of 1985, cocaine seizures had doubled and Interpol agents had taken to describing the fledgling British market as 'an unpicked plum', warning that the 'profiles' used to spot potential hashish and heroin smugglers were failing to catch out the more upmarket travellers bringing in a few kilos of nose candy.

A week after Scotland Yard's drug squad made their biggest-ever seizure – 6 kilos – the *Sunday Times* dubbed cocaine 'the new threat' and detailed how the saturation of the American market was leading to a surge in European seizures. A little later, the *Financial Times* nervously noted that the power of the cocaine barons was becoming 'unassailable'.

The following year, David Mellor, then Home Officer minister, toured Bolivia and Peru to distribute cocaine-fighting aid aimed at helping to prevent the drugs reaching the UK. Shortly after his return, John Dellow, Assistant Commissioner of the

Metropolitan Police, warned that 'violent and evil' criminals from South America were about to organise a drug distribution network in Britain.

By 1988, Richard Lawrence, then Chief Investigation Officer of HM Customs and Excise, was describing cocaine as 'the greatest concern for the future' because of signs that 'South American organisations' were trying to 'create an infrastructure in the UK to market their product'.

By the time of Claudia Goldsworthy's midnight flit, British seizures of cocaine had increased tenfold to 362 kilos, overtaking those of heroin for the first time in history. At the time the two developments seemed entirely unconnected and no one thought of Claudia as anything more than a typical gangster's moll. This could not have been further from the truth.

Far from having arrived by chance, she and her husband had been sent to London by her cousin, a certain Jorge Luis Ochoa, in order to initiate, develop and co-ordinate the British end of what quickly became the largest and most profitable criminal conspiracy in the world: the Medellin cartel.

The masters of what Colombians call *la otra economía* – the other economy – have a long tradition of profiting from their nation's natural wealth. Even today, smuggling remains the sole source of income for thousands of coastal- and border-town *contrabandistas* who trade everything from emeralds and coffee to gold, sugar and cattle, receiving black-market (and thus duty-free) jeans, cigarettes, electrical appliances and whisky in return.

During the late sixties, the most entrepreneurial and opportunistic among them, particularly those based in the Antioquia province of which Medellin is the capital, had tried to cash in on the growing American appetite for high-quality cannabis but found themselves crowded out by Mexican dealers, even though the Colombian product was far superior.

Then, in 1976, concerned at spiralling domestic usage, the Mexican government began spraying marijuana fields with the toxic weedkiller paraquat. The spraying itself barely dented production, but fears over poison-laced pot being sold on the streets of California meant that soon the Mexicans couldn't give their dope away.

Thus, by 1978, three-quarters of all the marijuana being sold in the United States was the Colombian 'gold' brand, with most sales at the American end of the trade being controlled by the thousands of Antioquian immigrants who had moved to New York following the sudden collapse of Medellin's textile trade a few years earlier.

This efficient, lucrative enterprise grew steadily until a massive increase in the 'home grown' dope scene in California all but killed off the market for imports. Some of the smugglers returned to the old ways but others switched to trafficking cocaine, a drug that was rapidly becoming the vogue in America thanks to songwriters and film-makers idolising its virtues.

There was certainly no shortage of the raw material: the coca plant has been cultivated in South America, particularly Peru and Bolivia, for more than 3,500 years. Traditionally its leaves, rich in vitamins, calcium, iron and fibre, are chewed by peasants and farm workers in order to alleviate the symptoms of altitude sickness and fatigue. There is also a huge industry which turns them into non-narcotic toothpaste, chewing gum, and the hugely popular *mate de coca* – coca tea – drunk by a least eight million South Americans daily.

Refining the leaves into pure cocaine in family-run 'factories' in Medellin, the smugglers (initially aided by the massively corrupt secret police) began supplying the Cuban dealers who controlled the fast-growing trade in Miami and New York.

But not all the Colombians were content to play second fiddle. It was while in Miami in 1977 at the age of twenty-eight that Jorge Luis Ochoa, one of three sons of a once-wealthy cattle ranching family that had fallen on hard times, witnessed the market beginning to change. At first, the Cubans had sold mostly to other Cubans but slowly, thanks to a series of FBI raids on amphetamine 'factories' pushing up the price of the closest alternative, more native

Americans began turning up in 'Little Havana' for their bags of snow.

Jorge's sharp mind was also quick to note that, while the finished product was retailing on the city streets in 1978 for up to $800 a gram, a whole kilo of pure cocaine could be bought in Colombia for only a little more. The way to make big money, he surmised, would be to take control of the smuggling, reduce the price and thus open up the user base: far better to sell 500 grams at $100 a time rather than 50 grams at $500.

Back in Colombia, Jorge, with the support of his brothers Juan and Fabio and their friends Gonzalo Gacha and the infamous Pablo Escobar, set about revolutionising the cocaine trade and restoring his family fortune.

By cultivating contacts with local criminals in major American cities, Jorge set up a series of satellite distribution networks; sent representatives to Peru and Bolivia (where massive overproduction meant coca plants were everywhere) to negotiate the best prices for the raw leaves; and used his own mules, vehicles and corrupt officials to ensure that the finished product got through.

Hundreds of other Medellin gangsters followed his lead and, within a year, a worried Drug Enforcement Administration noted that cocaine trafficking had gone from cottage enterprise to 'quasi-industrial status', employing thousands of people and making millions of dollars of profits for those in control.

The cartel itself was born proper in December 1981 after Jorge's sister, Martha, was kidnapped by members of Colombia's M-19 guerrilla movement. Kidnapping was (and remains) a frighteningly common occurrence in Colombia, but this was the first time the offspring of one of the major traffickers had been involved.

To pay the ransom would have been to invite a string of copycat attacks, so instead, Jorge called an emergency meeting of Colombia's most influential traffickers. A few days after the conference, leaflets began appearing all over the country announcing that, following discussions between

223 mafia bosses on the subject of kidnapping, the gangsters had launched a new operative group – Muerte a Secuestradores (Death to Kidnappers) – to even the score.

The group was true to its name. Amid widespread publicity, homes were invaded in the middle of the night, suspected guerrillas were shot, tortured and humiliated. Three months after her abduction, Martha Nieves was released unharmed and M-19 (and other guerrilla groups) had humbly agreed to work for the traffickers, carrying out their killings and protecting their refineries in return for guns and money.

But though the problem had been solved, the one-off co-operation had worked so well that the once-rival mafia bosses decided to make it permanent. The Ochoa brothers, Escobar and Gacha became self-appointed overlords of the cocaine empire, allotting coca paste for refining, organising huge shipments to America, and laundering the final profits.

(Like any good businessman, Ochoa reinvested his capital. He built huge refineries deep in the Colombian jungle to enable him to step up production. One, discovered at Caqueta in the south in 1984, had seven landing strips, accommodation for 100 people, workshops for car and aircraft maintenance, and even a club for pilots. It was capable of producing 20 tons of cocaine per month and 11,500 kilos of cocaine worth £1.2 billion were found during a raid.)

But by 1984, the American market had become saturated. The price had fallen to just $100 per gram as Ocha had hoped, but the user base had stopped growing, leaving the cartel's income static at an estimated $1.5 billion per year. It was time to expand so, while Jorge himself travelled to Spain to oversee things there, the Goldsworthys were despatched to London, closely followed by the youngest Ochoa brother, Fabio, and several others.

(Jorge and his colleague Gilberto Rodriguez Orejuela, who had started out laundering money for the cartels before becoming a trafficker in his own right, were both arrested in Madrid but later released without charge when the chief witness against them was assassinated.)

Within a few months of Claudia's arrival, the DEA had identified at least six top cartel figures travelling in and out of Britain, including Ochoa's lieutenant, Teodoro Castrillon, and chief co-ordinator, Cesar Arango. Travelling in pairs, they posed as legitimate businessmen and flew into Heathrow via connecting flights from Paris or Barcelona in order to ward off any suspicion.

They began by establishing a demand for the new product. Hundreds of Yardie-sponsored couriers were joined by hundreds more poor South Americans risking their liberty for the chance of earning enough from a single trip to feed their families for months.

Once the market was primed, the deliveries began in earnest. At first, multi-kilo loads would arrive concealed among consignments of fresh flowers from Europe, but once that method was discovered the smugglers quickly found new ones.

Wooden statues and *objects d'art* were hollowed out, stuffed with cocaine and glued back together, then coated with a mixture of resin and pigment. Such concealments could actually defy sniffer dogs and could only be discovered if the customs officers had total faith in their hunches and were willing to break the items apart.

Fruit was another popular method, with plastic apricots, peaches or pears stuffed with drugs hidden among boxes of real fruit. Regulations governing the transport of perishable goods give customs little time to search such containers and, with thousands entering Britain every day, the chances of being discovered are slim.

Other methods relied on more ingenuity. Cocaine powder could be mixed with plaster of Paris and moulded into bathroom fittings or mixed with fibreglass and made into dog kennels.

Cocaine oil has also been found soaked into the rubberised backing of carpets to be extracted on arrival while jumpers and other items of clothing have been impregnated with a cocaine solution.

Then there was the case of José Hernandez-Gomes, who

would have walked right through customs had it not been for the fact that the dye on his suitcase was seen coming off on his hands. It later emerged that his case had been dipped in a cocaine solution and then allowed to dry. The bag was worth an estimated £300,000.

As well as arranging smuggling, the cartel representatives also set up legitimate import companies in order to help launder the profits and arranged dozens of meetings with established British villains keen to make the profitable move out of armed robbery and into the drugs trade.

The Colombians also met a number of established British-based drug smugglers anxious to gain a foothold in the new market, including a certain Nikolaus Maria Chrastny. A Czech-born German national and still on the run for a 1973 gems robbery committed in Munich, Chrastny had worked his way up the drug-smuggling ladder, starting out guarding other people's runs and graduating to smuggling in his own right.

For eighteen months from the beginning of 1985, Nikolaus Chrastny, aided by his wife, travelled between Colombia and England to hold meetings with the Ochoa family and Pablo Escobar over the purchase of cocaine for the new UK market.

'I originally planned on getting between one hundred and fifty and two-hundred kilos of cocaine,' Chrastny later told customs officers, 'but they liked the idea of opening a further European market so much that they asked me how much I could take. I ended up with three hundred and ninety-two kilos.'

He paid just $190,000 for the first 38 kilos, taking the rest on credit. The Ochoas had dealt with Chrastny in the past and felt he was trustworthy; besides, Fabio travelled to Britain to help out.

Having successfully smuggled the cocaine into the country, Chrastny, who used the alias Charles Flynn, started distributing it from a house in Victoria, handing out 5–10-kilo packages to well-known London villains Roy Garner and later Mickey Henessey, collecting the money and then paying back his 'debt' to the London representative of the cartel. One day, outside London's Tara Hotel, he handed over plastic carrier bags containing $2,300,000.

(Charlotte Chrastny was another money-laundering expert. However, unlike Claudia, she preferred to buy clothes, furs and jewellery. In one month alone, she spent more than half a million pounds in Bond Street boutiques.)

But not everything was going as smoothly as Chrastny liked to think. Customs had been on his trail and he was eventually arrested. Most of the cocaine, however, had already been distributed – only 57 kilos were recovered. (Chrastny later escaped custody, having charmed the guards into trusting him, and remains at large.)

The (temporary) loss of a strong contact, and the subsequent loss of the Goldsworthys themselves, did little to dent the cartel's enthusiasm for the UK. Indeed, by 1989 the cartel's direct targeting of Britain was becoming so serious that a Colombian police expert was seconded to work with police and customs.

It was the first time an officer from Colombia had been sent into Europe, and the fact that Britain was chosen above Spain (then as now a major transshipment point for cocaine entering Europe) is a testimony to just how much worth both sides were placing on the UK market.

The first intelligence reports compiled after his arrival told how the cartel had invested in a number of businesses including restaurants, nightclubs and mini-cab offices.

While many senior members of the Medellin cartel passed through London at one time or another during the mid-eighties, the most famous member of the clan, Pablo Escobar, never did. However, his money was more than at home here.

The great man himself had an account at the Cannon Street branch of the disgraced BCCI, while millions of pounds' worth of his and the Ochoa family drug profits bounced back and forth between Britain and America in a bid to frustrate efforts to follow the paper trail.

The cartels have been forced to become masters of money laundering because of the vast amounts of cash their business generates. And while they have learned a great deal and employ some highly skilled people to assist them, the money laundering stage is often where the cartels are at their weakest.

For example, when professional money launderer Robert Musella, who acted on behalf of the Medellin cartel, arranged a meeting in Miami with senior BCCI directors, he left them in no doubt as to the nature of his business: comparing his client to a major motoring retailer, he noted that the only difference was that 'they sell cars and we sell cocaine'.

Far from balking at this, BCCI's laundering expert, Amjad Awan, personally recommended the safest routes for laundering the drugs cash: it could be collected in the US and then wired to the Florida resort town of Tampa.

From there it was to be telexed to a BCCI branch in Luxembourg and from there to London, where it would be used to purchase fixed-interest certificates of deposits, a kind of super-banknote.

These, in turn, would be used as collateral to obtain loans on behalf of various cartel-controlled shell companies which would be set up in Britain, the funds from which would then be transferred into current accounts for daily use.

The only problem with the slick plan was that, even with a bank with BCCI's legendary flexibility, cartel members would still need to travel abroad to open accounts in person. In May 1988, bearing letters of introduction, a party of Colombians that included Escobar's personal financier, Rudolph Armbrech, and his right-hand man, Javier Ospina, arrived in London and opened numerous accounts to set the scheme in motion. They also oversaw the formation of a London-based shell company, Capcom Financial Services, run by a former BCCI treasury manager, and over the next few months, some $20 million of drug money passed through the bank and company accounts.

In October 1988, Robert Musella announced to his colleagues that he would be marrying his girlfriend Kathleen Erickson at a plush golf club in Florida. The guests arrived and took the lift to the penthouse on the top floor, only to find themselves getting out at the second where they were promptly arrested by federal agents.

Musella had, in fact, been working undercover for US customs as part of Operation C-Chase, infiltrating the cartel, and BCCI, to prove the bank's involvement in laundering money on behalf of the drugs barons.

Operation C-Chase was the beginning of the end for the Medellin cartel and the group was effectively dead long before Pablo Escobar was brought down in a hail of bullets in December 1993.

The bad times began in 1989 when Luis Carlos Galan began his campaign for the presidency on a platform of extraditing the cocaine traffickers to America. He was a popular man, compared frequently to JFK, and the cartel made its biggest ever *faux pas* when it assassinated him in August that year.

Up until then, the traffickers had been able to enjoy their spectacular wealth openly. Escobar in particular spent his days relaxing at his vast ranch and zoo complex, surrounded by teams of heavily armed guards and co-ordinating his cocaine business from the comfort of his armchair.

But Galan's murder forced his successor, Virgilio Barca, to launch a crackdown. Escobar and Gacha declared themselves 'The Extraditables' and launched a bloody campaign of 'narcoterrorism' against the government using bombs and bullets in a bid to persuade them to drop the extradition law.

Among those who refused to join in the bombing and shootings were brothers Miguel and Gilberto Rodriguez Orejuela, whose small Cali-based organisation had progressed beyond being a Medellin subsidiary to a cartel in its own right. Once firm allies (Miguel had been Escobar's main money launderer, while it was Rodriguez who had been arrested in Spain with Jorge Ochoa), the brothers believed it would be impossible to defeat the state and distanced themselves from the attacks.

A little later, a dispute over ownership of the lucrative New York market had driven a further wedge between Cali and Medellin with Escobar swearing he would 'kill them all'. But in the end, the bullets were all travelling in the other direction. By December 1989 Gacha had been killed in a police shoot-out and a worried Escobar offered the government a deal: make extradition illegal, guarantee a short sentence and various other privileges, and he and the other traffickers would surrender.

The government reluctantly agreed. The Ochoa brothers, who had all but relinquished leadership of the cartel in favour of Escobar for a number of years, came in first to test the waters and to this day continue to reside in a comfortable prison in a satellite town just outside Medellin.

Escobar came in a little later (allowing the Colombian government to take out full-page advertisements in the *Washington Post* and *New York Times* boasting that every leader of the Medellin cartel was 'either dead or in jail') but escaped after a few months when political realignments caused him to lose confidence in the government's ability to stick to its promise.

Back on the run, his enemies were many. A terrorist group, People Persecuted by Pablo Escobar, allegedly funded directly by Cali, began waging a guerrilla war on Escobar's family and friends. But having spent a considerable amount of his fortune on (somewhat cynically) trying to eradicate Medellin's slums, Escobar also had friends in unlikely places.

Shortly after escaping from prison, Escobar agreed to answer a list of 127 questions from Colombian journalists. His responses covered twenty-three typewritten pages, each one authenticated by his thumbprint.

How would you like to end your life? 'I'd like to die on my feet in the year 3047.' *Do you not feel you are now alone after many of your old allies disappeared or have been killed?* 'It causes me great sadness and grief to have lost loyal and dear friends, but I am certain that in the streets and countryside of Colombia, there are thousands upon thousands who support and love me.'

(He was right. At his funeral, so many of Colombia's poor

wanted to pay their respects that the cortege was held up for more than two hours. 'He was a good man, he was like a God to me,' wept one elderly woman. 'He built me a house and he has never even met me.')

While Escobar bombed and blasted his way into self-oblivion, the Cali cartel tried the more subtle approach. Instead of lead, they used silver to keep their empire intact, bribing people at the highest level to ensure that their enterprise continued undisturbed. The Rodriguez brothers, along with their friend José Santacruz-Londono, now control 80 per cent of the world's cocaine trade.

According to a DEA spokesman: 'The Cali people are gentlemen – the most creative, technological and virtually impenetrable criminal organisation in the world.' A particularly graphic indication of their sophistication and influence came in late 1993 when it emerged that they had only just been prevented from hiring a spy satellite which would have put a stop to the CIA and DEA listening in on their conversations.

But then the Cali operatives have always been smarter. Back in 1984, when Jorge Ochoa's 'cocaine for the masses' product realignment had brought the price down as far as it would go, Ochoa decided to expand while the Cali men again took a more philosophical approach to the problem.

The drug had still only captured a fraction of the market – American ghettos had still failed to get excited about it, preferring heroin, which, dollar for dollar, produced a far stronger effect.

Smoked cocaine looked like the answer but the problem was finding a way in which the cocaine would burn, permitting its fumes to be inhaled. West Indians had traditionally sprinkled cocaine powder into their joints but this is ineffective as the drug simply vaporises at high temperatures and few fumes are actually inhaled.

Freebasing – which involves dissolving cocaine powder in ether then inhaling the fumes of the heated product – was one possible solution, but thanks to a series of well-publicised freebasing fires, one of which caused the 1985 plane crash that killed rock star Rick Nelson, the process had an extremely unsavoury reputation with even the most hardened addicts reluctant to try it.

No one quite knows who first came up with the simple process of converting cocaine into crack, but in a pre-trial deposition made in 1989, a young Colombian, Mario Villabona, recalled how, while working for the Cali cartel in Los Angeles in late 1984, he was summoned back to Colombia to meet a chemist known only as Oscar.

Oscar, using a couple of coffee-makers and a hot-plate, showed Villabona how to convert cocaine powder into a smokable form by mixing it with baking powder and water then heating the mixture. Oscar also explained that by selling each individual 'rock' for just $10, the profits on a kilo of cocaine could be multiplied by a factor of four.

Villabona took the magic formula back to Los Angeles and introduced it to one of LA's black street gangs, who control the street-level drugs trade not only in that city but also across much of America. The devastation caused by America's crack epidemic is the sad legacy of Villabona's success.

Unlike its Medellin rival, the Cali cartel has no real British representation. There are a handful of money launderers working on their behalf, and occasionally senior representatives may visit briefly to supervise the final stages of a delivery, but there is no equivalent of the Goldsworthy family overseeing the group's interests.

There have been dozens of agents, including Peruvians, Bolivians and Americans such as David Lemieux and Thomas O'Donnell, caught with 43 kilos of Cali cocaine and £2 million cash as part of Operation Green Ice in September 1992. The drugs turned out to be 'leftovers', with at least twice as much distributed in Britain by the pair in the months before their arrest.

There was also Antonio Teixeira, a Colombian businessman

who acted as the middle-man for former sixties gangster Eddie Richardson's ill-fated foray into narcotics. Teixeira, who had the most tenuous of connections to the Cali cartel, used his Blackheath home as a base for negotiating with Richardson to deliver 153 kilos of cocaine and two tons of cannabis concealed in a container of balsa wood shipped to Southampton.

Two Colombian colleagues of Teixeira's had earlier managed to smuggle in around 44 kilos of coke, but Teixeira himself was so incompetent and careless that he virtually led customs officers to the main haul which had been provided on credit as a (misguided) sop to Richardson's former reputation as a leading underworld face.

After Teixeira's demise, the cartel had no one at all looking after its British interests. When 1,300 kilos of high-purity cocaine were discovered on the Polish-American ship MV *Jurata*, which had berthed at Liverpool *en route* to Poland in January 1984 to unload some legitimate cargo, undercover officers managed to contact the Cali representatives in Poland (which has a growing Colombian population and is fast becoming the new European centre of the drug trade), telling them falsely that the drugs had not been discovered but that the ship would be stuck in Britain.

The only Cali men in London were a pair of low-ranking money launderers who had absolutely no idea about how to deal with drugs. In response to calls direct from Colombia, they tried to make their way to Liverpool to off-load the produce.

Thoroughly unfamiliar with travel in Britain, they made their way to Liverpool Street Station, thinking this was the place to catch a train to Liverpool. A few farcical days later, their bosses realised that the men simply weren't up to the task. Cali decided to abandon the drugs and cut its losses.

In the course of carrying out the research for this book, I spent a good deal of time trying to track down either Britons or Colombians who had dealt directly with representatives of the cartel and would be willing to talk about it.

I came tantalisingly close. At the lowest level there were dozens of couriers like Raul, currently serving six years for attempting to smuggle 2 kilos of cocaine through Heathrow, strapped to his legs in a pair of plastic bags. He claims to have known that what he was doing was illegal but says he had no choice, such was the level of poverty he and his family were being forced to endure.

Then there were more pathetic stories: women like Maria, another poor peasant woman who believed the trafficker who told her that, if she was caught, British customs would simply confiscate the drugs and send her back home. Instead, after they found the forty double-packed condoms containing 400 grams of cocaine that she had swallowed, they sentenced her to ten years.

At the next level there were extraordinary tales from the likes of Dave Hemingway, a middle-aged mini-cab controller approached while eating dinner in his favourite Spanish café by some friends of the owner and offered £15,000 to go to Colombia to bring back 5.5 kilos of cocaine worth more than £600,000.

Hemingway (who immediately told customs of the plot and agreed to go ahead with it so the organisers could be caught) spent six terrifying days in a Colombian border town where his hosts would get drunk, snort cocaine, then shoot their guns in the air.

Eventually he was fitted for a bulky body belt and a pair of oversize trousers before being taken to Bogotá airport (he had originally flown to Venezuela and then driven across the border) by a bent policeman who ensured that he was not frisked by the security police and that the immigration officer stamped the desk rather than his passport.

The biggest British coke dealer I came across, an affable and phenomenally rich man whom I shall call Albert, had a regular weekly order for 10 kilos. He would not tell me exactly who his suppliers were ('I really don't think they'd like it') but assured me they were not Colombian.

'I know a lot of people in this game, but no one who actually deals direct with the Colombians,' he explained. 'Those guys are only really interested in hundreds of kilos at a time. You're just asking for trouble if you try to shift that much gear.'

This was confirmed by the one man who was willing to talk. Well into his late fifties, slight and grey-haired, Peter looks like an archetypal bank manager. As I sat down in his functional Manchester office, he explained how he had recently been involved in direct negotiations with the number-six man in the Cali cartel to open up a major new drug pipeline in the UK.

Leafing briefly through the papers on his desk, Peter pulled out a postcard bearing Colombian postmarks, with a simple handwritten statement: 'The donkeys have come down from the mountains.'

'That was the signal,' he explained. 'The processing plant they were using was incredibly remote and because of bad weather, there was this huge delay before they could get our cocaine down to the airport and on to the plane.'

It took Peter a year to set up the deal during which time he made two visits to Colombia and also spent a good deal of time entertaining two cartel representatives in Britain.

'I was negotiating with them for two hundred and fifty kilos of ninety-six per cent pure cocaine for which we would be paying sixteen thousand pounds per kilo. The second it landed in Britain, it would have been worth more than twice that and the final street value would have been somewhere around fifty million pounds.

'They will only deal in bulk and for this reason they will only deal with people who actually appear professional and look like they know what they're doing. There is no point for them otherwise.

'They will also only deal with people they know or who have been sponsored. Someone has to put their neck on the block and say "this person is okay to trust, I guarantee it". In this case, that was Francisco who had been introduced to me by a contact in Amsterdam. They feel they have to take these kinds of precautions. They don't want to risk their merchandise with just anybody, especially not over here.

'The truth is they'd really rather not operate in Britain at all. When we first started talking, they wanted to deliver to Holland and leave it to us to sort out getting the drugs over the final stage. The problem for them was that there was no infrastructure in place.

'It's no trouble at all for them to get any amount of drugs on to a plane in Colombia, and no trouble at all for them to get them off again at Amsterdam. They've got people paid off left, right and centre. But in Britain, they don't have anything.

'It was only when I told them that I could easily sort out getting the drugs off the plane undetected at Manchester airport that they suddenly became more keen about the whole deal. They realised they could finally begin to off-load huge amounts of coke directly in Britain.

'Immediately, they started planning follow-up deals. Francisco offered to supply litre bottles of cannabis oil at eight thousand pound a bottle ("a little sideline of mine") then started planning weekly deliveries of half a ton, the first arriving just three days after the two hundred and fifty kilo shipment.

'They also offered me a three-tonne shipment at manufacturers' prices – just three thousand pounds a kilo. They were going crazy and got particularly excited as they would be able to use air freight. By ship, their usual method, it takes four or five weeks for each consignment to arrive. Suddenly they had a way of moving the same amount of drugs inside a day, thanks to our airport insiders.'

But the only reason that Peter was able to guarantee trouble-free unloading at Manchester was that he was an undercover customs officer and that the Colombians were slowly being drawn into a major sting operation which at the same time was highlighting their enthusiasm for, but lack of direct penetration into, the British drugs scene.

As the size of the deal grew, so did the level of concern from the cartel. Towards the final stages, the head of European operations was despatched from Madrid to review every last detail of the plan.

'That was quite a tense moment,' says Peter. 'Carlos was an incredibly sharp cookie. He wanted to know timings, to see warehouses, to meet our drivers and distributors, examine the accounts of our front company, everything.'

In order to prove their ability to pay, the team arranged to borrow £2 million in cash from a Manchester bank which was then driven (under discreet escort) to the warehouse where Carlos carefully examined it.

'We also had to ensure we practised anti-surveillance whenever he was around. Obviously, we were being watched, taped and filmed all the time, but we had to convince this guy not only that we weren't but that we were taking precautions to make sure that we couldn't be. If we hadn't, he'd've been on to us instantly.'

Indeed, Carlos routinely practised such techniques himself. One day, he took the Manchester shuttle train to the airport but got off two stops before and stood in the middle of the platform, watching and waiting. He hadn't seen the two customs officers, posing as a young couple, further back in his carriage; he was simply testing the waters. Even so, it was decided it would be best to abandon the pursuit for that day as Carlos was unlikely really to be going anywhere.

Dozens of additional undercover officers were drafted in to ensure that the ruse held steady, and Carlos seemed satisfied but stuck around for a few days to get to know Peter a little better.

'He wanted to come round to my house and meet my wife and family – he said it would be a sign of trust. But I said that I hadn't met his wife or family so why should I allow him to meet mine? He seemed to accept that, especially when I explained that I would be more than happy to invite him around once the deal had been completed by way of celebration.

'It got quite amusing on a few occasions,' says Peter. 'When we went out to dinner, I had to keep all the receipts in order to get the money back on my expenses. They were very impressed by this – they thought I was charging the money through the front company that we had set up and liked the idea of me working in such a methodical way.

'Carlos eventually went back to Spain and we were left with Francisco, the Cali man, and Borja, who was in charge of processing. They had agreed to accompany us to the warehouse to examine the delivery and check the purity of the cocaine before we handed over the money.

'We were driving back from the warehouse when the arrest team struck. The road was blocked off. The armed police had those guns with the laser sights. The main thing I remember is seeing the red dot appear on my chest – your natural instinct is to try to wipe it off, but it just stays there.

'They pulled us out of the car and threw us on the floor – at the time they didn't want to give away the fact that I was on their side so they had to make it look authentic. Once they got Francisco to the station, they explained exactly who I was and played him a little of the video evidence. He confessed immediately and asked to be allowed to make his one phone call.'

As the man who had put his neck on the line for the deal, Francisco knew that his life, and that of his family, could never be the same again. As the customs team watched him make his call, they couldn't help feeling a touch of sympathy.

As though he had prepared himself for the nightmare scenario a million times before, Francisco calmly dialled the number of his wife in Cali and summed up the future in a few short words.

'Peter has betrayed me. Get out of the house. Now.'

Having led to the seizure of 250 kilos of cocaine valued at £50 million, Operation Begonia was hailed a great success. 'We have destroyed their credibility in the UK,' boasted a senior customs officer to the local Manchester press shortly after the bust had been made. 'A seizure of this size must be a major setback for them.'

Yes and no. Had the Cali cartel really lost £50 million, the value of all the cocaine seized *at street level*, Begonia would certainly have been a considerable blow, but the reality of large-scale drug trafficking is that no one organisation receives the full value of the product.

In reality, the undercover customs agents would only have paid £4 million for the cocaine. Had they travelled to Colombia themselves to pick it up, the same amount would have cost just £750,000. In the end, the total loss to the Cali cartel was (leaving aside a senior operative) less than £150,000, hardly enough to bring an organisation that makes £4 billion a year to its knees.

And so despite such occasional slip-ups, the Cali cartel shows no signs of collapsing. In fact, thanks to its contacts in high places, it appears to be going from strength to strength.

In December 1993, four of the Colombian Attorney General's bodyguards were charged with cocaine trafficking on the cartel's behalf, while two months earlier a top prosecutor in charge of drug cases was arrested after police taped him talking to a Cali cartel leader.

Allegations of being in the pocket of the drug barons have haunted Colombia's current president, Ernesto Samper, since 1981, when Pablo Escobar claimed he had accepted $1 million from him while running the losing presidential campaign for fellow Liberal Alfonso Lopez.

In March 1994, when the country went to the polls, the ruling Liberal Party held on to power, winning 60 of the 102 seats despite only 30 per cent of the electorate turning out. The Cali cartel is believed to have compromised many of the parliament's members though bribery and intimidation.

In June, tapes emerged in which Cali cartel bosses appeared to be discussing paying £2.4 million into Samper's campaign account, and the CIA has since declared Colombia a narcodemocracy – a country where politicians appear to rule but in fact the drug lords pull the strings.

There is also concern about changes made to the law by the current regime. In May, possession of small amounts of hard drugs was legalised because the existing law 'violated rights to privacy and the free development of the personality'.

Internal cocaine seizures are also down dramatically. In 1990, Colombian police seized a creditable 55 tons followed by a record 81 tons the following year. But in 1992 the amount fell to 37 tons, in 1993 to 27 tons, and, by the end of 1994, just 10 kilos had been captured. Over the same period, production in the area rose from 550 to 700 tons.

There is also widespread corruption. In the last three years, 7,000 members of the police force have been dismissed or jailed for drug-related misconduct, and Colombian papers are full of farcical stories of attempts to catch the Cali barons.

In one case, the police who finally managed to track down José Santacruz-Londono managed 'accidentally' to raid the house of his neighbour, giving him plently of warning of what was going on and thus plenty of time to make his escape.

Pressure from the United States (among others) forced Samper to clean up his act. In June 1995, Rodriguez Orejuela was found hiding in a secret compartment behind a television set at his luxury safe house in southern Cali. Other key members of the cartel were arrested a few weeks later, but no one is pretending it will go any way towards stopping the trade.

Having successfully distanced themselves from the increasingly out-of-control Pablo Escobar long before his death, the Ochoa brothers are likely to be released from their low-security prison close to Medellin very soon and are ready to pick up whatever pieces of the Medellin cartel are left.

Spending their time making saddles and eating meals freshly cooked by their mother (she cooks all their meals in jail, partly because she used to run a restaurant and partly because she fears someone might try to poison them), the three brothers claim that their one-time fortune has all been spent on lawyers and security. Now they have a chance to make it back.

And even if they do not accept the challenge, there are plenty of wannabe cartel leaders waiting in the wings who would jump at the opportunity but the smart money is on the Ochoas.

'Do you really imagine that they are going to give up the most profitable business in the world?' asks the editor of one Colombian newspaper. 'They can't give it up. As soon as they lose the profits from the trafficking, they lose their ability to pay the police and army, to buy the politicians, to maintain the apparatus that keeps them alive. Once they stop, they are dead.'

Even the most successful corporation in the world can't afford to stand still or rest on its laurels. As any business school professor will tell you, the state of the market, competition and political climate must all be monitored if you want to maintain your premier position.

So, having successfully breathed new life into the cocaine trade with the introduction of crack, the men from the marketing divisions of the cocaine cartels are now focusing their attention on the future of the drug trade as a whole.

The chief problem they have to tackle is that the stimulant effect of cocaine, and particularly crack, is so powerful that regular users simply cannot cope with it all, burning themselves out after around five years.

A depressant drug such as heroin, on the other hand, can be taken over a much longer period of time. While many intravenous users suffer sores, ulcers and horrific abscesses, these are caused by impurities in the street-level product, not the drug itself. Thus, addicts with access to good-quality heroin can maintain their habits almost indefinitely without any ill-effects: many doctors believe the almost pure heroin to be less dangerous and addictive than nicotine.

By a bizarre twist of fate, the remote mountain regions of Colombia situated between Bogotá and Cali – utterly hopeless when it comes to coca cultivation – provide near-perfect growing conditions for opium poppy plantations and, having assessed the trends, the Cali cartel has, in recent years, become involved in what the US State Department describes as 'an aggressive effort to diversify' into the heroin market.

As well as protecting their long-term income, there are numerous other advantages for the traffickers. The chief coca-producing countries, such as Peru and Bolivia, are currently clamping down on production, spurred on by the promise of increased US and British aid.

Being able to grow poppies on their home soil means that Colombians will not only have greater control over the basic raw material but also that they can keep that additional profit for themselves and forgo the costs of transporting and smuggling leaves and paste into the country for final refining. Additionally, a coca crop needs at least eighteen months to reach full maturity, while opium poppies can be harvested every three to five months.

Ease of processing is another bonus. Although heroin is technically much harder to produce than cocaine, it requires a much smaller volume of chemicals, therefore reducing the need to smuggle thousands of gallons of strictly controlled 'precursor chemicals' such as ether and ammonia.

Finally, and perhaps most importantly, heroin is far more profitable than cocaine. In mid-1994, a kilogram was selling for $60,000 on the streets of New York, compared to just $8,000 for a kilo of cocaine.

But being able to grow poppies is only half the equation. In order to sell heroin on the open market, it needs to be of sufficient quality and, at first, no one in the cartel had sufficient technical know-how to make that happen.

Most of the world's heroin currently originates in one of two areas: the Golden Crescent of south-west Asia, comprising Afghanistan, Pakistan and Iran, and the Golden Triangle of south-east Asia, comprising Burma, Laos and Thailand.

At present, the best is produced in south-east Asia. Known as No. 4 (there are three grades in all, but no No. 1), it is supplied as a pure white crystalline powder and, uncut, is the closest thing to pharmaceutical heroin available on the street. Thanks to the skill and expertise of generations of Triad-controlled Thai and Burmese chemists, No. 4 has ruled the streets for two decades with nothing else coming close – until now.

According to the Drug Enforcement Administration: 'The first products coming up out of South America were sometimes humorous, but the stuff we see now is very high-quality – better than that being produced in Afghanistan and Pakistan where they have been at it for generations.'

As with all things Cali, the cartel simply bought the expertise it needed. Heroin cooks were illegally imported from all over the world to perfect the Colombian recipe. Those that failed to help found themselves abandoned and ended up being expelled from the country.

The source of a particular batch of heroin can be determined by identifying its characteristic chemical signature, a combination of factors derived from the manufacturing process. While the general chemistry is similar, slight modifications combined with different strains of poppy and different manufacturing processes leave a 'fingerprint' which, in the case of Colombian heroin, is distincly south-west Asian.

And having perfected the formula, the Cali cartel is now engaged in marketing the new product. Colombian heroin already accounts for 20 per cent of the American market and small amounts are now routinely included with deliveries of cocaine in order to force the market further.

In America, as in Britain, the authorities are ill prepared for this. Resources – both police and clinical – have been concentrating on the cocaine threat. According to a US embassy official based in London: 'Heroin is still the big worry. For the last few years, our major resources have been concentrated on crack and whenever you do that, the drug that you've been letting the pressure off builds up.'

The effect of the influx of the new product has been a general increase in quality all round, and a desperate attempt by Triad, Mafia and Turkish syndicates to maintain their grip on the market. So far as the users are concerned, the effects are often disastrous.

In January 1994, a batch of unusually pure heroin (63 per cent as opposed to the usual 40 per cent) led to the deaths of up to nine addicts. One, twenty-one-year-old Samantha Bultitude, a bright former public-school girl, died after collapsing outside a squat in the heart of the St Paul's district, Bristol.

The following month, eight heroin users died in one week in Glasgow after supplies of unusually pure heroin surfaced there. The previous year, seven dealers died from excessively pure heroin in London's King's Cross, all found within 250 yards of the mainline railway station in a single nine-day period.

Some blamed the deaths on inexperienced dealers who had failed to cut the drug – and therefore failed to maximise their profits – properly. But for the police and customs officers who pointed the finger of blame at a 'cynical marketing ploy' by new dealers . . .

In the park bordering on the city's St Paul's district, one heavy user summed up the mood. 'I haven't come across any of this killer stuff yet,' he said with a noisy sniffle. 'But I wouldn't mind getting hold of some . . .'

Chapter Seven

New Kids on the Block

The Russian Mafia

'Who do you believe is in control of the country?'
The Mafia 28%
The Government 21%

Result of Moscow opinion poll, June 1994

It's late on a Thursday afternoon and I'm leaning against a musty armchair in the corner of a dingy flatlet in Earl's Court, listening to the rain, staring at the floor and trying hard to think of a reason not to remove my trousers.

The pale, flawed beauty of Natalia stands opposite in stockinged feet and a well-worn housecoat, growing more impatient by the second. She thinks I'm trying to decide between straight sex (£30, condom mandatory) or the optional oral extra (£50) but in fact I'm just wondering whether she's the type who'd agree to an interview if I told her I was a journalist investigating the rise of East European organised crime.

So far I've discovered little about the woman whose bright yellow card – 'From Russia With Love' – was wedged into the corner of a telephone box promoting the dubious delights of a willing Moscow teenager. She claims to be nineteen (debatable), admits that she is not really from Moscow but Odessa in the Ukraine, and says that she used to work 'clubs' but prefers being her own boss. That aside, it's clear that she'd rather get down to business than spend time 'getting to know' her clients.

At the time, these snippets of information seemed to fit in with what my law enforcement contacts had told me. Apparently, around the beginning of 1993, a troupe of twenty or so upmarket Ukranian prostitutes had arrived in Britain and attempted to infiltrate London's casino network.

Travelling under the guise of 'public relations consultants' and 'dancers', the newcomers supposedly represented the Russian Mafia's first attempt to replicate the vast and lucrative sex industry it currently presides over in Moscow, which has already been successfully cloned in Frankfurt, Helsinki and Hong Kong.

Attaching themselves to likely-looking clients, the girls would charge upwards of £250 a night with the greater proportion of their money going back to their gang bosses to pay back the phenomenal debt they would have built up for the privilege of being transported to Britain in the first place.

Others arrived shortly afterwards from a wider catchment area – Russia, Poland, Czechoslovakia and the former Yugoslavia. Most were duped into believing they would be working as highly paid models, but found themselves steered towards the streets and trashy brothels within a few hours of arriving.

Tracking down the women was said to be virtually impossible. Because of the high level of intimidation employed, Russian-run prostitution rings have proved notoriously difficult to crack. 'Even though the women are treated very cruelly,' says a Czech detective who has been monitoring his country's own vice scene, 'they never turn to the police for help . . . and they never talk.'

Little wonder when, elsewhere in the Russian mafia's vice empire, girls who attempt to welsh on their 'contracts' of employment are routinely beaten and occasionally murdered.

In March 1995 it was announced that the year-long Project Ivan, a joint analysis by the National Criminal Intelligence Service, the Metropolitan Police, MI5, MI6, Customs and the Immigration department failed to find a single Russian prostitute operating in the country.

Although Mafioski connected to the vice trade elsewhere have been spotted in London, they are few and far between and seem to be working far more as underlings to Turkish syndicates (see Chapter Ten) than striking out on their own.

'The evidence and intelligence obtained by Project Ivan does not bear out what has been said in newspapers or on TV or even by some police officers. There is a threat, but not an extensive one, and it is only in London – not in the UK as a whole.'

So just who was Natalia and what was she doing in Britain? Sadly I will never know. As her impatience rapidly turned to discomfort, I made my excuses and left.

When I called the number again two weeks later, another woman answered. Natalia had gone. She did not know where.

The Russian Mafia or *Mafioski* or *Organizatsiya* is the largest and fastest-growing of all the world's organised crime gangs.

It is a monster that has seemingly come from nowhere: a decade ago crime – officially dismissed as a product of class inequalities nurtured by capitalism – was widely believed to have no place in the communist Utopia that was the Soviet Union.

Pre-*glasnost*, crime figures were never published, prostitution wasn't illegal because the state pretended it didn't exist, and the few criminals that did emerge were always portrayed as hopeless, vodka-sodden recidivists whose minds had been corrupted by Western influences.

As for the word 'mafia', it was only ever used in anti-government circles as an ironic, almost comical reference to the activities of the cadre of corrupt high-ranking officials who claimed subsidies for non-existent products and made fortunes in hard currency from illegal exports.

But this was nothing more than window dressing. Behind the Iron Curtain, Russia had a huge and well-organised criminal fraternity. Its origins dated back to the late 1800s, but the group first gained prominence during the Bolshevik revolution when terrorists and gangsters joined forces to spread public disorder.

Out of this grew an alternative underworld society with its own laws, regulations and values. The code of the Thief involved rejecting any dependence on the state, earning a living wholly through crime, never deceiving other Thieves, and not owning any property.

Entry to this élite band was through a formal 'coronation' – a ceremony available only to those who had distinguished themselves in criminal circles, proved they could organise rackets and commanded the absolute respect of their followers.

Operating under the banner of *vori v zakone*, which translates literally as 'Thieves in law', it was these same men who went on to control Russia's vast black market – often the only place where many commodities could ever be purchased and used by an estimated four out of five consumers.

Such regular, close contact between members of the public and members of the underworld, combined with the mainstream popularity of numerous *blatnaya* – criminal songs – cultivated the image of the Thief as an honourable rogue. Rather like Japan's Yakuza, Russia's gangsters became an accepted and tolerated part of society.

But when the law changed and the black market became the free market, many of the younger Thieves, who held the old ways in a lesser regard, took the opportunity to make the switch to Western-style organised crime. The prospects were excellent: in any normal economy, the mafia control drugs and prostitution – the activities on the edge of society. In Russia, thanks to chronic shortages, the new gangsters could control virtually everything – a prize well worth fighting for, even among themselves. So they did.

Since 1989, the murder rate in Russia alone has more than tripled and currently stands at 20 per 100,000 head of population per year – double that of the United States. Over the same period, the number of recorded crimes rose by more than 100 per cent to over three million as the outlaws once again spread public disorder, but this time in the name of profit, not politics.

In all there are believed to be between 3,000 and 5,000 criminal gangs operating throughout the former Soviet Union with a total annual income estimated at an incredible £15 billion. The latest indications are that some 40 per cent of Russia's Gross Domestic Product is now under the direct control of the Mob, as is much of the Army, security service and police force.

In February 1993, Boris Yeltsin declared that 'organised

crime has become a direct threat to Russia's strategic interests and national security.' He ordered a member of his presidential staff to investigate and the subsequent report, released at the beginning of the following year, confirmed all his worst suspicions. 'Every, repeat every owner of a shop or kiosk pays a racketeer,' stated the report, adding that between 70 and 80 per cent of banks and major businesses were paying out protection money – often up to half of their profits – rather than suffer violent reprisals at the hands of the mobsters.

The report also found that the most efficient gangs had their own informers within the police, teams of contract killers on permanent stand-by to settle scores, and even employed computer experts to hack into finance systems to facilitate money-laundering operations. The goal of every top gangster was said to be to escape from Russia and live on riches accumulated in a foreign bank account.

(Many had been doing so for some time. In the early seventies thousands of Russian Jews were allowed to emigrate to America. Along with the legitimate came hundreds of convicted criminals travelling with false papers issued by the KGB who hoped their presence would discredit the new community. New York's Brighton Beach – home to 40,000 émigrés – is now the *Mafioski*'s main stronghold outside Russia itself.)

Thanks to inaction in the early days, this push abroad has now advanced so far it seems impossible to stop. Ex-KGB officers have told how they received urgent instructions to crack down on the vast network of new criminals in the late eighties after the government realised they were a greater threat to communism than political violence.

Meanwhile many of the older Thieves – disturbed by the sudden increase in capital available to their younger colleagues and the growing links with politics, industry, finance and international lawbreaking – have also tried to dissuade the new groups from expanding overseas. But for both, it was too little, too late.

The new syndicates quickly updated their methods of operation, learning new skills such as money laundering, fraud and drug trafficking and linking up with the world's top gangs including the Colombian cartels and the Chinese Triads.

In an already crowded underworld, they have carved themselves a new niche and built a reputation for ruthlessness, efficiency and outrageous violence: torturing and mutilating before killing is considered the norm, while a favourite method of execution is to tie someone to a bed, place an iron on their bare chest and plug it in, literally roasting them to death.

Nowadays when you mention the word 'mafia', Russians react in the way you'd expect them to. With sheer terror.

In March 1994, dozens of terrified British businessmen working in Moscow held an unprecedented meeting with Russian police chiefs to discuss ways of defending themselves against an epidemic of mugging, murder and extortion.

Many complained of persistent 'visitors' who would bang on the doors of their flats in the early hours of the morning, demanding entry on the grounds that they wanted to discuss 'business'.

It was just such a visit that left Greg Kusztan, a thirty-one-year-old British telecommunications expert, dying from multiple stab wounds in his hotel room in August 1993.

Three months later, Michael Dasaro, who worked in the Moscow office of accounting firm Ernst and Young, was found dead in his hotel bath. His visitors had kicked down the door to his room. Officially, the shock was said to have brought on a massive heart attack; in private, many friends and colleagues insist he was murdered.

The threat is seen as a very real one. The British Embassy currently provides security briefings for all those working in Moscow. As well as receiving general advice on how to deal with the gangs, those who attend are urged to buy reinforced steel front doors and avoid taking the same route to work each day in order to thwart potential kidnappers.

Because of the gangsters' need to launder money and the status attached to a foreign bank account, those working in the finance sector are at greatest risk. In the two years prior to mid-1994, eighteen bankers were shot dead on their doorsteps in Moscow, St Petersburg and Yekaterinburg, as the gangs attempted to gain control of the banking sector. Some banks have gone so far as to form private armies to defend their staff.

But even working in a more mundane environment offers no protection – anyone who can provide the gangs with hard foreign currency is a potential target.

When fifty-year-old British Gas worker David Edwards was mown down by a car in the early hours of 3 October 1994 as he made his way to his Moscow hotel, it seemed like a simple hit-and-run tragedy.

However, his colleague, Michael Christie, who was walking with him and suffered two badly broken legs and numerous other injuries, graphically recalled how the vehicle – a police car, no less – had deliberately aimed at them and then speeded up. It was, without doubt, nothing less than a premeditated murder attempt.

Indeed, from the time he arrived in Russia on 6 June, the work log that Edwards kept recorded the campaign of intimidation and corruption he faced. He was regularly threatened with death or beating unless he stayed in mafia-'approved' hotels – usually horribly decrepit and vastly overpriced – and was strongly encouraged to make use of a particular taxi firm.

On 10 June he wrote: 'We have been threatened by two guys with guns – we are coming home.' Once alerted to the problem, British Gas made new board and lodging arrangements and Edwards returned to Moscow a month later. But soon his log recorded how he had to pay bribes to the police (who were being controlled by the gangs) to avoid arrest for trumped-up offences and to the mafia to avoid physical confrontations. When the money stopped flowing, they took their revenge.

Had Edwards seen a report by the security consultancy

Control Risks, in London, released earlier that same year, he might have been forewarned. Based on interviews with hundreds of company directors, it identified Russia as the leading 'gangster economy', noting a 'colossal' amount of official corruption throughout the former Soviet Union.

An estimated 7,000 extortion demands were made to foreign businesses based in Russia in the first six months of 1993 alone, while paying out bribes and protection money to avoid the threat of kidnap was considered part of everyday life.

'With the rouble and the dollar running parallel, overseas companies are seen as good vehicles for money laundering,' warned the report. 'It is causing considerable alarm for British businessmen.'

And as Russia's gangsters increasingly attempt to coerce Britons based overseas into helping them expand their criminal empire, the sense of alarm is quickly spreading to police, customs and government officials.

One businessman, identified only as Brian, told a BBC documentary how, following the collapse of communism, he went into business with a small group of Russian entrepreneurs. He helped them set up a network of offshore companies and bank accounts, and bought three properties in Kent and a number of luxury cars on their behalf.

His suspicions were first aroused when he noticed that his contacts each had access to dozens of forged passports, some even giving them diplomatic status. Brian also became alarmed at the vast amounts of money flowing into some of the accounts: £3 million passed through one alone in a matter of days.

But it wasn't until a few weeks later that his business partners finally showed their true colours. 'They asked me to sell arms to anybody I could find, particularly the IRA. When I refused they produced a pistol, loaded it in front of me and placed it against my head. They said they doubted whether I'd be leaving Moscow.'

His life was spared only after he agreed to take the list of weapons – which included anti-tank artillery, anti-aircraft guided missile systems, detonators and plastic explosive – to England and attempt to contact the terrorists. Instead he went straight to the police and remains under their constant armed protection.

This easy access to cheap, seemingly endless supplies of high-quality weapons – a legacy of the partial dismantling of the massive Soviet Army – is an aspect of the Russian Mafia that causes particular concern in British law enforcement circles, which fear that weapons-grade uranium and plutonium liberated from nuclear weapons could find its way into the hands of terrorists.

Attempts at smuggling this kind of material have risen steadily since the collapse of communism, with Germany emerging as the main arena. In 1990 there were just four seizures; by 1993 there were 241, though a significant number were scams involving, say, soil from Chernobyl, which would be just potent enough to get the geiger counter of a gullible customer clicking.

However, the ninety-odd cases that came to light during the first five months of 1994 were most notable for a significant 'quality leap', with genuine plutonium appearing for the first time.

While no seizure has yet yielded anywhere near enough to make even the most crude nuclear weapon, there has been more than enough material for a terrorist group to contaminate the water supply of a major city.

At the time of writing, nothing has been seized in Britain and weapons of minor rather than mass destruction remain the biggest worry. At an organised crime conference held in England in May 1993, David Veness, then head of Scotland Yard's specialist operations department, warned that gun-smuggling Russian crime syndicates were threatening to bring about an explosion in armed crime which, coupled with the increasing number of Yardie-style street shoot-outs, would rapidly accelerate the need for a fully armed police force.

'In five years' time there is absolutely no doubt that the

major problem threatening the inner cities of this country will be central and east European criminals,' Veness warned the delegates. 'Their trafficking activities and kits of drugs and weapons will be the equivalent of the current problems posed by the Triads, Mafia and Colombians combined.'

Kalashnikov AK-47 assault rifles, weapons so powerful that the shock of the bullet's impact is often sufficient to kill, regardless of the location of the wound, and a range of Eastern Bloc submachine-guns and pistols, are now being uncovered during raids on British crime gangs with startling regularity. Andrew, the underworld armourer from the first chapter, claimed to have one the day before I visited and commented on the increasing numbers of ex-army weapons that were passing through his hands.

(In September 1994, a Kalashnikov was, for the first time, used in an attempt to rob a bank. Surprisingly, this didn't occur in some depressed inner city but in the sleepy town of Kendal in the heart of the Lake District.)

Any doubts that such weapons are coming direct from representatives of the *Organizatsiya* evaporate when you speak to men like André – one of hundreds of Russian businessmen living and working in London who have discovered that, far from escaping the clutches of the mafia by moving to Britain, the organisation was waiting for them when they arrived.

'They try to be subtle but they fail,' he sighs. 'They telephone or visit and ask if it is possible for them to do business with you. They say you must be doing well, making a lot of money; that there are many dangers which you need protection from.'

Those who refuse are subjected to the usual threats of having their homes burned down or their children kidnapped. Anecdotal evidence suggests that as many as 60 per cent of Russian businessmen in Britain err on the side of caution and opt to pay up.

Wealthy executives are a particular target and, in the case of those with good connections, the gangs will often prefer payment in kind rather than cash. The executives can find themselves providing financial arrangements, fixing insurance and opening bank accounts of behalf of the mafia, often unwillingly assisting in the movement of ill-gotten gains.

But as is the case in Russia, some businessmen end up positively encouraging the mafia. 'If I have a problem with someone who has not paid a debt, I call them in,' says André. 'If I am paying them anyway, I may as well get some benefit. They collect the money and keep a percentage.'

Emigré stall-holders selling Russian artefacts around Petticoat Lane have also been targeted by the protection squads, but worst hit are the thousands of Russians who are in Britain illegally, often working in Turkish sweatshops throughout London's East End where conditions and salaries are akin to those of slave labour.

Under the threat of being reported to the Home Office and thus deported, as well as more physical punishment, many hand over virtually all their meagre salaries to mafia hoodlums. The Turkish factory owners themselves have also been targeted.

In April 1994, police announced that four men had been identified as spearheading the main *Mafioski* push into the UK. The quartet had all bought expensive homes, formed front companies with the help of unsuspecting British business partners, and were believed to be setting up a system whereby millions of pounds' worth of drugs, arms and racketeering profits could be laundered.

However, separating the legitimate from the illegitimate is proving almost impossible. In recent years, Russian investment in Britain has soared: at the time of writing, the value of Russian assets being held in British banks is around £3.1 billion, and some £50 million is believed to have been spent on London properties alone.

During 1993, under regulations that require banks and other institutions to notify the police of 'suspicious financial transactions', 13,000 cases were reported. Of these, only 200 involved Russians (up from four the previous year) but they were distinguished by the sheer size of the transactions. While many of the other reports dealt with amounts around £20,000, the smallest involving a Russian was in excess of £500,000, while the largest ran to several million pounds.

With capital flight from the former Soviet Union to the West running at an estimated £12 billion each year, hundreds of millions of pounds are known to be passing through the City of London, second only to Switzerland as a favoured laundering conduit because of the size and relative stability of its banking industry.

Just how much of this money belongs to the mafia no one can say. With Russians, perhaps more than with others, appearances are often deceptive.

It took Harrods three days to deliver everything they had bought, including a £20,000 sofa, a £9,000 double bed, and £37,000 worth of high-class reproduction furniture. 'I've never seen anyone spend that kind of money in so little time,' recalled one lorry driver who helped shift the goods.

But it was only the tip of the iceberg. From the time they had arrived in London in October 1992 – ostensibly to arrange the printing of stamps and currency – Ruslan Outsiev, Prime Minister of the renegade Russian republic of Chechnya, and his brother Nazarbek had eschewed their modest communist roots to live a life of ostentatious luxury.

Having first enjoyed the best suites in a string of top hotels, the pair eventually set their sights on a four-bedroom penthouse flat in Bickenhall Mansions close to Baker Street, on the market for £750,000. The brothers offered to pay in cash.

Alarmed at such a prospect, the owners of the mansion block in which the flat was based decided to check out the Outsievs' credentials during negotiations. They eventually received a statement from the Foreign Office which detailed the make-up of Chechnya's ultra-violent criminal gangs and explained how the country was rapidly becoming known as Russia's Sicily. But the brothers were given a clean bill of health (though as a cautionary measure they were placed under police surveillance).

Once the brothers were settled into their new home, the spending showed no sign of slowing down, Ruslan became notorious in local restaurants for shelling out up to £2,000 a night on tips, handing every passing waiter £100 or so, while together, the pair would arrange for up to six high-class prostitutes to visit the flat each evening.

The Special Branch team assigned to monitor the brothers rapidly discovered that, although they were spending freely in public, their biggest shopping expeditions were being conducted well away from prying eyes.

One private but lucrative venture involved taking control of the London market in stolen antiques and artworks from Eastern Europe, something that Ruslan (who had been a middle-league racketeer when he was younger) found well within his capabilities. Another involved selling off thousands of barrels of Chechen oil – the country's only natural asset – for personal gain.

But the main 'secret' project was on a far grander scale. From the comfort of the opulent master bedroom, Ruslan had been negotiating with a certain Joseph C. Ripp – an American financier and former convict with known links to the Cosa Nostra – for a £173 million loan to enable Chechnya to purchase 2,000 Stinger surface-to-air missiles.

Ordering the weapons, intended to tip the balance in the long-expected full-scale battle with Russia over independence, turned out to be Ruslan's downfall after his interpreter, a patriotic Armenian émigré named Gagic Ter-Ogannisyan, leaked details of the plan to friends in the republic's government. Ter-Ogannisyan had lived in London for five years and had married BBC journalist Alison Ponting, but his nationalist sympathies remained as strong as ever.

Terrified of the prospect of such firepower being passed by the Chechens to their fellow Muslims in Azerbaijan, with whom the Armenians had been fighting a bitter five-year war, the decision was taken to try to stop the deal at all costs.

In late February 1993 the Outsievs attended an 'urgent'

meeting at London's Langham Hotel with Ashot Sarkyssian and Mkrtitch Martirossian, both identified as Armenian KGB agents. The brothers were implored to go no further with the negotiations. They refused.

A week later, two removal men, Patrick Johnson and Patrick Marsh, were tempted by the generous offer of £450 to work on their day off, carrying a refrigerator box from the Bickenhall Mansion penthouse to a house in Harrow. 'We were trying to lift it – it was heavy and if it was a fridge-freezer it shouldn't have been that heavy,' said Johnson. 'It smelled like everything inside had gone rotten and there was a lavender fragrance trying to disguise the smell, whatever it was.'

After thinking about the odour all weekend, the men finally called the police. When they opened the box officers found Ruslan's decomposing body inside. He had been shot in the head three times. Breaking into the Baker Street flat, they found Nazarbek's body on one of the beds. He had been executed in an identical fashion. The following day Ter-Ogannisyan and Martirossian were arrested as they attempted to re-enter the flat.

The media went crazy. For months, organised crime experts across the globe had been chronicling the rise of the Russian Mafia, predicting that it was only a matter of time before their reach extended across Europe and into Britain.

But once details of the arms plot were made public the furore calmed down. While on remand, Mkrtitch Martirossian made a full confession to the killings before hanging himself and leaving Ter-Ogannisyan, who had helped to dispose of Ruslan's body, to face the music alone. He is now serving life.

Six months after the trial, Karen Reed, sister to Alison Ponting, was shot dead on the doorstep of her Woking home by an unknown 'professional' assassin. Alison had been sharing the house at the time and at first it seemed that, but for a case of mistaken identity, the Chechens had taken revenge for the death of their Prime Minister.

But new evidence has since emerged which suggests firstly

that there may have been other reasons for the bungled attempt on Ponting's life and secondly that the initial mafia references may not have been completely redundant.

In addition to his day jobs, Ter-Ogannisyan also ran an import-export company, Alga International, trading various goods – from clothes and computers to antiques and artworks – between the UK and Russia. Because of the dominance of Russia's black market, this work, which generated a turnover well into six figures, would undoubtedly have brought them into contact with the underworld.

(The *Organizatsiya* is known to be heavily involved in the plundering of the rarest of paintings, icons and antiques from all over Eastern Europe. One Interpol estimate puts the value of art stolen from Czechoslovakia alone in 1993 at £18.5 billion.)

Over the years, the Armenian had built up a personal collection of rare Eastern Bloc art worth an estimated £1 million, and was said to have received 'threats' from 'foreign sources' laying claim to it. Some of the items had been acquired during Gagic's time in Britain, but the most valuable went back further.

Ter-Ogannisyan had in fact run a similar antiques business in partnership with none other than Mkrtitch Martirossian back in Russia and Armenia before the pair moved to Britain in the late eighties. This, coupled with a little-known detail that emerged during Martirossian's confession – that he had been forced to join up with the KGB to avoid prosecution for illegally selling valuable artworks – puts a very different spin on the whole episode.

While the death of Ruslan and Nazarbek was greatly mourned by their fellow countrymen, they were even more missed by the mafia gangsters who had relied on them to co-ordinate the movement of stolen art treasures through the London underworld.

Thanks to Ruslan stashing dozens of irreplaceable items in places where no one can now find them, millions of pounds have been lost – the Russian Mafia's motivation for a revenge killing which is as strong, if not stronger, than any.

But new 'controllers' have now taken up residence in London and the stolen art trade, along with the money laundering, gun running and toxic waste disposal, shows no sign of slowing down.

In January 1995, a farm in Northamptonshire was sealed off after 50 kilos of uranium off-cuts were found dumped on the site. The material is believed to have originated in the Eastern Bloc where the *Mafioski* is known to have infiltrated the lucrative toxic waste disposal industry, but tighter rules on fly-tipping on the European mainland make Britain appear a softer target.

In September 1995, a second draft of the Project Ivan report showed that, away from the prostitution arena, the doom-laden rhetoric seemed to be holding true and the links between British and Russian gangs growing ever stronger. Three suspected arms deals were identified including one in which a consignment of hand grenades were purchased by a London-based crime family. There was also evidence of attempts to smuggle in high-tech weaponry including night sights and sniper rifles and one report of a British gangster who, from a base in a Moscow casino, supplied arms to gangs across Europe.

The most over-used newspaper headline of the nineties – 'The Russians Are Coming' – may yet bear bitter fruit.

Chapter Eight

Storm from the East

The Triads

'I shall not disclose the secrets of the Hung family,
not even to my parents, brothers or wife. I shall
never disclose the secrets for money. I will
be killed by a myriad of swords if I do so'

*One (number five) of the 36 oaths common
to all Triad societies. Hung was the original name
given to such societies*

E ven if English were his mother tongue, Kan would not rank among the world's most eloquent men. As it is, with only a handful of words at his disposal, it is difficult to convey the sheer terror and desperation in his voice when he talks about the day the Triads came.

The squat forty-six-year-old, who moved to England from Hong Kong in the early eighties, currently runs a compact but elegant Chinese restaurant well away from the George Street heart of Manchester's Chinatown. For the first few years his business was trouble-free but then, in March 1994, a scruffy letter was pushed under his door one afternoon asking if he was interested in 'investing' in a local company.

Such letters are now widely accepted within the Chinese community as signalling the start of a modern-day Triad extortion campaign. They promise an abundance of good luck and good fortune for those who subscribe but warn of bad times ahead for those who do not.

But while they bring many of their superstitions and rituals with them, few Chinese who have lived in Britain for any length of time are willing to make a financial sacrifice on the strength of a letter alone. So when, as was the case with Kan, this initial softly, softly approach is ignored, a chain of events is set in motion to ensure that all that is promised comes true.

A week or so after the letter arrived, three Chinese youths turned up at Kan's restaurant just as he was locking up for the night. 'They said they were 14K [the name of one of the four

main Triad gangs currently operating in Britain]. They looked
. . . bad,' he says, struggling for words.

'They told me I had done bad things and that evil would
happen. They said I had to pay to be protected from this. They
asked for two hundred and fifty pounds "tea money" a week.
I had no choice. I could not afford what they were asking . . .
I tell them too much, but no [he shakes his head vigorously].
They leave, but very angry. Swearing.'

A few days later, Kan arrived at the restaurant to find that
human or dog excrement had been thrown at and smeared
around the main doorway. For the next few days he received
threatening phone calls telling him he would be 'chopped' –
attacked by men with meat cleavers – and that his business
would be burned to the ground unless he paid what he 'owed'.

Three times in the month that followed staged yet beautifully
choreographed fights suddenly erupted between groups of
bogus customers just when the restaurant was at its busiest.
Legitimate clients scattered while regulars were left with the
distinct impression that their once-quiet lunchtime retreat had
gone to the dogs.

In between fights, other 'customers' would suddenly stand
up and loudly denounce the quality of their food ('This is dog
food; I see rat shit'), push their plates on to the floor and walk
out. There were also times when table-loads of youths who had
eaten heartily would suddenly realise they had 'forgotten' all
their money and leave without paying.

Just when it seemed things could not get any worse, Kan's staff
began to complain of harassment. Some had been approached on
their doorsteps and told bluntly that they should find new jobs.
A few quietly suggested that Kan pay up and allow them to get
on with their lives. Others opted to leave their jobs altogether
and work for employers who were more 'safety'-conscious.

Kan thought he could ride out the storm, but then, while
opening up one April morning, he was rushed by six men wearing
balaclavas. 'They had bars of iron. They hit me here, here, here,'
he says softly, pointing to his head, knees and groin. He then

holds his hands either side of his ears like an Egyptian dancer. 'Swell up like ball,' he whispers, wincing at the memory.

The beating was just a warning. Next time he knew that he would be 'chopped' – attacked with meat cleavers or melon knives. While the Triads have ready access to guns and other weapons, 'choppings' are considered particularly symbolic as they relate to the death by a 'myriad of swords' warnings in many of the Triad oaths.

Such attacks are rarely intended to be fatal – the principal targets are the main muscles including the calves, thighs, forearms and biceps, though the scalp is often slashed too – but the hideously scarred amputees who survive serve as a warning to others in the community that failing to give the Triads sufficient 'face' – the Chinese equivalent of respect – will not be tolerated.

Enough was enough. Today, like an estimated six out of ten Chinese businessmen working in Britain, Kan pays protection money to the Triads. He will not say how much, though he is adamant that it is considerably less than they originally asked for. To his mind, this is a victory, albeit a small one.

However, gang members now often stage their informal meetings at Kan's place, eating and drinking for free. Kan is also obliged to buy most of his food supplies, his linen and cleaning products through Triad-run companies. He pays way over the odds for a service that could only be described as shoddy and, while once the restaurant's balance sheet was healthy, he now only just manages to scrape a living. But at least his staff are happy.

In 1985 the House of Commons Home Affairs Committee on the Chinese Community in Britain reported the total absence of Triads in Britain. In what appears to have been a particularly hasty conclusion, it stated:

'The myth flourishes despite the absence of any evidence whatever to sustain it. It is true of course that any Chinese criminals in Britain are likely to have contacts in Hong Kong.

But no one was able to provide us with any evidence or even reasonable suspicion of links between criminal activities or organisations in Britain and Hong Kong and Macao.'

In fact the Triads have had a presence in Britain since the beginning of the century and, as one of the oldest of all criminal groups (many say the Chinese practically invented organised crime), the Triads are undoubtedly the best established of all the international gangs currently operating in the UK.

There are about 156,000 Chinese in Britain. One-third live in Greater London, around 4,000 in Barnet alone. A further 3,000 have made their homes in Northern Ireland while the rest are spread throughout Manchester, Liverpool, York, South Wales, and central Scotland.

More than a quarter are self-employed – among ethnic communities they have the highest rate for starting their own businesses – and this is one of the reasons why the community is seen as such a suitable target for gangs seeking extortion money.

Like the Asian mafia, the structure of the Triads is akin to a series of concentric circles. On the outermost level are the street gangs. Their members are generally young, often unemployed males trying to identify with the culture their parents grew up with, despite having lived here all their lives.

Most of the gangs are led by individuals who have travelled over from Hong Kong, often illegally, to stir them up into a frenzy and organise them into teams in order to target restaurants and businesses with extortion demands. Although they will refer to themselves as Triads, the vast majority of street gang members will not have taken any formal oaths or passed through the initiation ceremony.

The next level is made up of more upmarket, institutionalised gangs, composed of men in their late twenties upwards. Formally inducted into the Triads, the members of this group will be involved in a wide range of criminal activities including loan sharking, illegal gambling, assault, prostitution, racketeering, credit card fraud, illegal immigration, and VAT evasion.

Finally, there is the innermost circle, which contains strictly controlled, highly professional Triads who function as an international business. They control a huge drug-trafficking empire, dabble in commercial fraud, and have a sophisticated money-laundering network in order to 'wash' the profits of their crimes.

All three levels are highly active within the UK, though by virtue of the age and experience of those involved, it is the first two which tend to be the most noticeable and, so far as the individual victims are concerned, the most worrying.

If all the youths who preyed on Kan's place and the other restaurants were strictly Chinese, then eventually their faces would become so well known that it would become increasingly difficult for them to gain access to places in order to play the intimidation game.

The Triads wised up to that problem long ago. At first, they employed disenfranchised Vietnamese youths to 'bang tables' for them. Now, as the former boat people increasingly form gangs of their own, the low-level Triad thugs are more likely to be Japanese. Or Thai. Or black.

'Having established themselves in the UK, they have found they simply can't recruit enough willing young Chinese to work their rounds,' says one detective close to the London community. 'The youngsters that do join are growing up on the same housing estates and going to the same schools as loads of other white, black, Japanese and Greek kids.

'They also meet up at the same local martial arts clubs and they all want to hang out together. So increasingly, these non-Chinese are being allowed to join but only at the very lowest level. They become "Hanging Blue Lanterns" – non-initiated Triad members – and they're never allowed to go any higher. They basically don't trust the round-eyes.'

For the past year, teams of teenage recruiters have appeared outside the gates of schools in most major cities, particularly in the London boroughs of Southwark, Lambeth and Croydon.

Simple graffiti publicising the gangs has also been spotted close to some of the recruiting sites.

Under the watchful eye of their adult controllers, the youngsters who join the gangs start off in petty crime – stealing handbags and breaking into call boxes, before moving on to shoplifting and extorting money from shops and restaurants who are under Triad 'protection'.

'Most kids join because they are being picked on,' says Yeung, a pupil at the Lillian Bayliss School in Kennington, 'and they want the back up. Either that or they just like the image that goes with it. It started off being just Chinese or Vietnamese kids but now it's anyone.

'You have to pay to get in. The amount varies but it is usually £3.60 [the numbers three and six having special significance in Chinese mythology] each week. You get a red envelope and the money goes in that, then you write your name and address on the back and that's it, you're in. If you want to get out, it is a big problem. You either have to pay out big time – £30, £40 a time, or you get rushed – beaten up really badly.

'The person who gets you in is called your Dai Lo [Big Brother] and that's who you turn to if you have trouble. There was one time that I met up with a member of a rival gang in Chinatown. He got on his mobile – they've all got them – to call in some back-up. I realised I wouldn't stand a chance against them all so when my mate passed me a knife, I didn't hesitate. I stabbed him in the arm but I would have killed him if I had to.

'It sounds vicious but you have to be vicious. Either you are going to end up in hospital or they are. If you leave it and let them walk away, they will just come after you for the rest of your life. You have to end it.'

Police have recorded a number of vicious attacks including an incident outside the Lillian Bayliss School in June 1995 which left a 14-year-old black kid with his hand almost completely severed at the wrist following a blow from a machete. A 15-year-old of Chinese origin was charged with the attack.

Police were first alerted to the growth of the gangs, dubbed the Teeny Triads by the tabloids, after a string of pitched battles at the Trocadero centre in London's Piccadilly Circus. Arrests showed that unlike most youth gangs, kids on the same side went to different schools and came from different areas. Among the gangs identified were the Nam Boys, the SW Triads and the Gremlins. Although the problem is most recognised in London, similar gangs are flourishing in Manchester, Birmingham and Southampton.

Schools across the south east have been aware of the growth of the gangs for months – the Headteachers Association in Croydon estimates that at least 100 pupils in the area have become members – but the true scale activities came to public attention with the death of headteacher Phillip Lawrence, stabbed with a machete outside his school in Maida Vale, London, after he attempted to save a pupil who was being attacked by members of a Triad-style youth gang. Police are keen to play down the links to organised crime but admit that the recruiters who wait outside the school gates to attract newcomers into the gangs have at some time had links to the Triads. Gang members also model themselves on the real thing, wearing Chinese-style clothes – baggy black trousers and oversized white shirts with zips instead of buttons.

The principal effect of this sudden and dramatic increase in manpower has been a corresponding rise in the amount of extortion taking place. Demands for 'tea money' had started to die down towards the end of the eighties but in recent years, initiated by the teams of Blue Lanterns, they have escalated alarmingly.

Over the same period of time, the Chinese community has managed to lose a little of its reluctance about speaking to the world at large about what is going on, though a basic mistrust of authority remains.

In June 1990, fifteen businessmen, led by outspoken restaurateur and President of the Chinatown Association, Tim Yau, held an unprecedented meeting with officers of Scotland Yard's Chinese liaison unit. Over cups of jasmine tea, the delegates spoke of the growing intimidation problem, of the threats and the beatings, and called for the law to be changed (in Hong Kong, Triad membership itself is illegal) in order for them to be better protected.

Four main gangs were identified: the Wo Shing Wo, the Sui Fong (also known as the Wo On Lok), the 14K, and the San Yee On. The traders also complained about the growing activities of an unknown number of Vietnamese gangs.

The police, however, could only suggest that the businessmen upgraded their security systems, and handed out a confidential telephone number to which they could give information, anonymously if they so desired. The police also suggested installing secret video cameras so that any future threats could be filmed and the tapes used as evidence.

The new measures, along with publicity generated by the meeting itself, appeared to act as a deterrent but only for a short time. The 'tea money' gangs simply switched to using letters and ensuring that any physical attacks were carried out at the target's home, well away from any video surveillance.

Yau – whose open defiance of the Triads has earned him the nickname 'walking death' – says that in the five years since the meeting not only has the gang problem got worse but the gulf between the police and the Chinese community has widened more than ever. 'The police say that we are not co-operative, but there are many people who want something to be done, they are just not receiving any help,' says Yau through an interpreter.

'The same thing that is happening here is happening in Manchester, Southampton, York and Glasgow – every Triad stronghold in the country – on a daily basis. Everyone, even the authorities in Hong Kong, are aware just how serious the situation is over here but the British police know they cannot beat the gangs so they would rather pretend they do not exist.

'Every now and then, you get a group of young kids in the restaurant say between ten and fourteen years old, who demand a lot of food. If you do not give it to them, they attack your staff there and then. If you do, they say they have no money. I call the police and they tell me the boys are too young to be prosecuted.

They say maybe they simply forgot to bring their wallets. But if you go into a restaurant and you know you have no money, how can you ever have intended to pay?'

Yau's frustration doesn't end there. He complains that he knows of several restaurant owners who have been brutally assaulted by well-known Triad members but that the police have yet to make a single arrest.

He also cites the more personal example of a fracas which occurred the previous November when seven Vietnamese thugs came into his restaurant, demanded money and then began attacking him and his staff. Yau fought back, knocking one of the men to the floor and holding on to him until the police arrived.

'But when they came they arrested me! An old man. They tried to charge me with assault,' he says bitterly. 'Me who had done nothing except tried to defend my business.'

Then there was the case of the two Chinese businessmen who joined forces to go to the police and tell them about the threats they were receiving. 'The police said they would protect them but the men were beaten up anyway. The police simply cannot be there all the time,' sighs Yau.

'And it's not just the restaurants. The bookshops, the super-markets, the hairdressing salons, the video stores – all have to pay extortion money. If you try to reduce the amount because of the recession or because you have some other problem, they just beat you.

'If you are in conflict with the Triads, your staff will desert you. The manager of the [he names a prominent eaterie in Gerrard Street] was threatened by Triads who gave him ten minutes to make a decision about whether he would pay. The next day, he went to his boss and demanded a one-way ticket back to Hong Kong.

'The local Chinese newspaper used to write about Triads regularly until it had its windows broken three times in one week. Now no more. Everywhere is the same. The police know who the people are but they do nothing.'

Not surprisingly, the police see the situation somewhat differently. 'The simple fact is that many of the people in Chinatown don't want to talk to us,' says one detective with the Chinese liaison unit. 'They have an irrational fear of authority which they bring with them from Hong Kong and of course they have an enormous fear of the Triads themselves. A few, like Yau, are willing to talk, but even he will not make written statements and sign them which is what we require.

'They don't like the idea of a permanent record of what they have been saying being held by a government agency. They would certainly never testify from the witness stand. They don't understand that we just can't go and arrest these people for no reason.'

But with so much Triad activity taking place under the guise of normality, firm evidence of wrongdoing is often virtually impossible to come by.

The extravagant Chinese New Year celebrations are a poignant example. While tourists and bystanders marvel at the spectacle of the traditional lion dance, the restaurateurs outside whose premises the teams perform fret as they ensure the 'lion's food' – a red envelope stuffed with cash – is handed over as quickly as possible.

Stand close by at the right moment and you can often witness the owner swapping the red packets around according to which lion appears first – of the five dance teams operating in the capital, four are linked to the Triads; three have high-ranking members in their ranks; one is led by the second in command of the Wo On Lok.

And while most see such festivals as a time for celebration and relaxation, for Chinatown businessmen (there are few businesswomen) it is often a time of severe financial strain. During New Year, extortion demands escalate out of all proportion – payments of five or ten times the usual rate, often equivalent to more than £3,000, are not unknown.

'Tea money' currently accounts for the greatest proportion of

Triad income, but until relatively recently the sources were far more diverse. One particularly lucrative, though seemingly unlikely, area was the video rental business.

For years, only one British company had the franchise for programmes made by Hong Kong's ATV and TVB Pearl networks, and up-to-date copies of Hong Kong Chinese soap operas and films (the colony has the third-largest movie industry in the world after Bombay and Hollywood) were in great demand.

The Triads quickly discovered that a stolen or smuggled master tape could be used to produce around 5,000 copies which, when distributed around the country by networks of couriers and rented out for around £2 per week, could return gross annual profits of up to £520,000 per pirated film – easily equal to a year's major drug trafficking but with a fraction of the risk.

The vast sums of money involved inevitably led to dozens of violent confrontations. When video shop owner Tai Kik Tsin attempted to sue some of the pirates, he received repeated threats from Wo Sing Wo representatives, advising him to drop the action.

He ignored them and, while leaving his office one evening, was attacked from behind by a man using a specially made two-pronged knife. He was left with a 'Y'-shaped wound on his left buttock that needed more than thirty stitches.

He was not alone. A spate of attacks in London, Manchester and Nottingham during the late 1980s, including one in which a man lost a leg and part of his thumb, another where the victim was left with seven cleaver wounds to his skull, and another simultaneously involving no less than forty combatants, were, according to police sources, directly linked to disputes over 'video trade territory'.

However, by the start of the decade, income from pirating had started to drop off sharply, thanks chiefly to the rapidly increasing popularity and availability of Chinese-language cable television.

Other long-established forms of underworld income have also

suffered. In bygone years, hundreds of thousands of pounds would change hands in the dozens of Triad-run illegal gambling dens that would spring up above or below restaurants close to the heart of the local Chinese community.

Such premises were generally tolerated by the police who considered them a useful way of keeping tabs on local villains. They would be raided periodically but it was never more than a token gesture.

For the Triads themselves the advantages were numerous. As well as all the money from gambling losses, they would cream off a 1 per cent table tax on all bets. Overheads were minimal and there was no need to pay tax, though periodic fines of around £1,000 tended partly to compensate for this.

Normally any non-Chinese attempting to enter one of these joints is immediately ejected. My one visit to a basement club in London's Gerrard Street lasted only a little longer because I had an ulterior motive – I was attempting to gain an audience with a certain Mr Sang, head of the London branch of the Wo Sing Wo.

Mentioning such a name in the right circles always provokes a strong reaction. The young guards who worked the den's spyhole mistakenly thought I had an appointment and therefore must be some very important gangster from out of town, and I was allowed to hover by the entrance for a few minutes while they faffed about.

I knew from my informants that Sang was inside but there was little chance he'd agree to see me. Two weeks earlier, he had been confronted outside his home by four masked men armed with machetes. A karate expert, Sang attempted to chop and kick his way to safety but suffered numerous cuts to his hands, arms and head in the process.

Because of his status within the Wo Sing Wo, Sang would normally be surrounded by a posse of bodyguards, but his attackers had done their homework well. Ostensibly a dedi-cated family man, Sang had taken a mistress and had been to visit her that evening, dispensing with his guards and returning home alone at 3.30 a.m. to find the ambush waiting for him.

The attack had been organised by representatives of the rival Sui Fong Triad, which has its London power base in the 'alternative' Chinatown that can be found along the streets of Queensway. They had been called in after Sang, who has been charged but never convicted of Triad-related offences, had personally attempted to get protection money from a Gerrard Street restaurant, slapping a waitress and causing the owners to lose face in the process.

Within a week, Sang was back out on the streets, eating each evening in his favourite restaurant on Gerrard Street and then gambling the night away in the basement den where I now stood waiting.

The lighting was harsh, almost surgical, and the room was totally dominated by two pristine tables, around which were gathered a mixed bag of punters – businessmen and blue-collar workers – who occasionally eyed me with a mixture of suspicion and derision.

The first table was playing *pai-kau*, a domino-like game where each player receives four tiles and has to arrange them in pairs that have a higher value than those of the dealer.

The other table was devoted to the more popular and distinctly downmarket *fan-tan*. In this simple but highly addictive game, punters bet on the number of buttons that will be left when the croupier up-ends a dishful and then begins drawing them off with a fan in groups of four.

(A rarer beast is the *mah jong* den. Played with 144 ornate 'tiles', the game requires each player to collect four sets of three identical tiles from a pack, throwing out one tile every turn. The winner is the first to collect a complete hand. Such games are strictly private, played for vast stakes between members of the Chinese business élite.)

On a wall shelf under a placard bearing Chinese script, a knife had been stuck into a pile of raw ginger, a device used to ward off evil spirits. This aside, there was nothing in the room. There were no spectators or hang-arounds – this was a place in which to bet, not to socialise. If someone wanted to stop gambling, they simply had to leave.

All too quickly, the guards returned with the news that the great man was not about, and that even if he was, he would not want to talk to me. I was politely but firmly shown the door.

In December 1994, the Metropolitan Police's Gaming Unit announced that twelve of the fifteen illegal gambling dens run out of the basements of buildings throughout the West End had been shut down.

This is by no means all down to detective work. Increasing numbers of Chinese blue-collar workers can be found at the legitimate casinos all across London and Manchester. By way of cutting their losses, the Triads have begun to target such venues, watching out for anyone who has lost and then encouraging them to borrow money to try to win something back. Annual interest rates on these 'loans' are often as high as 3,000 per cent.

The dens are missed most of all by the remnants of the first generation of Chinese immigrants. 'The older ones, they don't want films or videos,' one sympathetic restaurant waiter explained to me. 'When they finish work, they want to relax among friends in a place where they think they may have a chance of winning some money, so they go to the clubs. Now, they have nowhere.'

The Triads too have found the squeeze on their operations somewhat painful. Little wonder that they have begun looking at pastures new.

Ever since the workings of the City of London were transformed by the Big Bang, there have been law enforcement fears that organised crime could try to muscle in on the securities and commodity futures markets. When, in January 1994, the first hard evidence of an attempt to do just this emerged, it surprised no one that the Triads were behind it.

For Paul Lamb, who runs the London and Global currency trading company in Soho, it all began innocently enough one

Wednesday afternoon when the receptionist called his office to inform him that two men were waiting for him.

'They didn't have an appointment but said they wanted to see me about possible currency deals,' says Lamb. 'They were well dressed and in their late twenties. They were also both more than six foot tall – big for a Chinese – and physically threatening.

'They explained that they wanted to trade in currency without putting any money up. I said that this was not possible – you have to put money in first – but they were very insistent. They wanted between three hundred thousand and four hundred thousand pounds' free credit. If they had lost the money, my company would have been liable for the lot.

'They said straight away that they were from the Wo Sing Wo. If they hadn't there would have been nothing to be afraid of. I would have just sent them away without a thought and maybe hired a couple of security guards. But when you know you are dealing with the Triads, you just can't do that.'

However, the gang had not reckoned on Lamb's cool head. 'I tried to put them off. I showed them that it just couldn't be done. I even brought my wife, Margaret [she is Irish], into the room with us. These people only like dealing with the Chinese community – after all, we are the ones that fear the Triads. When other people are involved, there is the fear that they may go to the police, so I brought her in in an attempt to put them off. She was someone who would not play the game.'

But the ploy didn't work. 'They gave me a telephone number and said that I should telephone a man called "Kenny" within a week to tell them what I was going to do.'

(Kenny is a well-known face on the London Triad scene, known particularly for his capacity for extreme violence. He was once caught on a police surveillance camera drawing a meat cleaver out of his trousers as he entered a basement in Gerrard Street. Minutes later, a man was badly injured in a 'chopping'. No one has ever been charged with the crime.)

'The truth is, if they had only wanted a small amount, I would have been in much more of a dilemma. If they had asked for just five thousand, I would have had to think hard about whether to pay it. I would have tried to pay less, two thousand five hundred maybe, anything to sort it out. But because the amount was so enormous, I simply had no choice. There was no alternative but to say no.'

In the week that followed, the Triads tried to ensure that the decision would be made in their favour. On two occasions, thugs forced their way into Lamb's offices, threatening staff and screaming abuse. Three days after the initial approach had been made, ten of Lamb's thirty staff decided to 'work from home' until the problem had been solved.

The reaction of some of the other staff was a little more surprising. Lamb explains: 'After the first incident, two of them came up and asked if I wanted them to speak to their "connections" and get it sorted out. It turned out they were members of the Sui Fong.'

Lamb was quick to turn down this offer of inside help. 'Had I said yes, first I would be in the middle of a war and then I would owe the Sui Fong a favour. They would simply have taken over where the Wo Sing Wo had left off. But I now know that several members of my staff are Triads. It is not a problem. Everyone has some connection. If you took fifty of my friends, I wouldn't be surprised if twenty-five of them were Triads. It is a very common thing. Everyone knows a Triad or two.

'The whole movement has quite noble origins and many people still see it in that way. Even today, many join simply to be protected from any problems. Families will often encourage one person to join to the benefit of them all. You don't necessarily have to get involved in crime: the codes which you have to live by are very strict – in effect, you can be a good person and still be a Triad.'

(Like the Sicilian Mafia and the Yakuza, the Triads claim roots in a romantic movement sworn to fight oppression and injustice. According to Chinese legend, the original Triads were a group of Buddhist monks who invented the art of Kung Fu and became the symbol of opposition to the Manchu dynasty.)

'However, they are now starting to spin off into street gangs. It is not the same. Even if Triads have to do bad things, they have codes which dictate the way they must do them. But these youngsters don't take these oaths so they don't follow the codes.'

Feeling he was backed into a corner, Lamb opted for a totally new approach. He wrote to John Major and Hong Kong Governor Chris Patten and contacted the *Evening Standard*, which ran a full-page story on his plight the day the deadline was up.

If the idea was to make himself so prominent that the Triads would not risk paying him further attention, it worked. But as time moves on, so the threat of reprisal increases.

'I hope I have done the right thing in standing up to these people, but I am afraid that this is all going to end in violence,' sighs Lamb. 'I don't expect anything will happen to the company but I may have to suffer some form of personal attack to pay for the Triads' loss of face.

'Since then, many people come up to us and whisper "thank you" yet they are almost relieved when we are off their premises. I suppose they fear reprisal while we are among them.

'If anything does happen, the police know who the men are. Everyone in the community will know who did it but there will be no revulsion. They will simply believe that we were in the wrong and that we should have paid or allowed them to trade.

'It will just go on and on. Even if the men who came to my office are caught tomorrow, that will not stop it. You cannot control the Triads, you can only try to control the things that the Triads do.'

The most detailed recent account of life as a fully fledged Triad in the UK emerged during the October 1992 trial of twenty-eight-year-old Wai Hen Cheung, who appeared at the Old Bailey charged with conspiracy to inflict grievous bodily harm as well as various assault, arson, firearms and drug offences.

Cheung – George to his friends – was a distinctly unremarkable character who had achieved nothing of note during his adult life, yet his court appearance constituted a landmark in criminal history as he opted not only to plead guilty, but also to tell all he knew about the inner workings of the Chinese criminal empire.

After decades of speculation, fantasy and falsehood, a Triad supergrass had finally emerged to set the record straight.

But from the moment he took the witness stand, Cheung, who had been described as a 'sadistic assassin', a 'thug steeped in crime', and a man with 'strong hatreds and uncontrollable violence', shattered everyone's expectations of what a leading Triad 'enforcer' would be like.

Just five feet four inches with thick glasses and a severe acne problem, Cheung's hesitant, agitated performance in the witness box soon earned him a less welcome nickname – Chicken George – but, appearances aside, his information turned out to be first-class.

Born in Leicester of Chinese parents who ran a take-away restaurant, Cheung had first been drawn into the underworld in March 1990 when he and his flatmate were badly beaten up outside their home by a group of masked men.

It transpired that an ex-boyfriend of Cheung's flatmate's latest girlfriend had been so upset over her starting a new relationship that he had paid some Triad thugs to exact revenge. Fearing further attacks, Cheung, on advice from his uncle, approached members of the Sui Fong Triad, from whose ranks the attackers had come, to find a possible solution.

A meeting was arranged at a gambling den in a basement in Gerrard Street and Cheung and his flatmate were introduced to a man called Fei Yan or Flying Man.

'He told me the problem was not serious and could be sorted out if we joined the gang and called him *tai lo* [big brother],' Cheung told the court. 'I understood this meant we would have to be loyal to him and do what he asked. In return he said he would look after us.'

Three weeks later Cheung, along with nine other young men,

was taken to a Chinese restaurant in Fulham, west London, at 2 a.m. to undergo the ritual initiation ceremony.

The recruits were made to remove all jewellery and strip to their underpants before being taken to a room in the restaurant's basement which had been cleared of furniture except for a single table in the centre covered in red paper on which a knife, wine and a paper cut-out in the shape of a man had been placed.

A makeshift 'altar' made of more red paper had been taped to one bare wall and beneath it were nine or ten sets of pieces of paper laid out in triangles. The air was heavy with the scent of burning joss-sticks.

The restaurant owner, Lo Ng, then appeared and began to conduct the initiation ceremony in an ancient Chinese dialect. 'We were told to kneel on the pieces of paper on the floor and hold joss-sticks between our fingers,' said Cheung.

Ng then began to call out the thirty-five oaths of allegiance, again in ancient Chinese, among them:

(1) 'After having entered the Hung Gates I must treat the parents and relatives of my sworn brothers as mine own kin. I shall suffer death by five thunderbolts if I do not keep this oath.'

(12) 'If I have lied about my past, my identity and my motives for the purpose of joining the Hung Family, I shall be killed by five thunderbolts.'

(23) 'I shall not cause discord or alarm among my sworn brothers by spreading false reports of them. If I do, I shall be killed by myriads of swords.'

'I didn't understand the oaths at the time but I repeated them anyway. Later I learned they meant I was never to betray a brother, never to steal from a brother and never to commit adultery with a brother's wife.

'Everyone in the gang was seen as family and everyone in it was a brother. If we broke these oaths we were told that we would be punished severely. We could be crippled or we could be killed.

'The owner then asked me, "If one of your brothers was in trouble and the police were seeking him and willing to pay for information, do you want money or your brothers?" I answered my brothers. I then got slapped with the back of the flat blade of a knife.'

The middle finger of Cheung's left hand was then pricked with a pin and, as it bled, the restaurant owner placed it in a glass of wine. 'I was then told to place my bleeding finger in my mouth and he asked me how it tasted. I said it was sweet.

'After this, the teacher took the piece of paper cut like a man and said it was an informer, somebody who had betrayed his brothers, and the penalty for this was death. He asked us what we would do and everyone said "Death". He said "Louder" and we all shouted "Death". He took the knife and hacked the piece of paper to pieces.'

From that moment on, Cheung was a 49 – a fighter member of the Triads. According to Triad mythology, he had died in his former life and been reborn a gang member. For Cheung, whose life before had been something of a non-event, it was a concept that he readily embraced.

He eagerly carried out a number of vicious attacks for his new bosses, each one earning him slightly more kudos and respect among his peers. In one incident, he stalked a man for two days before slashing his face with two razor blades taped together. This type of injury is particularly difficult to stitch and even when healed leaves an ugly scar. It is as much a warning to others as a punishment to the victim.

On another occasion Cheung and two others burst into a Chinese restaurant in north London armed with iron bars in order to teach a lesson in humility to the owner who owed money to one of Cheung's Sui Fong brothers. But when the owner pulled a gun, the three hitmen fled.

Cheung also admitted attacking the boss of a video shop in Cardiff and travelling to Glasgow to give a man a 'good hiding', all on the instructions of his superiors. His clean record also came in handy – he was asked to sign the lease for a Bayswater flat which was later converted into a brothel.

As his standing within the gang increased, Cheung found himself singled out for a mission of vital importance.

The Hong Kong branch of the Sui Fong had been unhappy with the way the London bosses were running things, particularly with regard to the gang's battles with the Wo Sing Wo, and had decided to send one of their own high-ranking officials, Ying Kit Lam, to take over.

When the head of the London branch, an eleven-year veteran of the Hong Kong police, got wind of the plan, he decided to teach Lam a lesson he wouldn't forget. Cheung was ordered to cripple Mr Lam by shooting him twice in the back and 'four or five times in the backside or the groin, depending on how he fell.' He was told specifically not to shoot to kill but that: 'If Mr Lam died, it would be his own fault.'

In early September 1991, Cheung was flown to London from Guernsey (where he had been 'hiding' so that Lam would not recognise him on the day of the shooting – Chinatown is, after all, quite a small place) and given a grey blazer with a specially adapted inside pocket in which to keep his .22 pistol which had been fitted with a silencer.

Additionally armed with a set of photographs, Cheung – backed up by several other Sui Fong members who wanted to ensure that the hit was carried out – made his way into Gerrard Street to seek out his target. It did not take long to find him. 'I saw Fishball Tak talking to Lam. I was about fifteen yards behind. Lam turned round and looked straight at me. I did not know what to do.

'I was scared. I started to feel dizzy. I looked around and looked away from him. I saw Jason standing outside a car park. He was with two other Sui Fong members. Jason was looking at me. He nodded at me as if to say "Go on, shoot him." I turned back around and Lam had disappeared.'

The second opportunity to carry out his mission came later that day. 'I saw him again. He had his back to me and was leaning into Fishball Tak's van. Jason was next to him and he saw me and tried to move away from Lam.

'I was just about to pull the gun out when Lam turned around and looked straight at me. He walked to the back of the van and I went to the front and then crossed the road and entered a video shop.'

Later than day, Cheung was asked by his bosses why he had not shot Lam. His big brother, Flying Man, rang in a foul mood. 'He told me the next opportunity I had of shooting Lam, I had to do it.'

On 7 September, Cheung again went into Chinatown. 'I got changed and prepared the gun. I decided not to be scared any more and made the decision to shoot. I decided to end it.

'I walked up close behind Lam, checked to see if anyone was watching and I pulled the trigger twice. I saw three marks on his trousers. I didn't see any blood. I thought he wasn't hurt.'

In fact two bullets had hit Lam in the spine but, despite this injury (he is now confined to a wheelchair), he managed to wrestle with Cheung in the street, eventually pinning him to the ground. Cheung tried to fire twice more but the weapon jammed. He fled to Manchester and went into hiding but was arrested soon afterwards.

While in prison on remand, Cheung was visited by two other members of the Sui Fong who warned him against co-operating with the police. They reminded him of his oaths of allegiance and loyalty and that the Triad penalty for informing was death. They said that if he was sent to prison, other Triads in jail would make sure he was seriously harmed, crippled or even killed.

Six alleged members of the Sui Fong stood trial with Cheung. All were acquitted, but police are convinced that Cheung's testimony was all true. Because of his co-operation, he was jailed for only five years for offences that would normally warrant a minimum of twenty.

Today, having been awarded permanent residency status in Britain and having been granted financial assistance with living expenses and a new identity, he lives in fear of the promised retribution.

As one policeman put it shortly after the trial: 'He will

probably never have any hiding place. He is going to be on the outside for the rest of his life and will always be looking over his shoulder expecting a bullet. As an outcast, he can never return to the Chinese community.'

In Sydney, Australia, Triad gangs are said to control 90 per cent of the heroin trade. In Vancouver, which has an enormous Chinese population, the figure is the same. In New York, where most people believe the Mafia is king, the Triads have 70 per cent of the trade.

During the mid-1970s, the Triads dominated the London heroin market, but this domination collapsed after the arrest of a major smuggling ring and the decision to concentrate on other activities that were unlikely to attract mass police attention in the way that drugs did.

However, the clampdown on other areas of income has led to a change of heart. In November 1987, British detectives posing as international drug dealers managed to infiltrate an Amsterdam-based faction of the 14K and foil attempts to re-establish the heroin supply lines to Britain.

Operation Takeaway discovered that vast quantities of opium and morphine being produced in Laos were being smuggled into Amsterdam where they were converted into heroin and then passed on to couriers for transportation to Britain.

The syndicate had decided to undercut the Turkish syndicates that currently control the trade, selling to dealers for just £6,000 per kilo as opposed to the usual £20,000. Had they succeeded, the street price of heroin in Britain could have fallen to as little as £25 per gram.

(Incidentally, the drug plan had been thrashed out on 7 March that same year when influential European-based leaders of Triad gangs assembled in London for a secret meeting. The summit was just one in a series held by the Triads in order to discuss ways of diversifying income.)

Having nipped the 14K's drug ambitions in the bud, both police and customs believed they had given up. This notion was supported by police forces across Europe who, particularly in Holland, where the Triads are particularly strong, had been finding less and less heroin of South-East Asian origin on the streets. The vast majority of the drugs currently being seized had been chemically identified as coming from Turkey and Pakistan; it was as if the Triads had dropped out of the market.

In Britain in particular the Triads are not now thought to be involved in drugs. In 1991 just 4 kilos of South-East Asian heroin were seized as compared to more than 500 kilos of South-West Asian heroin.

However, in two 1995 raids on heroin labs, Hong Kong officials were shocked to discover detailed directions enabling the chemist to make Chinese heroin look as though it had been processed in Lebanon or Mexico. Financially this was a sound move – the latter brands have far higher retail values.

As a result, the CIA now believes that South-East Asian heroin probably constitutes one half of all the heroin consumed in the United States and an even higher proportion in Europe. The British authorities are still being remarkably coy about accepting the fact that the Triads may be far more involved in the heroin trade than they have acknowledged.

And with the profits of drug trafficking available to back up the Triad coffers, the outlook for those already suffering from the attentions of the gangs is decidedly grim, with most insiders predicting a significant increase in the amount of inter-gang rivalry in years to come.

This is particularly significant given the increasing reports that the most vicious and bloodthirsty of all the Triad gangs, the Tai Heun Chai, is attempting to establish a base in Britain.

Also known as the Big Circle Gang, the group has become a virtual byword for violence and is believed to have wrested control of the Dutch heroin market from the 14K in a series of shootings, choppings and bomb attacks.

While most Triad members in Britain come from Hong Kong, those who belong to the Big Circle are originally drawn from members of the Red Guard who fled from China and are well armed and trained.

The first firm indication that they had arrived came with the murder of Cheung To and Lam Fei, who were found dead in an east-London house in May 1995. Both men were members of the Red Army who were seeking political asylum and Fei's body bore Triad tattoos which linked him to the new gang.

Meanwhile the other gangs are investing much of their drug money in long-term projects, particularly prostitution, which has long been a Triad staple. In the past, however, the brothels, usually situated in plush houses in areas like Mayfair, Bayswater and the like, have catered purely for a Chinese clientele.

More recently, police have noticed increasing numbers of Japanese businessmen entering these premises, many of whom are undoubtedly linked to the Yakuza, and there are indications that some of the brothels may soon open their doors to a non-oriental audience.

The drug money is also being used to corrupt officials, particularly those working in the immigration field, to facilitate the smuggling of key personnel into the country.

In one typical case a thirty-five-year-old immigration officer, Victor Matthews, was threatened by members of the Wo Shing Wo and persuaded to set up a system to enable those who had been refused permission to stay in Britain a chance to do just that.

It began when a Chinese friend asked him to help another friend remain in the country. After Matthews said there was nothing he could do, he was visited at home by a Chinese man who told him 'something had to be done'. The man revealed intimate knowledge of his life and friends, and it was then that a terrified Matthews devised the plan.

Usually a six-month stay is granted by immigration officers, who have sole discretion. Details of each visitor are then sent on to the Home Office and placed on computer. The paper records are then destroyed. Matthews devised a plan that allowed visitors to remain in Britian under 'sole company representative' status giving them a four-year limit. At the end of that time, the Home Office normally allows a person to remain indefinitely.

Matthews was discovered after immigration officers on a routine raid found a Chinese waiter with a four-year company representative visa.

Towards the end of 1993, a far larger scam was uncovered in Ireland. Working in conjunction with a network of corrupt Irish police, Triads had arranged for hundreds of illegal immigrants to be granted visas.

The scandal was hushed up by the Republic to avoid a diplomatic row with London, but there is evidence that several political figures in Dublin have dubious links with the Chinese underworld.

One hundred cases of illegally approved visa applications were detected, but hundreds more are believed to have passed through unseen. They mainly involved wealthy Hong Kong businessmen seeking a new life in Britain ahead of the communist takeover of the colony in 1997.

Although these people already hold British passports, a quota system prevents them from settling in the UK. But under EC law, an Irish work or residency visa stamped in their passports allows them to travel or live anywhere in the Community.

The alert was sounded more loudly when it was noted that one Chinese organiser of the racket had strong links with the 14K gang. He moved to the Republic in 1986 and is believed to be in charge of smuggling operations there.

There was also the case of twenty-four-year-old David Lynch of Brixton who was terrorised into illegally issuing hundreds of passports after being threatened with a gun by a group of Chinese men who accosted him outside his flat one day.

They explained that they knew Lynch worked as an examiner at the Passport Office in central London and said they would kill him unless he co-operated.

In the year that followed, he approved more than 400 applications, begrudgingly accepting televisions, cars and even a flat as 'payment' for his services.

He would receive calls from men, sometimes in Hong Kong, telling him to go to a car in a car park in Hampton Hill where he would find passport applications in the boot. Police found a further forty-eight completed applications when they arrested him after a tip-off.

While on remand, Lynch was warned by a Chinese prisoner that he would be wise not to say anything. At trial, he declined to give evidence against his co-accused.

So far as the future is concerned, one of the greatest threats comes from the unknown number of Vietnamese gangs operating across the country. Traditionally used by the Triads as enforcers, they are now beginning to strike out on their own, preying both on their own community as well as the Chinese.

In April 1994, the Old Bailey heard how three former Vietnamese boat people, part of a larger gang, had kidnapped two Chinese businessmen and threatened them with death and mutilation unless their families paid ransoms totalling £50,000.

Van Sang Bui, his brother Van So Bui and Dinh Tah were all said to have Triad connections but to have begun to operate independently. Their first victim, a restaurant owner, was snatched from the street and driven to a house in Peckham, south London, where he was told his hand would be cut off unless he paid over £16,000.

The terrified restaurateur was then forced to telephone his wife and beg her to borrow the money. Later, two of the gang visited his home and told her that two of her husband's fingers would be sliced off and her children attacked unless she came up with the cash.

During another telephone call she was told the whole family would be 'chopped down'. She was so scared she packed her bags and fled to a friend's home. Eventually the gang released the husband on condition that he raised the money within two days, but after he found out his wife and children were safe, he went to the police.

The second victim lived in Essex but ran a small clothing

factory in Tottenham. While driving home from Romford greyhound stadium he was forced off the road, threatened at knifepoint, and then bundled into the gang's car.

At a flat in Peckham which served as the gang's headquarters, he was blindfolded, handcuffed, and told to pay £30,000 to the 'big brother' otherwise his legs would be chopped off.

The man was held captive for three days during which time he was also threatened with a shotgun. Over the same period, one gang member visited the man's wife and made her listen to her husband's agonised screams over the telephone.

But on the final day of his ordeal, the man awoke to find his guard asleep and he fled barefoot into the street. A passing motorist took him to the police station and the three men were arrested shortly afterwards.

Detective Superintendent Roland Harris, who led the investigation, said that while some of the defendants were found to have strong Triad connections, both in London and Manchester, the specific crimes for which they were eventually jailed did not appear to be Triad-initiated or sponsored.

'There is no getting away from the fact that there are gangs which operate within the Vietnamese community though our feeling is that the vast majority of incidents go unreported.'

In 1987, seven people in a Chinese gambling club were burned to death after a petrol attack by members of a Vietnamese gang who were in dispute with the club's owners, while in August 1992 two murders were directly linked to disputes between Vietnamese gangs and Triads.

Now, with the twenty-thousand-strong Vietnamese community directly targeting the Chinese business community, the potential for conflict can only be even greater.

Chapter Nine

This Thing of Ours

The Mafia

'As a wiseguy, you can lie, you can cheat,
you can steal, you can kill people – *legitimately*.
You can do any goddam thing you want and nobody
can say anything about it.
Who wouldn't want to be a wiseguy?'

Soldier in the Bonnanno Family quoted in
Donnie Brasco: My Undercover Life in the Mafia

At first glance, Salvatore Di Prima seems an unlikely Don Corleone. The stocky Sicilian, described by *The Times* as 'the founder of the British wing of the Mafia', opens the door to his semi-detached Woking home holding a knife – but only because he's midway through dinner.

His record, however, speaks for itself. In August 1987 Di Prima was sentenced to seven years for attempting to smuggle 43 kilos of top-grade cannabis into Britain. The drugs had been cunningly concealed in the petrol tank of a specially adapted Lancia, driven by a young couple who had borrowed a baby in order to make themselves look like typical holidaymakers.

Di Prima was said to have masterminded the operation: providing the finance, liaising with the Mafia-run garage in Barcelona to get the car converted, using yet more Mafia contacts to acquire the drugs, and recruiting and vetting the rest of the team.

During his trial, Exeter Crown Court heard how Di Prima's Mafia bosses – fearing he might crack and name them – had issued a contract on his life. Indeed, while on remand he had received a threatening postcard: 'We are quite worried to hear your family are still on their own,' it read. 'Still, this only acts as a reminder that you too are on your own.'

While giving evidence, a prosecution witness choked with disbelief when accused of threatening to reveal details of an alleged affair to Salvatore's wife. 'You have got to be joking,' he gasped. 'No one would dare threaten Mr Di Prima. I wish I could say a few things more. Ask him about his associates . . .'

Before he can talk to me, Di Prima explains that he will have to seek 'permission' from those self-same associates. 'This concerns Mr D,' he says without a trace of an Italian accent, or emotion. 'So I'll have to check it's okay. I'm visiting him this weekend and I'll see what he says.'

Mr D is Di Prima's nickname for his former boss and self-styled adoptive father; a man described by *The Times* as 'the Sicilian Mafia's top operative in Britain' and by Italian detectives as 'the Butcher of Altofonte' – Francesco Di Carlo.

His record too speaks volumes. Back in his native Sicily, he has been convicted of Mafia membership (a serious crime carrying a mandatory eight-year sentence), firearms offences, and drug trafficking. Di Carlo has also been charged with the 1979 murder of Boris Giuliano, the head of Palermo's Flying Squad and the man credited with exposing the 'pizza connection' and also the 1980 killing of Emanuele Basile, the captain of the Carabinieri, after which he is said to have fled to Britain.

Basing himself in and around London, Di Carlo continued at a breakneck pace. Between 1980 and 1985 customs officers linked him to a least a dozen multi-million-pound drug hauls, only a handful of which were intercepted. In between, Di Carlo was said *personally* to have murdered the banker Roberto Calvi, whose body was found hanging beneath Blackfriars Bridge in London in 1982, in revenge for the theft of 'tens of millions of pounds' of Mafia money.

According to the late Judge Giovanni Falcone, Di Carlo has immense clout in underworld circles. The modern Mafia is organised on a system of tiers based on local families. At the top of the pyramid is a council of eight top bosses – the Commission – of which Di Carlo is said to be a member, making him one of the top ten Mafia bosses in the world and giving him the ability to reach anyone, anywhere.

Hence, when he was eventually brought to trial after being linked to an attempt to smuggle £60 million worth of heroin to

Canada through London, Di Carlo was said to have arranged the 1985 murder of Antonino Cassara, deputy head of the Palermo Flying Squad, who had caused 'annoyance' by attempting to extradite Di Carlo back to Italy while on remand for the drugs charge.

The following year, during Di Carlo's five-month Old Bailey trial, the word Mafia was not used once, the judge fearing that such an emotive term might prejudice the defence. However, a crucial customs interpreter who had overhead private conversations between the defendants was sent a copy of a book entitled *Unless They Kill Me First*, about a Mafioso turned informer. Two weeks later she was crippled in a hit-and-run 'accident'.

Court escorts also reported how, each morning as they were led from the cells, Di Carlo's co-defendants would bow and kiss his hand as they passed him, standard protocol for greeting a *capo*. An American Mafia hitman, remanded in Brixton at the same time as Di Carlo, reportedly told police 'it was an honour to be doing time in the same prison as Don Francesco'.

It is little surprise then that Di Carlo was given a sentence befitting that of a Mafioso, not a typical drug smuggler – twenty-five years. Having been 'ghosted' (moved from jail to jail at a moment's notice) a number of times, Di Carlo eventually settled into the maximum-security wing at Whitemoor before being moved to Belmarsh because of the 1994 IRA breakout. Since his own release, Di Prima has visited or telephoned Di Carlo at least weekly.

The following weekend I telephoned Di Prima as arranged to find out whether I would be able to interview him. I caught him just as he was dashing out to football practice. 'Yeah,' he said hurriedly. 'And Mr D wants to meet you an' all.'

Under long-standing Home Office regulations, it is forbidden for a journalist to interview any person being detained at Her Majesty's pleasure.

The general line is that prisoners are not allowed to discuss the particulars of their case with the media. Therefore, while it is possible (with a little difficulty) to arrange a visit to a jail to talk to inmates about conditions and so on, you cannot ask to talk to a specific person about the crimes they have committed.

Of course, there are ways around this. Journalists regularly pose as friends and family in order to sneak their way into visiting rooms, but this is generally only effective with low-grade convicts.

Anyone wishing to see a prisoner detained under Category AA – multiple murderers, IRA terrorists, Mafiosi – are subject to a range of additional checks and must be vetted by both police and Home Office in order to ensure that the visit will not constitute a security risk.

There are ways around this too. Legal visits – those made by a prisoner's solicitor or barrister – are generally less stringently checked so, if a journalist can find a friendly representative who will sneak them in as a clerk or assistant, the vetting procedure will not apply. It was this method I decided to employ in order to arrange my meeting with Mr D.

The only problem is that the visitor in question still has to provide his real name – a passport or driving licence is required to be shown at the prison gate in order to prove you are who you say you are, and the specific ID has to be announced in advance.

Two days before the visit, the solicitor called Belmarsh prison to announce that, on the day in question, he would be accompanied by his clerk, Tony Thompson. Three hours later the Duty Governor called him back.

'The visit's cancelled.'

'What? Why on earth . . .'

'Look, mate, don't try to play the innocent. You know.'

'Know what?'

'He's a journalist. There's no way he's coming in.'

Perhaps my name appears on MI5's F2(R) list of teachers, students, pacifists and journalists known to associate with subversives (I once interviewed several active members of the Animal Liberation Front); perhaps the Duty Governor at Belmarsh was just a fan of my work; either way, I'd been rumbled.

Furthermore, my friendly solicitor was left fuming – he was ordered to write to the Home Secretary apologising for his behaviour and promising never to attempt such a thing again or face being struck off.

I had desperately wanted to meet Francesco Di Carlo face to face. I had visions of starting this chapter with a description of how large his hands were, how firm his grip was: '. . . could hands such as these have strangled Roberto Calvi? Surely yes . . .' Now I would have to settle for third party answers to my questions. It is probably just as well.

The era of the pan-continental criminal was born with the signing of the 1958 Treaty of Rome which brought into being the European Economic Community, establishing free trade between West Germany, France, Belgium, the Netherlands, Luxembourg and Italy.

For the Sicilian Mafia, the EEC was a superb opportunity to begin expanding its business empire. It had already mastered the art of diverting regional subsidies and regeneration grants from Rome into its own coffers, and it quickly learned to do the same with monies from the Common Agricultural Policy, earning billions of lira by claming compensation for having cut down trees that never actually existed.

When in 1972 Britain voted to join the union, the opportunity became even more golden. As an island superpower, Britain's air and sea connections were significantly better than those in many other parts of Europe. More importantly, Britain's 'special relationship' with the United States and Canada made it the perfect staging post for smuggling drugs to both countries.

Whoever was chosen to be lord of this new empire had to have the experience and ability to run potentially the most

powerful Mafia satellite outside America. So it came as no
surprise when, after a series of discussions, the Commission
chose to appoint a leading light from the Cuntrera family.

Using a combination of theft, violence and arson, the
Cuntreras began their criminal careers by extorting money
from the owners of Sicily's landed estates, quickly becoming
powerful enough to take over complete fiefdoms. Once their
fortune – and their reputation for ruthlessness – was established, they moved to Montreal where, having failed to wait
for permission from the ruling Mafia family before beginning
their own operations, they soon found themselves embroiled
in a bloody war of superiority.

But the grounding they had received during similar battles
in their home town of Siculiano on Sicily's southern coast
stood them in good stead. When the shootings, stabbings and
bombings eventually stopped, it was the Cuntreras and their
close cousins the Caruanas who were left victorious, while the
boss of the Montreal Mob was left dead.

Once settled in Canada, the family extended their horizons,
turning their attention to the heroin trade and taking advantage
of the country's vast, porous border with America to smuggle
in tons of the drug and boost their personal fortune even
further.

More recently, as cocaine became America's drug of choice,
the Cuntreras moved to Venezuela, leaving the Caruanas behind
to supervise their Canadian interests. Caracas turned out to
be an ideal base for their activities. There was no extradition
treaty with any country, no exchange controls, and a myriad
of opportunities for dirty money to be invested in legitimate
businesses, allowing the Cuntreras to deal drugs and launder
the profits beneath a veneer of respectability.

The family established contacts with every major Sicilian
and American Mafia family, as well as with the Colombian
cartels, and acted as middle-men for one and all. By the early
eighties, around 80 per cent of all the cocaine leaving Colombia
for America first passed through Venezuela, and the Cuntreras

became billionaires by ensuring that they took a cut of every last kilo.

But it was back in 1975, while the family was still on its way to such wealth, that the eldest of the four Cuntrera brothers, Liborio, was despatched to Britain to set up a new Mafia stronghold in the heart of the Surrey stockbroker belt.

Woking was not quite so bizarre a choice for the centre of Liborio's operations as it might at first have seemed. During the Second World War, the West Byfleet Golf Club was a low-key prisoner-of-war camp for Italians and, when the fighting ended, many opted to stay, setting up homes and bringing their families over to join them.

As the Italian population started to grow, so the entrepreneurs followed, setting up specialist services to cater for the needs of the community. Today, Woking's 5,000 Sicilians outnumber every other ethnic group in the town, attend churches where all the sermons are in Italian, shops where all the foods are freshly imported, and enjoy the attentions of a host of native stonemasons, gardeners and restaurateurs who ensure that Woking is, as far as possible, a home from home.

Liborio immediately bought himself a £1 million mansion (for cash) on the edge of the town and set up a fake import/export company to launder some of his brothers' drug profits. He would order non-existent goods from one of his 'international offices' which would be paid for with dirty money that would turn clean the instant it appeared on the books as a legitimate sale.

The system was working beautifully, washing millions of pounds each year until Liborio unexpectedly died of cirrhosis of the liver in May 1982. According to the Mafia grapevine, he was expected to be replaced by his cousin, Alfonso Caruana, who duly arrived, along with his brother Pasquale, the following July.

Both settled in Woking, paying cash for their luxury homes. Alfonso bought Broomfield House, a palatial neo-Georgian mansion with a heated swimming pool, landscaped gardens,

six bedrooms, three bathrooms and two paddocks, which at
the time of writing is worth £1.5 million. Pasquale settled for
'The Hook', a detached house with an indoor swimming pool,
sauna, heart-shaped lily pond, four bedrooms, three bathrooms,
and a sophisticated security system.

Unlike Liborio, during the three years they spent in the town,
the Caruanas never bothered to establish a legitimate business
front. Instead they spent virtually all their time opening and
paying money into numerous bank accounts. Alfonso had one
at the local branch of Barclays but kept at least fifteen others
in London, Amsterdam and Canada. Pasquale had thirty-one
accounts in all, including some at banks in Panama, New York
and Milan to name but a few.

On one occasion, the brothers arrived at Barclays to deposit
$200,000 in Canadian bills. The manager was distraught –
not because he had suspicions that the money might be the
product of drug sales, but because it had arrived in plastic
carrier bags and he was worried about his customers' lack of
security awareness.

On another occasion, the pair brought in so many loose
notes that the female teller complained that she simply didn't
have time to count them all. 'You'll have to come back after
lunch,' she told them.

The closest Alfonso and Pasquale ever came to engaging in
any kind of seemingly authentic business transactions were the
numerous occasions when they asked the manager of Barclays
to remit money to a company in Thailand to pay for the
importation of exotic carved walnut furniture, for which the
pair seemed to have a particular affinity.

Yet despite their presence, and the suspicious nature of the
rest of their activities while in Britain, police and customs
officers believe the real replacement for Liborio Cuntrera was
none other than Francesco Di Carlo.

He too had settled in Woking, having first visited Britain
in 1976 to scout for talent to perform in his plush nightclub, Il Castello, on the outskirts of Palermo, which he ran

jointly with Sicilian aristocrat Prince Alessandro di Vanni Cavello.

Over the next four years, while regularly commuting between London and Sicily, Di Carlo set up a series of businesses that capitalised on the needs of the Woking community – a food import/export concern, a specialist travel agency, a bureau de change, an antique-exporting firm, a wine bar, and the Parco Hotel in King's Cross – all of which just happen to be ideal fronts for laundering money and smuggling drugs.

In January 1980, the Carabinieri issued a warrant obliging Di Carlo to remain in Italy pending the result of an investigation into alleged Mafia links. But when news reached him that his two elder brothers had received long sentences after being found guilty of 'Mafia association' and murder, Di Carlo decided to ignore the order and remain in Britain on a more permanent basis. 'There was an ill wind blowing for me back home,' he says.

Six months later, the Italian police stepped up the pressure, issuing an arrest warrant, furnishing the British police with Di Carlo's correct address, and demanding that he be extradited back to Sicily to face trial. The warrant further alleged that Di Carlo and his brothers were involved in a conspiracy to manufacture heroin and smuggle it to the US, and that Francesco was further suspected of murder and extortion.

What happened next is perhaps the most incredible and unbelievable part of the whole Di Carlo story. Thanks to a spiral of phenomenal incompetence, Mr D became perhaps the *least* pursued Mafia fugitive the world has ever known. Whether (as they later claimed) the British police failed to receive the extradition request or whether they simply ignored it has never been fully ascertained. Either way, life for Di Carlo continued exactly as before.

In the last week of July, the *Sunday Times* got wind of the story, publishing a front-page item – 'Mafia man in London' – repeating details of the arrest warrant and even tracking Di Carlo down from the address details it had provided. No action was taken and Britain's Mafia empire continued to grow unabated.

In December 1980, a van-load of peeled tomatoes was stopped for a routine inspection by customs officers stationed at Dover. The driver, obviously new to the smuggling game, panicked and ran off, leaving behind dozens of boxes of rotting vegetables and 348 kilos of cannabis. The man was never found but the van was traced back to Fauci Continental, a food import/export company based in south London.

Listed under the name of director Girolamo Fauci as a key employee of the firm was a certain Franceso Di Carlo, but the name failed to ring any bells with any of those involved in the investigation and again no action was taken.

In 1983, Di Carlo, now regularly 'networking' with the Caruana brothers, once more made the news back home. A 'soldier' in one of Palermo's leading Mafia families decided to turn supergrass. As part of his extensive testimony, Salvatore Contorno identified Di Carlo as one of the top men in the Altofonte (the name of the town where Di Carlo was born) crime family. 'He is a big boss and a millionaire who has murdered many times,' confided Contorno, but in London his claims fell on deaf ears and Di Carlo continued to enjoy his liberty to the full.

In December 1984, a suspicious consignment of carved walnut furniture from Bombay was given a thorough inspection by customs officers based at Felixstowe and was found to contain 250 kilos of high-quality cannabis resin. Impressed with the sophistication of the concealment, the customs officers removed the drugs, replacing them with a substitute, and followed them on their journey to their ultimate location, a warehouse owned by Elongate Ltd in Mitcham, Surrey.

There, an undercover surveillance team spotted two men carefully painting out the Indian markings on the crates to make them appear English in origin, then redirecting them to Montreal along with false papers claiming that the goods had been 'made in Britain'. Across the pond, a team of officers from the Royal Canadian Mounted Police tracked the shipment to a company called Santa Rita, well known for its strong Mafia connections.

Rather than make a few arrests, the British customs team decided to set up a big sting. They discovered that the same furniture company had previously sent loads to a south London food company, Ital Provisions Ltd, and that another shipment, this time from Bangkok, was on its way.

As had been the case with the cannabis, the smugglers hoped that by sending the concealed drugs to Canada from London rather than direct from Thailand they would arouse far less suspicion.

In May 1985 a container carrying the goods arrived at Southampton. Hidden inside a carved table were 60 kilos of almost pure heroin, worth around £15 million. This time, 24 kilos of the drug were removed and the rest sent on, via Ital Provisions, to Canada as a controlled delivery.

Over the next few days, raids were carried out on employees of Ital Provisions and Elongate and their associates. Di Carlo, who was a business associate of the directors of both companies, was picked up along with the others, although he was not immediately a strong suspect.

In fact, at first customs officers had no idea who he was until someone dug out the old Italian extradition warrant. Realising that they had a high-ranking Mafioso on their hands and that, because of the Canadian Mafia connection, he was almost certainly the mastermind of the entire smuggling operation, the customs team played for time.

The extradition was out of date and failed to comply with English law. It had as much chance of succeeding as a snowball had of surviving in hell, but they let it go ahead in order to give them time to gather more evidence with which to charge Di Carlo.

This eventually emerged in the form of statements from his American Express gold card which showed that he had purchased flight tickets to send associates to Bangkok and

Bombay, the very cities from which the drug shipments had originally been sent.

The extradition hearing took place in August and was thrown out after only a few minutes of debate. For a few seconds more, Di Carlo was a free man, but he was immediately rearrested and charged with conspiracy to import class A drugs. He pleaded not guilty.

Sentencing him to twenty-five years in March 1987, Judge John Hazan defended allegations of harshness (the usual maximum is fourteen years): 'In many countries, a smuggling operation of this scale would attract the death sentence.'

The trial had cost £6 million of which £1.5 million was taken up by jury protection. Despite his businesses, his £50,000 Ferrari and his own £250,000 five-bedroomed house in Woking, Di Carlo had pleaded poverty and received legal aid throughout.

'When I see the things that they write about me and I hear the things they say, I can only imagine they must be talking about some other Francesco Di Carlo, this is how removed I am, how unreal it all seems.'

When the opportunity to communicate with Mr D first arose, I wasn't quite sure what to expect. A full confession? Unlikely. A thinly veiled threat not to pursue the story any further? Possibly. A detailed look at life in the Mafia through the eyes of a senior member? Ideally. An impassioned plea that one of the world's most renowned and feared international organised crime figures was in fact the victim of a miscarriage of justice? Surely not!

'They say that I am a criminal, the man who killed Calvi, a grand drug trafficker,' Di Carlo told me. 'All I can say is that I wouldn't be able to raise my eyes from the ground if these things were true.'

That his two brothers have been convicted of Mafia association he does not deny; that the criminal elements in his family are said to have formed an alliance with the Corleone clan he cannot confirm. He does, however, admit to having grown up with the men who were later convicted of murdering Judge Falcone.

Many leading Mafiosi are, therefore, close friends of his family, though the relationships go no further; although he admits to having associated with the Caruana brothers (both lived close to him), he denies actually being involved in any business transactions with them.

He also admits to a long criminal record stretching back to 1962 which includes arrests for theft, extortion, receiving stolen goods, carrying a gun, and murder. However, he points out that he has actual convictions only for minor offences.

As for Calvi, Di Carlo writes that he is 'sick of that story' and complains that he has become a scapegoat for every major murder that has occurred in the last decade, bar that of Judge Falcone. 'If I hadn't been locked up at the time, I am sure they would have tried to pin that one on me too.'

The Calvi allegation first surfaced in 1991 when a Mafia supergrass, Francesco 'Mozzarella' Mannoia, now under FBI protection, recalled being told by another Mafioso while watching a television programme about Calvi that Di Carlo had been responsible. 'All hearsay,' says Mr D.

The story was given dubious creedence two years later when the man behind the £40 million Knightsbridge safe deposit raid, Valerio Viccei, announced that, during the robbery, he had opened a safety deposit box belonging to Di Carlo and found Calvi's passport and other documents.

'He has never shown those papers to anybody because they do not exist,' writes Di Carlo. 'He simply dreamt up this story in order to persuade the authorities to move him to a jail in Italy.

'Calvi had an insurance policy worth £9 million but his family cannot claim if his death was suicide. That kind of money cannot leave anybody indifferent. It could lead anybody to accuse anyone of anything.

'Criminal responsibility is a personal thing. Simply because a man belongs to a Mafia family, you cannot accuse him of being a Mafioso. There are other aspects that need to be considered. I cannot be convicted for crimes my family have committed.'

Di Carlo refers to his arrest for involvement in the heroin shipment as 'a trap' but does not specify who was responsible for implicating him or how it was done. As with many of his answers, one has to read between the lines of much of what he says because he is simply unable (or unwilling) to speak directly; not because of *omerta*, the Mafia's infamous code of silence, but simply because of his culture.

In his book *The Italians*, author Luigi Barzini explains this characteristic by giving the word mafia (with a lower-case M) a far wider meaning: it is a state of mind, a philosophy of life, a conception of society, a particular susceptibility prevailing among all Sicilians.

'They are taught in the cradle or born already knowing that they must aid each other, side with friends and fight the common enemy – even when the friends are wrong and the enemy is right; each must defend his dignity at all costs and keep honour by keeping secrets.'

Following Di Carlo's hints, the case against him does indeed, under closer scrutiny, appear less solid than customs would have the world believe.

For example, the only link between Di Carlo and the van-load of cannabis stopped at Dover in 1980 – supposedly his first major shipment – was the fact that he was employed by the company that owned the van, Fauci Continental.

However, two years later, while driving a second-hand British-registered van stuffed with 250 kilos of high-quality cannabis across the Italian-Swiss frontier, the director, Girolamo Fauci, was himself arrested. Therefore that first shipment could, quite conceivably, have been all Signor Fauci's own work.

As for the two loads of furniture packed with cannabis and heroin, these are known to have been ordered by the Caruana brothers. Indeed, when the Royal Canadian Mounted Police swooped on the four men unpacking the 60 kilos of heroin from the carved table that had been sent as a 'controlled' delivery, one of them was Gerlando Caruana, Alfonso and Pasquale's younger brother.

It is also worth noting that, while customs are happy to take all the credit for having 'taken out one of the Mafia's main units operating in this country', they are somewhat loath to explain just how it was that the Caruana brothers managed to get away.

The pair fled to Canada, evading charges there, and then to Venezuela a few days before the raids. Alfonso was even so bold as to return to Britain the following year to sign papers allowing his house to be sold and the half-million-pound profit to be re-exported.

The same sources that place Di Carlo on the Mafia's ruling Commission (though many say it is his brother Andrea who sits there) place Alfonso on the Triumvirate, the body that rules over the Commission. And while the Caruanas were always flush with cash, the accounts of Di Carlo's business interests show little sign of having been artificially bolstered by drug money.

But if Di Carlo is truly guilty of nothing more than having somewhat foolishly used his family name and its Mafia connotations to further his business career, then what of the man who calls him Mr D.

Salvatore Di Prima, a handyman who had lived in Britain since the age of two, first met Di Carlo in 1980 when he was employed to decorate his house. 'We got on really well so he kept on getting me back to do bits and pieces. He didn't speak any English so every time he had to fill out a form or something, he'd ask me along to help out.'

Di Carlo – who had two daughters but longed for a little boy – used to joke about Salvatore being like a son to him, and as time went on came to rely on his assistance more and more.

Soon, Di Prima was offered a job as manager of Leo's Wine Bar in Streatham, one of Di Carlo's alleged front companies, and was initially arrested along with the others on suspicion of having played a part in the heroin shipments. When no evidence was found, he was released without charge.

While Di Carlo was on remand, Di Prima did his best to look after his interests, continuing to run the businesses, doing odd jobs around the house for Mr D's wife, driving her to visit her husband in prison, and making personal use of the family BMW whenever he required it.

He was only too well aware that, as a fellow Sicilian and someone who had carried out maintenance work for the Caruana brothers, customs were keeping a close eye on him. Most of his friends knew this too.

Some time later, in August 1986, Di Prima received a worried telephone call from Gerrard Allen, a man he knew as a regular customer at the wine bar. 'He said he'd been to Spain on holiday but he'd run out of money and wondered if I could pick him up off the ferry from Plymouth.'

Di Prima set off in Di Carlo's BMW and was promptly arrested on the motorway by a joint police and customs team. It was a complete set-up. Allen, who had been supervising the drug run in Spain, had been on the same ferry as the Lancia with the petrol tank full of cannabis.

When this was apprehended (a similarly converted car had been discovered earlier in the year and the port authorities were on the lookout for similar models) he decided to implicate Di Prima, knowing that, because of his supposed Mafia links, it would divert suspicion from himself.

In court, Allen turned Queen's evidence and claimed that Di Prima had set up the entire operation using his Mafia contacts. A convincing witness, he alleged that Di Prima had dug up £50,000 from a safe in Di Carlo's garden to finance the job and that he had been introduced to Di Prima's Mafia contacts abroad.

The stories about a contract being taken out on his life were pure speculation and the threatening postcard was almost certainly sent by Allen rather than anyone else. Thanks to his co-operation, Allen received a significantly reduced sentence of two and half years. Di Prima got seven.

'They were convinced I had to be involved because of Di Carlo,' he says. 'I remember when they arrested me, the senior customs officer who got out of the car was the same one who'd arrested Mr D. As he walked towards me he was rubbing his hands with glee and said "You've made my day you have". I never stood a chance.'

The true origins of the Mafia have been for ever lost in a mixture of myth, speculation and fantasy.

One story claims that the organisation was born during Easter week of 1282 when Sicily was under French domination. According to local legend, a fracas developed after a group of church-going worshippers from Palermo was apprehended *en route* by treasury agents looking for tax debtors.

During the confusion, one young lady was brutally raped by a French soldier and her distraught mother ran through the streets screaming '*Ma fia*' – 'my daughter' in Sicilian. This cry of anguish soon became the rallying call of the resistance movement who adapted it into an acronym: *Morte alla Francia, Italia anela* – 'Death to the French is Italy's cry'.

Another tale dates back to the days of the Inquisition when thousands of Sicilians found that their only shield against the constant oppression was a secret brotherhood that upheld the true virtues of honour. The group took the name Mafia from the Arabic word meaning 'place of refuge'.

Yet another story says the name is a tribute to an Arab family living in Palermo, the Ma'afirs, who helped set up a society that avenged wrongs against Sicilian peasants by means of terror and vendetta. The group reached new strengths during the nineteenth century when it was employed by absentee landlords to manage their estates but quickly became so powerful that it became the unofficial ruling class.

Many Italian academics believe some of the stories aim to give the Mafia false respectability by according it ancient and noble origins. Whatever the truth, the Mafia today, they point out, is simply a conspiratorial system of criminal power that serves only itself.

Globally, the real power base has always been in Sicily, but it is often the exploits of the American Mafia which have brought the organisation the greatest degree of public attention.

US Mafia bosses travelled to Palermo in the autumn of 1957 to meet their Sicilian counterparts in order to agree a push into heroin trafficking and strategies for networking their money-laundering operations.

A subsequent meeting staged at Appalachin, New York State in November that same year to thrash out the details of the pan-American operation ended suddenly when a lone policeman stumbled across a hundred or so known gangsters from a dozen states as they converged on a woodland ranch-house.

The delegates were rounded up but no crime had been committed – they all claimed to have been visiting a sick friend – and they were subsequently released without charge. The press, however, had a field day. For years law enforcement, in particular J. Edgar Hoover's FBI, had denied that any such body as the Mafia existed. The Appalachin meeting proved beyond doubt for the first time that this was wrong.

It was the Americans who first coined the term *La Cosa Nostra* – This Thing of Ours – as an alternative name for the group, and it was also the Americans who provided the world with its first detailed look at the inner workings of the organisation, first through turncoat informers and later through more sophisticated means.

While undertaking routine surveillance on numerous leading underworld figures in New England early in 1990, hoping to get information on a recent murder, FBI agents found themselves listening in on one of the Mafia's most secret ceremonies – the baptism of new members.

Each recruit was brought separately into a room where they sat before local godfather Raymond Patriarca Jr, four lieutenants, a mediator, and eleven soldiers.

The ceremony began with the mediator reciting the words *In Onore della Famiglia la Famiglia ti abbraccia* – In honor of the Family, the Family embraces you. He then explained to the first candidate, a convicted loan shark: 'We're going to baptise you again. You were baptised when you were a baby, your parents did it, but now this time we're going to do it.'

The shark was then asked if he would be prepared to leave his mother dying in bed if he was called by La Cosa Nostra. 'Yes,' he answered. 'I want to enter this organisation to protect my family and protect all my friends. I swear not to divulge this secret and to obey with love and *omerta*.'

Through a system of counting fingers and matching numbers, a made member was chosen to sponsor the new recruit. Both men cut their hands to mingle the blood of their trigger-fingers, then a holy card bearing a picture of a saint was placed in the recruit's open hands and set alight.

As the flames rose he vowed: 'As burns this saint so will burn my soul. I enter alive into this organisation and I leave it dead.'

Afterwards, the mediator emphasised the importance of the code of *omerta*. 'It's no hope,' he said. 'No Jesus, no Madonna, nobody can help us if we ever give this secret to anybody. This thing cannot be exposed.'

Reaching such a stage is no mean feat. Outside direct recruitment within families, admission to the Mafia is by recommendation only and each applicant is carefully scrutinised.

He should be of proven courage, ruthless and decisive, be born of a 'respected' family and have no friendship or blood relationship with any member of the police. He must also maintain 'correct' relations with women – it is deemed acceptable to have a mistress but not to leave one's wife.

No one can be considered a true man of honour until he has proved his courage by committing murder. This is also an assurance that the group cannot be penetrated by undercover police officers.

*　　*　　*

The American Mafia first began working the British market in the balmy summer of 1962. That was the year in which Angelo Bruno, the widely respected head of the Philadelphia Mob, arrived to oversee the setting up of a number of international money-laundering schemes including the attempted purchase of a number of Mayfair gambling clubs.

News of his visit spread throughout the underworld and Bruno was advised that, if the Mafia wanted a quiet life while working overseas, they had better meet with London's top crime bosses in order to thrash out a few details.

The London villains were bluffing, but when Bruno eventually met up with Ronnie and Reggie Kray, he was sufficiently impressed to ensure that their firm became the principal conduit through which Mafia business in Britain was conducted.

'They needed our help,' explains Charlie Kray. 'When they first arrived they were trying to do things the way they did them back in America. They just wanted to buy their way into everything – cops, judges, you name it – so we had to take them to one side and explain that it didn't really work like that.'

As the level of trust grew, the Krays were also charged with minding the Mafia's newly acquired casinos, the 'Colony Club' and the 'Pair of Shoes', and protecting their many clients and business associates who periodically arrived from the States on gambling junkets.

Three years later, Bruno himself personally recommended using the Krays to help dispose of a backlog of $2 million of bearer bonds which the Mafia had stolen in a series of bank robberies in Montreal undertaken by a consortium of the Gambino, Bonnano and Columbo families.

The twins started cautiously, sending a representative to Canada to collect £20,000 worth. These were rapidly and easily sold and so, delighted with what seemed to be a way of making money with very little effort, the Krays launched themselves into what became a highly profitable sideline, earning them hundreds of thousands of pounds up until the time of their arrest in 1967.

Three decades later, the links are as strong as ever. Old-school villain Joey Pyle used his US Mafia connections to help keep him out of police clutches during his thirty-year stint in the underworld before finally succumbing to a US-style sting in 1992.

Elsewhere in the UK, there are hundreds of Mafia-run front companies and businesses. There is also a plush restaurant in Central London, the ownership of which is 'concealed' thanks to its having been registered on the Island of Jersey. However, the trail of those who set it up leads to a man with an FBI record for drug trafficking who is a member of New York's Genovese crime family.

In April 1987, the Old Bailey heard how an American Mafia family based in Detroit had attempted to set up a cocaine distribution chain in Britain which, if successful, would have pushed the street price down to half its current level.

Having made contact with a group of top Bolivian traffickers, the Lopez family, who agreed to supply large amounts of high-quality cocaine on a regular basis, the original aim of the Detroit-based Giacoloni family (who formed the Sicilian faction of the Detroit gang) had been to import the drugs into the US.

However, it was quickly ascertained that this market was becoming too flooded, so the plan was switched to Britain.

The specific details of the conspiracy would have remained unknown had it not been for David Medin, a nervous petty criminal and freelance financier who became involved with the Mafia after foolishly calling them in to assist a computer firm for which he was working in winning a new contract in Italy.

In return for providing the money and influence to clinch the deal, the Mafia took a fee and a sizable percentage of the profits. It also put pressure on Medin to use his financial expertise to assist them whenever they needed to set up new money-laundering operations, or any other favours.

And so it was that Medin found himself reluctantly in the back of a taxi on his way to a meeting at the Dorchester Hotel with two suitcases containing 36 kilos of virtually pure cocaine worth £10 million. When he was arrested by police acting on a tip-off, he took only a few hours to decide to turn supergrass, providing detailed information on the Mafia's plan, including supply routes and money-laundering facilities.

The drugs had been smuggled into Britain concealed inside bulldozer parts flown in from Venezuela which were then delivered to a garage in Chesterfield, Derbyshire. Once safely there, Medin and a member of the Giacoloni family used angle-grinders to cut open the box sections and remove the packets of drugs which were then taken by Medin to a safe house in Grays, Essex.

The following day, two members of the Lopez family arrived in London and, along with Mafia representatives, hosted a meeting at a Knightsbridge hotel of a consortium of major London villains (and representatives of the IRA), all of whom had expressed an interest in helping with the distribution of the drugs.

The plan was that, following a couple of successful 'test shipments' to check the security of the smuggling route, 100 kilos of cocaine would be delivered to Britain each month, significantly increasing its availability at street level and thus drastically reducing the price.

But one of those at the meeting, car dealer Peter McNeil, panicked on his way from the meeting, thinking he was being followed, and decided to go to the police, providing them with details of Medin's movements and allowing them to make the arrest.

Medin also revealed that he had set up a number of 'shell' companies, registered in Jersey, supposedly trading in computer parts, which would launder the profits of the scheme which had been estimated at around £1 million per week.

But not all the Cosa Nostra's attempts to take their business across the Atlantic have been quite so spectacular.

In early 1991, a slick American businessman named Ricky

Martino approached Northern and Shell, the London-based publishers of a range of soft-porn titles including *Penthouse*, *Big Ones* and *Asian Babes*, with a view to doing some business.

Martino's New York-based company, ATN, ran a successful telephone sex line business and he was keen to expand his operation overseas. Working through a go-between company called Harvest Advertising, Martino was interested in finding out what benefits advertising in N&S titles might bring.

Over the next few months, Martino, through Harvest, spent at least a million pounds on advertising his lines, but soon began to complain that the returns simply weren't big enough to justify continuing the deal. Keen to keep such a wealthy customer on the books, N&S executives wined and dined the head of Harvest, who eventually agreed to stick to the arrangement and look at means of changing the way the lines were being advertised.

After a revamp, the lines started to make a small profit, but still not enough to cover the cost of the advertising. N&S then suggested extending the reach by advertising in all the European editions of the company's magazines, but when this also failed to turn things around, Harvest stopped paying its bills and allowed the deal to lapse.

A series of angry telephone calls followed, with Harvest claiming that they had been misled and demanding compensation. N&S steadfastly refused, then in September 1992 Martino unexpectedly arrived in London for an emergency meeting with Northern and Shell's Chairman, Richard Desmond. Martino, so the story goes, informed the man: 'Don't fuck with me or you'll find out who I really am.'

Everything went quiet until the following month when Phillip Bailey, the managing director of Northern and Shell who was in New York on a business trip, was assaulted as he prepared to make his way back to London.

A limousine, supposedly sent by a business contact, arrived at his hotel to take him to the airport. But a few minutes into the journey, the vehicle stopped and two men jumped into the car. Bailey was pistol-whipped, electrocuted with some sort of cattle-prod, and his face was cut with a knife.

According to the report Bailey filed with the New York Police Department, as the men attacked him they shouted: 'Tell your boss Desmond he's a fucking dead man. The pond is a short trip across and we know his address.' Bailey was then thrown out of the car which sped away.

Back in London, Bailey and Desmond reported the threats to the British police and new security guards were hired to patrol the reception area at N&S.

Desmond has subsequently dismissed the story. As for Martino, a little digging through the FBI files reveals that he served time for attempted robbery and gambling offences during the early eighties and is currently a 'made' soldier in the Gambino family.

His telephone sex line business, along with the property company he runs with his brother Daniel, are said to be thriving.

With so many key personnel based in Latin America – most notably, of late, members of the Cuntrera and Caruana families – it comes as no surprise to learn that the Mafia has been working hand in hand with the Colombian cartels for a number of years.

The principal arrangement – the exchange of cocaine for heroin – dates back to the mid-eighties when America's drug market was showing the first signs of saturation. In Europe, cocaine was fetching a far higher price, but the fledgling distribution chain of the Cali cartel (which had closer links to the Mafia than its Medellin rival) simply couldn't compete with the long-established network that spread out of Italy.

Heroin, on the other hand, was widely available in Europe and, thanks to the Common Market, transporting consignments around the Continent was relatively straightforward. Unlike cocaine, heroin's price had held steady but, at around £35,000 per kilo (in Rome), was still around four times *lower* than the price in New York.

Following a key summit between senior representatives of both groups on the Caribbean island of Aruba in October 1987, the deal was struck. The Mafia would ship its heroin to New York and 'sell' it to the Colombians. But rather than receiving cash, they would take delivery of an equivalent amount of cocaine which in turn would be shipped back to Europe.

So successful was the Sicilian–Colombian alliance that it soon became closer and stronger. They shared transport and distribution facilities, jointly established front companies, and pooled their intelligence about law enforcement activities. The cartels are even believed to have assisted the Mafia in some of its more spectacular assassinations.

Hard evidence of just how close the two groups had become emerged during the Drug Enforcement Administration's nine-month investigation into the Cali cartel's money-laundering network. The forty-five undercover agents assigned to Operation Green Ice stumbled across details of a second Mafia–cartel summit, scheduled to be held in Rome in September 1992.

The investigators also found out that a number of fundamental decisions had already been taken: Italy, rather than Spain, was to be the main 'warehouse' for drugs entering Europe, and the Mafia were to take the lead role, placing trusted agents directly into Colombia to supervise cocaine being despatched back to Italy.

Once all this was known, Operation Green Ice was quickly expanded to include undercover officers from the Central Operational Service of the Italian police and, days before the main meeting was due to take place, José 'Tony' Duran, one of the world's biggest distributors of Colombian cocaine, and his colleague Pedro Villaquiran, were arrested while drinking cocktails in a smart café on Rome's Piazza di Spagna.

Duran, whose fingerprints have been found in various countries under at least twenty different names and whose true identity has never really been estalished, had been appointed to represent not just the Cali and Medellin cartels but also the emerging contenders based in Pereira, Costa and Valle del Norte.

The arrest of Duran and Villaquiran was the signal for hundreds of police and customs officers across the world to go into action. Picked up in Rome at the same time were many of those who would have been sitting on the other side of Duran's negotiating table: members of the Corleone clan, the Calabrian 'Ndrangheta and the Alfieri family from the Naples-based Camorra. (The latter two are satellite Mafia organisations wielding great power in their home towns but still bowing to the will of Sicily.)

In Spain four more Mafia launderers were arrested; in Canada millions of dollars generated from drug sales were liberated; in Colombia the office of Gilberto Rodriguez Orejuela, head of the Cali cartel, was raided, while in San Diego two of his top lieutenants were picked up having been lured there with the promise of a meeting to discuss laundering £14 million.

In Britain two Americans, David Lemieux and Thomas O'Donnell, who acted as joint envoys of the Cali cartel and the Mafia, were arrested in Queensgate, west London. The customs officers who picked them up also found 43 kilos of Cali cocaine worth around £7 million and a further £2 million in banknotes.

Overall, thirty-six hours after Operation Green Ice reached its climax, 201 suspects had been arrested in seven nations. Drugs and cash worth more than £40 million had been seized and some fifteen front companies had been shut down, including a Corleone-based wine export agency, a frozen-fish franchise, an office cleaning contractor, and the Rome-based European Institute for the Protection of Animals.

'We have driven a stake through the heart of the illegal drugs business by attacking their financial operations. We have reduced their capacity to do evil,' said US Deputy Attorney-General George Terwilliger. 'Never has the Mafia suffered a blow on such a scale,' added Vincenzo Parisi, chief of the Italian police.

Yet within a few months, all the damage caused by the operation had been repaired: new front companies had been formed, new distribution networks established, and deputies had been promoted to take the places of their imprisoned bosses. Business quickly got back to normal and the pact remained as strong as ever.

One year on, during a raid on the Palermo home of fugitive Mafia boss Salvatore Gallina, documents were found which indicated that a very large shipment of Cali cocaine was being despatched to Italy. The tone of the correspondence seemed to indicate that many other such shipments had already been made.

With extensive use of police informers and telephone taps, the consignment was followed 'inch by inch' and, just before Christmas, 850 kilos of high-quality cocaine, worth a phenomenal £226 million, were seized at an Italian port.

At the same time, a further 263 kilos – £70 million worth – a slice of the original batch which had been diverted to Britain on board the Monrovian-registered container ship MV *Maipo*, were seized at Felixstowe.

The drugs had been concealed in the false bases of two containers full of coffee with a layer of lead to prevent X-ray detection. Douglas Tweddle, then chief investigations officer for Customs and Excise, admitted that, without the tip-off from Italian police, the drugs would have been almost impossible to detect.

Among those arrested in Britain was Pietro Soggiu, a Sicilian with strong contacts with the Corleone clan, one of Palermo's most feared families, while in Colombia, Giuseppe 'Old Man' Triolo, who had replaced the Cuntrera brothers, was finally brought to book.

That Soggiu had been living in Britain without ringing any alarm bells for several months before the bust posed the question of just how many other Mafiosi might be in Britain.

Certainly, at the lowest levels, they are known to be numerous. That the streets and squats around King's Cross are streaming with junkies and prostitutes is well known; that the heroin trade is in the hands of the Mafia's elder cousin, the Naples-based Camorra, is not.

When police launched Operation Welwyn against user/dealers in the area, they arrested some sixty Neapolitans, many of whom had come to England for legitimate reasons such as to study but ended up becoming embroiled in minor criminal culture because of a lack of finance.

(There are more than 2,000 Italian heroin addicts in London alone, and many agencies have set up special Anglo-Italian clinics to deal with the problem.)

While the majority of those arrested were addicts dealing purely to support their own habits, a few were highly successful, making thousands of pounds a day selling large quantities of high-quality heroin. Many of them alleged that they were being supplied with their drugs by members of the Camorra, and another team of Neapolitans is known to be conducting a campaign of extortion against Italian restaurants across London and the south-east.

But there is also concern about higher-level operatives heading for Britain. According to a confidential report published in 1993 by the National Criminal Intelligence Service: 'There have been a number of incidents recently when fugitives from Italian justice have been located in this country.

'This phenomenon will undoubtedly continue and reliable intelligence indicates that the United Kingdom has been identified by Italian organised crime as a country suitable as a haven for such persons.'

A week after Soggiu was arrested, the *Sunday Times* stuck its neck out, publishing a list of potential fugitives hiding in Britain which included Giovanni Brusca, the man said to have set off the remote-control bomb that killed Giovanni Falcone; Leoluca 'The Colonel' Bagarella, brother-in-law of the Mafia's long-time leader Salvatore Rina; and mass murderer

Bernardo Provenzano, Rina's right-hand man and probable successor.

The report was immediately shot down by leading Sicilian anti-Mafia magistrates. 'A boss outside his territory is like a fish out of water,' said public prosecutor Lo Forte. 'To abandon Sicily for Britain would be as if the Mafia had suddenly conceded defeat.'

Indeed, when Rina was finally caught after twenty-three years on the run, he was found to have lived in Palermo all that time, protected by nothing more than a false ID card and a conspiracy of silence. At the time, he was living just 400 yards from Falcone's home.

Therefore, it is far more likely that a Mafioso setting up home in Britain would do so only for some 'tactical' purpose like setting up a new drug distribution channel or supervising a major shipment.

Giovanbattista Maganuco, an alleged member of the Iani Cavalo clan, was extradited back to Italy in late 1993 to face charges of extortion in his home town of Gela. He was tracked to a house in Rochdale where he had set up home, having come to Britain to work as a chef.

Anti-Mafia detectives believe he too was sent to England in order to establish a presence for the clan which is known to want to expand its drug activities.

Italian police and British customs officers have also carried out covert surveillance on Antonio La Torre, the owner of an Italian restaurant in Aberdeen whose name has been linked to the Camorra.

At one point, La Torre was on the run from Italian justice. An international arrest warrant had been issued in connection with offences of 'criminal conspiracy of a Camorra kind'. A subsequent remand tribunal overturned the custody order so he is no longer a fugitive.

The La Torre clan are notoriously violent, not particularly large, but notorious. In April 1990, six of their men burst into a local bar in the town of Mondragone, eighty miles north of

Naples, and executed a group of North African immigrants who had been undercutting local drug prices and not paying a cut to Camorra bosses.

A Criminalpol report on the clan compiled in 1991 lists them as specialising in 'extortion, robberies, drugs dealing and arms trafficking'.

Telephone taps have allegedly shown La Torre to have been in contact with two known Camorra drug traffickers based in Caracas, Venezuela, while initial surveillance showed him travelling long distances, sometimes up to 200 miles, for meetings that would last just a few minutes.

Since his name became public, such travels and telephone calls have ceased, but there is no suggestion that La Torre has committed any offence in this country.

Another member of the Italian community in Aberdeen has also been named. He is described by police in Naples as having 'interests in Zurich' and as being the 'Ambassador' in the organisation of – if not the actual courier of – drugs travelling between South America and Holland. According to his lawyer, the man is flabbergasted and bemused by the suggestion.

Few Mafiosi hold down mundane full-time jobs purely for the love of working. Running a cash-based business such as a restaurant, or being the managing director of a small company that trades across international borders, are both ideal positions from which to launder the proceeds of criminal activity.

Increasingly, however, the profits of the Mafia's worldwide empire have become so great that they require the assistance of specialist launderers in order to allow them to make use of the money they have earned illegally.

Britain has always figured high in the plans of such operatives and, as a major financial centre, is well suited to the task of making dirty money clean.

Although the methods have changed, the basic problem every launderer has to address – how to turn large quantities of small-denomination banknotes into small quantities of large ones or into bank drafts, letters of credit or traveller's cheques – remains the same.

In the early days, they would simply change money over at high-street bureaux de change or, as the Caruanas did, pay it into the bank. However, new legislation introduced in the late eighties and recently updated means that all banks, solicitors, accountants and the like must report any 'suspicious' transactions to the National Criminal Intelligence Service.

In 1987 there were less than 300 reports. By 1993, there were close to 13,000, with the number showing no sign of decreasing.

Hence launderers have had to seek out other outlets. They currently make extensive use of casinos, particularly in London. A launderer will build a reputation for gambling large amounts at the tables. Then, at some later date, he can go in and hand the cashier £100,000 in cash without raising eyebrows and get chips in return.

He can then play for a little while before cashing in his chips for a cheque drawn on the casino's respectable bank which, because it will appear to be the result of a legitimate transaction, will not lead to a report being submitted to the police.

For this popular method of laundering, Britain is ideally placed. Despite restrictions introduced in the 1970s, Britain has more casinos than any European nation except France. Unlike almost every other country, casinos can be found in most big British cities: London has twenty-one casinos while Paris, New York and Washington have none.

Furthermore, keeping tabs on these kinds of transactions is almost impossible. The last available figures indicate that around £2 billion is converted to gaming chips in Britain each year, two-thirds of it passing through London casinos alone.

The Mafia launderers have also infiltrated the fine-art market. Early in 1993, the Phillips auction house in London was forced to purchase a cash-counting machine because its sales staff were unable to process the millions of pounds' worth of notes being handed over to pay for purchases.

The increasing trend towards cash payments in auction rooms across the capital was said to be almost entirely down to a new breed of buyers, young, well dressed and obviously Italian, who would bid up to four times over the estimates in order to ensure that they got the pictures and antiques they wanted.

It is said by some observers that, without their money, the London art market might not have survived the recession, though there is no suggestion that Phillips or any other auction house ever knowingly accepted 'dirty' money as payment.

For this method of laundering, money is simply smuggled into Britain inside suitcases. It is then used to buy pictures which are then transported back to Italy with bona fide bills of sale from some of the world's most prestigious auction houses, putting them way beyond the reproach of law enforcement. The paintings are then either resold for clean money or held in reserve.

(It is said that the world's most famous missing painting, Caravaggio's *The Nativity of San Lorenzo*, stolen from a Palermo church in 1969, has spent the past twenty years in Sicily in the hands of different Mafia families being used as collateral for drug deals.)

The use of the art market as a means of money laundering accelerated at the beginning of 1993 when border restrictions within the European Community were ended. Previously, any painting bought in Britain and transported back to Italy would have been subject to a hefty levy, but this has now been abandoned, making the process even more profitable.

In a bid to curb the trade, some auction houses now require all new arrivals to hand over their passports so that their names can be checked against the register of bidders. Others read out a new regulation at the beginning of each session, explaining that the name and address of each bidder must remain the same throughout the purchase, preventing paintings being 'switched' to lesser-known clients immediately they are sold.

Such is the success of these and many other Mafia schemes

that increasingly other groups are expressing an interest in getting involved.

In November 1990 Judge Giovanni Falcone warned a police conference in Germany that the great crime syndicates of the world were coming together. The Mafia, the Triads, the yakuza and the Russians were involved in what he called 'operations welding' and had 'stipulated a sort of non-aggression pact, dividing up the world.'

As the team working on Operation Green Ice discovered, numerous conferences and summits have already been held (with many more scheduled for years to come), with the most significant to emerge so far being the universal agreement that it will be the Mafia which takes premier position within the new global gang, chiefly because of its strength and influence in both Europe and America.

Scotland Yard, the FBI, DEA and others publicly agree that the fight against drugs and organised crime is really the fight against money laundering – if you deprive people of the ability to benefit from their activities they will be forced to stop. In private, however, they also admit that, while they may win the occasional battle against the Mafia and its increasingly sophisticated launderers, they are still losing the war.

Chapter Ten

To Be Somebody

Miscellaneous Organised Crime

'To join a gang or not to join a gang
That is the question
For if I do not, I will be all alone
And if I do, I will surely die'

*Former member of Los Angeles' Crips gang
after studying Shakespeare in reform school*

Land of Opportunity

David Rollings hated letting the bad guys win. The sixty-one-year-old Tory councillor and professional troubleshooter relished the role of knight in shining armour, seeing himself as a wannabe John Harvey Jones with just a touch of James Bond. Given a choice of sides, he'd always back the underdog.

So when he learned that some of his business associates in Bristol had been fleeced of more than £2 million by a slick Nigerian fraudster, Rollings had little hesitation in volunteering to do what he could to set matters right.

Having worked as an export consultant to the water industry, Rollings had made dozens of trips to Nigeria over the years and was well known to the staff at his favourite hotel, the five-star Ikoyi in the heart of the capital, Lagos.

On this occasion, he arrived on the evening of Friday, 26 July 1991, had an uneventful weekend, and then left the hotel early on Monday morning for what he described as a 'business meeting'. But when he arrived back half an hour later, it was clear that all was not well. 'It was obvious that something was very wrong,' the Ikoyi's manageress, Fatima Mohammed, said later. 'He was sweating profusely and appeared to be very upset.' Rollings demanded his key. When the clerk gingerly enquired if everything was okay, Rollings snapped back that he was fine and marched across to the lift. He stabbed at the button a few times then, fed up with waiting, made for the stairs.

Just after 11 a.m., a shot rang out. 'There was a terrific bang,' said Mohammed. 'Everyone in the hotel heard it and we all ran about knocking on all the doors trying to find out where it had come from. For a few minutes there was chaos, people everywhere.'

When Rollings failed to reply to the frantic knocks on his door, staff entered his room with a pass key. They found him sprawled on the bed with a bullet hole in the back of the head.

The room was still neat and tidy – there had been no attempt to rob him. No gun was ever found in the room and his killer or killers almost certainly slipped away during the moments of chaos that followed the gunshot. They have never been caught.

Had Rollings read the previous months' Nigerian newspapers, he might have been forewarned.

A few weeks earlier an American finance consultant, Gerald Scruggs, had also visited Lagos, staying in the five-star Sheraton in the city's suburbs, to oversee what he thought was a legitimate multi-million-dollar 'business opportunity' that had fallen into his lap by way of a wealthy Nigerian lawyer.

However, once Scruggs had arrived in the country the lawyer, whom he had never met, kept on demanding more and more cash to help 'sweeten' the final deal. After handing over thousands of dollars, Scruggs perhaps began to suspect that the glittering opportunity was only fool's gold and refused to pay any more.

When they found him, just outside the hotel grounds, he had been necklaced – a car tyre had been strung about his neck, doused with petrol and then set alight. His killers have never been caught.

The following May, Wigan-based engineer John Hillman arrived in Lagos to close a seemingly legitimate deal arranged by his friend, Darrell Purchase, who ran a Midlands packing firm. The day after Hillman arrived two men claiming to be friends of Purchase asked him to fly up-country to Enugu to 'sort out a few problems'.

The forty-nine-year-old was lured to a flat on the outskirts of Onitsha on the pretext of signing a few papers, but once he was alone with them the two men demanded money. Not just his wallet, but hundreds of thousands of pounds from Purchase's company accounts. When Hillman failed to comply the men threatened him with a shotgun and repeatedly beat him with the flat side of a four-foot machete until he was virtually unconscious.

In a five-day ordeal, the kidnappers – who were involved in a larger plot to defraud a string of British businessmen of £35 million – told Hillman they were going to cut out his eyes, stab him in the stomach, then throw him in the bush. They didn't allow him to move from the sofa for three days, except to make telephone calls to demand a £20,000 ransom from his family and a further £270,000 from Purchase.

He was eventually freed after Nigerian agents working for Interpol tracked down the gang's hideout, using the contact numbers they had provided to his family in order to facilitate payment of the ransom.

Despite such highly publicised incidents, hardly a week goes by without an American or European diplomat being called to escort some terrified scam victim from their Lagos hotel room to the airport in order to remove them from what the US Consulate calls 'potentially life-threatening situations'.

Invariably, like Rollings, Scruggs and Hillman, they have fallen prey to the nameless, ruthless international organised crime syndicate which, through a combination of highly sophisticated fraud, cunning deception, first-class counterfeiting and large-scale drug trafficking, rakes in at least £3 billion each year, principally from Britain and America.

With no single leader, little inter-group loyalty, technical expertise that is second to none, and a vast workforce that includes dozens of government officials, judges, police and military personnel, the fifty or sixty major 'families' and hundreds of smaller gangs that make up the Nigerian mafia are, collectively, one of the richest, most powerful criminal organisations in the world.

The success and wealth of the syndicates have continued to grow despite a sizable, well-co-ordinated multi-agency campaign aimed at curbing their activities. In Britain, banks, building societies, trade associations and local councils are only too well aware of the threat of Nigerian fraud and, along with the police, customs and immigration authorities, have introduced special (some say draconian and racist) procedures to prevent it.

But such is the sophistication of the syndicates that these policies have succeeded only in making life hell for Nigeria's many legitimate entrepreneurs and driving the name of the country ever further into the dirt.

In a cover story entitled 'Why are we so fraudulent?' the *Journal of Nigerian Affairs* notes with disdain: 'Our main contribution to 20th century civilisation is fraud. From Canada to Zimbabwe, from the remote Asian highland of Katmandu to the celebrated streets of New York City, Nigerians abound and wherever they are, corruption hangs over them like a cloud they cannot shake off.'

Nigerian businessmen attempting to operate in Britain are routinely refused permission to open accounts at high-street banks because of the fear of fraud. Huge deposits are demanded for even the most mundane business services, and the majority of purchases have to be paid for in advance, preferably with cash – credit might just as well be a four-letter word.

Yet the syndicates continue to skim hundreds of millions out of banks each year. A report by the Association of North

American Bankers suggested that US financial houses were being defrauded of $1 billion each year by gangs of organised Nigerian criminals. The report further estimates that: 'out of 100,000 Nigerians living on the East Coast, some 75,000 are engaged in fraudulent activities.'

Problems with bogus student loan applications have led the Department of Education in the UK to insist that local councils – duty-bound to award grants to all those who are eligible – tighten up procedures and also apply a far greater degree of scrutiny to applications with some link with Nigeria than those of any other national.

In the London borough of Waltham Forest, for example, original copies of documents rather than photocopies must now be supplied. National Insurance numbers are now painstakingly checked against dates of birth and all applicants must supply photographs of themselves.

Yet the syndicates continue to submit thousands of fraudulent loan requests each year, backed up with near-perfect forgeries of all the necessary documents from exam certificates and job references to union cards and National Insurance numbers. Exactly how much is lost is not known, but one man, Michael Olusoji, acting alone, was found to have tricked seventeen universities into offering him places on degree courses. His grants totalled £89,373.

In a bid to reduce the £2 billion cost of benefits fraud, dozens of councils have been forced to employ additional staff to check housing and social security claims while the government is considering introducing a central computer register to collate claims and cross-check names and addresses.

Yet thousands of bogus payments are made each week, often on a grand scale. One investigation in 1993 led to the discovery of a seventeen-strong unit operating from a three-storey house in Kensington and receiving £150,000 per month in benefits using more than two thousand false identities. As well as the Kensington residence, the group had more than five hundred other addresses to which cheques were being delivered.

Another group, operating out of twenty grand houses in the Bayswater area, lived in luxury. One of the houses commanded rent of £60,000 per year. The team had been using the identities of people who died between 1972 and 1982 or of living students who had 'clean' National Insurance contribution records. Two of the women involved were daughters of Nigerian tribal chiefs, another was the daughter of a judge. They had made more than £1 million.

In March 1992, the Home Office announced the formation of a special immigration squad specifically to target the problem of Nigerians entering the country on false papers, a move which the country's High Commission described as 'extreme, unfair and humiliating'.

Yet thousands of Nigerians still manage to enter the country illegally each year, using bogus passports, visas or often on the basis of fake applications made to universities and colleges.

A further three thousand Nigerians are estimated to gain indefinite leave to remain in Britain each year through sham marriages. One ring uncovered in 1989 was found to be approaching homeless men and offering them £1000 plus a suit to marry women they had never met. The women themselves were paying between £2000 and £3000.

Others made use of false documents to allow them to marry many times under different identities. One British woman was found to have married thirty separate Nigerian men over a two-year period.

The ring was uncovered only when registrars in several towns reported the same brides, bridegrooms and witnesses appearing at different weddings, sometimes in the same week. The immigration authorities say they know the scam is still going on but admit they don't have the resources to combat it.

The Metropolitan Police, in common with most other major forces, have a detective working full time on deception cases originating in Nigeria, while the International Maritime Bureau, a trade association that investigates international shipping fraud, splits its work into four main categories:

container investment, phantom cargoes, Nigerian oil, Nigerian investment.

On top of this, the Nigerian government itelf advertises widely in leading British and American publications, warning the business community about the danger of fraud, and the Central Bank of Nigeria has issued warnings to 'gullible victims' that it is not possible to 'reap where you did not sow'.

Yet, thanks mostly to the greed of British businessmen hoping to make a fast buck at the Third World's expense, the fraudsters continue to flourish, with reports of new, more diverse and ever-more lucrative cases being uncovered almost every week.

And at every turn, the name of Nigeria seems to become increasingly synonymous with sharp practice and chicanery.

In December 1993, British Telecom and Mercury both announced bans on pay-phone credit card calls to Nigeria because of 'a clear pattern of fraudulent use'. Nigerians even top the list issued by the Foreign Office of diplomats who fail to pay parking fines, more than 20 per cent ahead of their nearest rivals.

In the league table of countries stigmatised by institutionalised crime, Nigeria is second only to Jamaica.

And while the country has established new laws and a special police squad to target the gangs, corruption is so widespread (a recent crackdown led to the dismissals of thirty senior officers, twenty-nine inspectors and 101 constables in Lagos alone) that it surprises no one to learn that, after more than two years of operation, the squad has yet to secure a single conviction or return a single penny to a foreign businessman.

There could be no doubt about it, Femi was destitute. The last time his former schoolfriend Peter, a Nigerian businessman now based in Birmingham, saw him, he was 'so wretched, he couldn't even buy shoes. I gave him some money to buy a pair.'

Fourteen months later, when Peter was back in Lagos on

a business trip, a sleek BMW sounded its horn as it passed, then pulled up alongside the pavement. It was Femi.

As the pair cruised the streets, Femi talked of the extraordinary change in his fortunes. How he now had a large mansion in the affluent suburbs, two such cars, a sizable collection of Italian suits, and enough shoes to open a shop of his own. 'He told me he was on his way to buy a plane,' says Peter.

And, as a favour to a kind friend, Femi passed on the secret of his route to wealth as, a few months earlier, another friend had to him.

Firstly, as a one-off to get him off the ground, Femi had agreed to act as a drug 'mule', swallowing ten condoms each containing around 20 grams of cocaine, a haul worth around £16,000. He had spent weeks preparing for the journey, acclimatising his gullet by swallowing whole grapes smothered in honey so that he would not gag when it came to ingesting the drugs.

The morning of his flight, he took half a pack of diarrhoea treatment to prevent his bowels moving until he was safely in the country. As a further precaution, each drug-filled condom had been smeared in charcoal, an attempt to make it invisible to X-rays should a customs officer become suspicious.

On the plane, Femi was careful to follow the instructions he had been given. When the coast was clear, he slipped the contents of his meal tray into his sick bag and hid it under his seat – airline staff regularly tip off the authorities about passengers who fail to eat during long flights on known drug-trafficking routes in case they are carrying drugs.

For the same reason, Femi was careful not to dawdle in the lavatory, avoided leaving packs of diarrhoea tablets or painkillers around, and tried to appear happy and relaxed throughout the journey.

Unlike many mules, Femi was only too aware of the risks he was taking. Dozens of Nigerians are imprisoned each year. Many have agreed to take drugs on the false understanding that, if they are caught, they will simply be deported, whereas in reality they face sentences of four to fourteen years. Other mules have suffered at the hands of unscrupulous traffickers who fail to wrap the drugs properly, causing the packages to burst in the courier's stomach, leading to a slow, agonising death.

There are some former mules who believe this is deliberate – creating enough of a distraction to enable other couriers on the same flight to pass through customs unhindered. Certainly there have been cases where the drug barons themselves have tipped off customs about one or two of their own couriers on a flight, knowing this will divert attention from the half a dozen others.

Femi knew the £800 he was being paid for his smuggling trip was nothing compared to the gamble he was taking, but for him the most important aspect of the deal was that he would get free passage to Britain, a country where, by following the advice of those who had been there before him, he knew he could make his fortune.

Unable to get a job in a post office sorting room – the ideal scenario – Femi compromised and approached a fellow Nigerian who already worked in one. He offered the man a £200 down payment and then £1,000 per month to redirect 'promising'-looking letters to an accommodation address Femi had set up.

'Promising' letters take only a little practice to spot. Unmarked, firm on one side and flexible on the other, they are highly likely to contain credit cards or cash cards. Each time the sorter came across one, he would dip into his pocket, pull out a pre-printed address label, and stick it over the original address.

Every other day, Femi would collect his mail, using the credit cards to purchase electrical goods (often on monthly credit schemes so that only a small amount would be debited from the card), hire cars, withdraw cash and buy food and clothes.

Each card was 'safe' only for two or three days, after which the issuing company would get around to cancelling it and the risk of using it become too great, but by then Femi had dozens of other cards waiting for him.

As the money began to roll in, Femi refined the scheme. He employed a network of sorters at different post offices across the country; rented half a dozen cheap flats (all paid for by fake housing benefit claims) to which the letters would be sent. Despite all the 'free' accommodation his scheme produced, Femi was careful to ensure that he lived some distance away as an additional precaution.

To avoid suspicion about the large amount of post, he addressed the labels in the names of bogus companies – Nu Vox Home Products and the like – and to double his chances of being able to spend other people's money, he employed a team of women to use the cards registered to female owners.

After ten months, he moved back home, where his new-found wealth provided all the credibility he needed to mix it with the best of the Nigerian aristocracy. Femi's parties are now the talk of the town, and he fully expects to be awarded a chieftaincy in the near future.

He is far from unique. According to a comprehensive report by the US Immigration and Naturalisation Service, there are dozens of similar 'cells' operating all over Britain and the US.

Typically, each cell will be run by an 'officer' and be composed of between five and twenty 'soldiers'. To ensure maximum security, only the officer can make contact with other cells, and he is also responsible for ensuring that adjacent operations don't encroach on one another's territory.

Each member of the gang has a specific role. One will be appointed to act as a facilitator, taking a job within a building society, government department or benefit office. Once inside, his task is to provide detailed information on how that particular system works in order for schemes to be thought up to defraud it.

Others will take jobs as security guards or cleaners in the targeted companies and spend their spare time going through rubbish bins and filing cabinets, looking for letterheaded paper, official stamps and other items that can be used to produce or support bogus identities.

In addition, the most sophisticated cells will usually have their own counterfeiter (though these are sometimes shared between groups), a bank clerk to assist in the opening of accounts in false names, a housing worker to establish mailing addresses, and a recruiter to approach other Nigerians working in 'useful' organisations and offer them money in return for their co-operation.

If they can be of particular benefit, these new recruits may be asked to join the organisation proper. There are impromptu 'colleges of crime' both in Nigeria and Britain where newcomers are taught the tricks of the trade with all the conviction and professionalism of a university degree course.

After raiding one such premises, police discovered a make-shift training manual which advised those setting up new lives for themselves: 'All ID starts with a birth certificate. With this document you can obtain all the other forms of official ID.'

The manual also included tips on how to create multiple bogus identities, using 'tried and tested' methods such as scanning the obituary columns of newspapers for details of deaths and then applying for a copy of the person's birth certificate.

Rather than making use of stolen credit cards, which only have a few days' useful life in them, the manual further suggests that syndicate members apply for their own simply by placing £250 in a bank account – using an assumed identity – for a few weeks to build up a reputable 'credit history'.

'The idea that there are just a few people operating on their own who have only turned to crime in order to make a meagre living is a complete fallacy,' says one detective who specialises in Nigerian fraud cases. 'There is a highly organised, highly professional body at work and they have as many scams as there are pebbles on a beach. You name it, they've found a way to make money from it.'

*   *   *

The clouds of corruption that now haunt Nigerians first formed in 1979 when Shehu Shagari became the country's first civilian president and fired the starting pistol on the African equivalent of a gold rush.

With the country's oil industry pushing out millions of barrels each day, money was everywhere, and foreign and local businessmen were quick to exploit the booming demand for imports from all over the world.

For a time, Nigerians were seen as the latest and greatest international entrepreneurs. Everywhere they went, financial doors swung open for them. Everybody wanted a piece of the action. It was then that the 419 gangs started.

Named after the section of the Nigerian penal code which it infringes, the typical 419 scam begins with a relatively innocent letter, faxed or sent through the post and bearing the official crest of a Lagos-based bank, government office or major corporation.

In pidgin English, the letter will explain how the recipient has been selected/recommended as 'a trusted international businessman' and will request 'absolute confidentiality' over an urgent 'business transaction' they would like to carry out.

The individual stories differ widely but in essence there are two main themes. One offers the recipient a lucrative government contract while the other relates how a large sum of money has become available, either by legitimate or illegitimate means, and how, because of government restrictions, a foreign bank account is required in order for the senders to make use of the cash. In the latter case, the recipient is offered a huge commission fee for assisting.

A batch of 419 letters which hit numerous British businesses in the late eighties purported to be from a Dr F.O. Rufai of the Technical Committee for Privatisation and Commercialisation. The doctor explained how he and his colleagues had been given the task of selling off all government-held shares in loss-making companies.

'During this exercise, a substantial amount of money was

realised, part of which we did not remit into the government's purse for the obvious reason of transferring it overseas into a foreign bank account for onward disbursement amongst ourselves.'

But, says the letter, government officials are not allowed to open foreign bank accounts so: 'We are now soliciting your assistance for the use of your account facility into which we can transfer this money, for which we are offering you an unconditional 20 per cent of the total sum.'

With a total of $42.6 million up for grabs, this commission amounts to more than £11 million.

The fraudsters go to extraordinary lengths to reassure those who feel such offers are simply too good to be true. The telephone numbers that accompany the bogus letters will be seemingly genuine, answered brightly by people claiming to represent whatever company is in vogue that week.

Even those who do not wholly believe the scenario will often go along with it all as there seems to be little risk. After all, the letters do not ask for money, merely a signed, blank company letterhead, a signed blank invoice, and full details of the company's bank accounts so that the money can be quickly and easily transferred.

However, the signed letters are used to ask the company's bank to transfer money *out* of the account. An unfortunate few have lost hundreds of thousands of pounds literally overnight. The blank invoices, meanwhile, are reproduced and submitted to numerous companies around the world as bills for goods or services. Many simply pay up.

As the business world becomes aware of one set of scams, so new ones are developed. In the early 1990s, hundreds of victims of earlier 419 frauds found themselves being contacted by the Presidential Task Force on Debt Repayment.

To qualify for a full refund – a gesture of goodwill from the Nigerian government – all the business needed to do was to send their full financial details within two days. The end results were inevitable.

The fraudsters are also targeting an ever-wider audience. In January 1994 it emerged that Cafod, the Catholic aid agency, had received a fax from a man called Mr D. Mba from Lagos announcing that the charity had been left £150,000 in the will of 'the late Dr Mrs Rosaline Ellis-Okafor'. The woman was said to have been a devout Catholic who had married a Nigerian and lived in Nigeria for twenty-three years before passing away the previous summer.

Fax messages went back and forth with the directors of the charity naturally being pleased at the bequest. Just before Christmas, Cafod received a cheque by courier for £150,000 drawn on the Central Bank of Nigeria.

A fax sent shortly after the cheque arrived delivered the *coup de grâce* – asking for Cafod to send £6,000 by immediate direct transfer to pay death duties.

The aim of the fraudsters would have been to get their hands on Cafod's money before the charity discovered that the cheque was bogus. But before the 'death duties' were paid, a sharp-eyed worker in the accounts department noticed something odd about the bank identity code on the cheque. Investigating further, it turned out to have been 'borrowed' from a branch of Lloyds in Oxford Street.

The 419 letters are a massive industry. Scotland Yard estimates that around 500,000 were sent out around the world in 1993 alone. But although the scheme earns the fraudsters millions, the biggest of the illicit bucks have always been made from the country's greatest natural asset. Oil.

'The problem', says Eric Ellen of the International Maritime Bureau, 'is that myths are developed which no one is prepared to shoot down: myths that the Central Bank of Nigeria is holding development funds exclusively for British companies; myths that there are short-term bank accounts paying 25 per cent interest; and most of all myths that it is possible to buy tanker-loads of Nigerian crude oil outside official government channels.'

The IMB currently receives reports of three or four new cases of Nigerian fraud each week, the tip of an iceberg believed to be earning the top gangs a sizable share of an estimated £2 billion each year.

Theoretically, fraud is virtually impossible thanks to a complex system of internationally recognised documents that ensure that the right goods are delivered to the right people and that the right people are paid for the right goods.

However, on the back streets of Lagos, all manner of fake documents from passports and birth certificates to land deeds and treasury bills are available for as little as fifty pence per set. In many cases, the quality of the forgery is so high only experts can tell them apart from the real thing.

And as the Nigerians have proved time and time again, with a touch of forgery and a way with red tape, it's possible to fool almost all of the people almost all of the time.

There are two key documents needed to trade sea cargo: the bill of lading, which gives details of the goods being carried, and the letter of credit, which authorises payment from the receiver's bank accounts once the goods have arrived.

In the classic Nigerian oil sting, a well-dressed, well-spoken and utterly plausible fraudster will seek out a medium-sized company and offer the deal of a lifetime.

He will claim to have at least a million barrels of high-class crude to sell at, for example, $2 per barrel below the market price. This bargain price, the fraudster will explain, is because the oil is a special consignment being offered by the state-controlled Nigerian National Petroleum Corporation.

But, explains the seller, if the corporation's regular customers found out about this, they would be deeply upset. Best to keep it completely confidential.

Reassurance that the deal is bona fide is available in abundance. The seller will provide the name of a ship which, if checked out with Lloyd's of London, will always be going where it is supposed to be going and always be filled with crude oil.

The buyer will also receive a copy of the bill of lading – a skilful forgery – which 'proves' that the seller owns the cargo and in return will provide a letter of credit. This carries no risk – the money will not be paid until the cargo is delivered – so the buyer feels safe.

Inevitably, though, a couple of days before the ship is due to dock, the buyer will be told that there has been some problem, some unforeseen extra cost which needs to be covered. The usual request is for $250,000 to be paid immediately or risk losing everything.

With millions of dollars in profit just a few hours away, the buyer will usually not hesitate to issue a cheque. The money is cashed, the ship arrives, and the buyer turns up at the quay only to discover that the documents he has are fakes and that the oil actually belongs to someone else.

Despite a long history, the first successful prosecution for this kind of fraud anywhere in the world did not take place until April 1990 when Nigerian chief and barrister Tunde Ibikunle was sentenced to four years for falsely claiming he had $22 million of oil for sale. He had managed to persuade two London brothers who ran a small, independent oil company to part with $150,000, money he claimed was needed to 'charter a tanker'.

From a base in Rotterdam, Ibikunle had contacted the brothers with the story that he was an agent for gift cargoes of crude oil – supposedly awarded to army chiefs by the Nigerian President in return for their loyalty.

As well as providing all the usual fake documents, Ibikunle even allowed one of the brothers to speak to the captain of the tanker to confirm it was on its way to Amsterdam with a hold full of Ibikunle's oil. But in fact the man was just an acquaintance of Ibikunle's playing a role.

When police raided his flat in Ealing, west London, they found thousands of documents relating to oil frauds and dozens of law books, open to sections on fraud and the Fugitive Offenders Act.

*   *   *

'When it comes to drug trafficking,' says a senior customs officer, 'the Colombians will send over a ship with 500 kilos of cocaine because that to them is a cheap commodity. The Nigerians will send over a thousand couriers, each carrying half a kilo because to them, people are a cheap commodity.'

Nigeria is fast becoming the premier point of entry for both cocaine and heroin entering Europe and Britain. With widespread corruption among all law enforcement agencies, it is relatively simple for major cartels to arrange for large shipments of drugs to be delivered to Lagos.

More importantly, there is a ready, sizable workforce of cheap labour ready to move the stuff on. Nigeria is roughly the same size as other African states such as Angola, Mauritania and Niger. But while these have populations of ten million, two million and eight million respectively, Nigeria is home to nearly ninety million people.

Because they are considered virtually expendable (and, frankly, because many of them are inexperienced and completely unsuited to the task of being couriers), Nigerian 'mules' are now massively over-represented in the British prison system. Around one in three females convicted of drug trafficking is of Nigerian origin.

The majority say they only agreed to take the drugs because of extreme poverty and because they had little or no idea how harshly they would be treated. Many want to co-operate with the authorities to help catch those higher up in the organisation who supplied the drugs and arranged their passage, but there have been few prosecutions.

In 1991, embarrassed by the growing number of traffickers held in foreign jails, the Nigerian government introduced Decree 33 – a mandatory additional five-year sentence for all those returning to Nigeria at the end of their original sentence.

But rather than staunching the flow of couriers, the decree led instead to a spate of escapes among British-based prisoners. Many are still on the run.

In April 1994, a US State Department survey of drug cultivation and trafficking stated that Nigerians, with the help of their government, had created a global drug trafficking network in Europe and Asia which dealt with around 35 to 40 per cent of all heroin shipments.

But it's not just Nigeria – nearby Ghana is also emerging as something of a force on the international drug scene, while on the other side of the continent a new, perhaps even more sinister threat is emerging.

One night, as Ahmed Jama slept, a team of officers from Special Branch raided his east London council flat and planted tiny microphones in the hallway.

Buried deep within the walls, the state-of-the-art bugging devices recorded not only Ahmed's words but also his thoughts, transmitting them via satellite to a central recording station.

During the day, undercover agents would follow his every move. Men, women, even children were on his trail, pointing him out and whispering into the microphones concealed in their lapels. 'He's on his way to the launderette now,' he'd hear them say. During the night, they'd monitor the inside of his bedroom by shining powerful lights through the windows and walls.

He was irritated by his flatmate who pretended not to notice that there was anything strange going on. He suspected she was one of them, controlling the voices. 'I've got all the world shouting in my head,' he told her.

On 20 April 1994 he tried to admit himself to St Clement's Psychiatric Hospital, but the staff turned him away, telling him to report instead to the accident and emergency ward at the Royal London Hospital. As he made his way there he heard a voice telling him he was worthless. His friends tried to stop him, but he threw himself under a train at Mile End station. He died instantly.

Ahmed was suffering the classic symptoms of paranoid psychosis, usually associated with over-use of cocaine or amphetamines. But the root of the twenty-seven-year-old Somalian's problem was a drug like no other available in Britain.

Khat is inexpensive, highly addictive, widely available, and has a proven potential to inflict massive social and physical harm. But the real reason it stands apart from other drugs is far more surprising. It's legal.

Khat is one of nearly forty names for the green-leafed shrub *catha edulis*, cultivated mostly in the Horn of Africa. Each day, millions in Somalia, Ethiopia, Yemen and Djibouti chew twigs of khat to release a substance that produces an amphetamine-like high which, according to local mythology, is akin to a state of spiritual fulfilment.

Khat has been used in this way for more than seven hundred years, but during the last three decades use of the drug has exploded, particularly in Somalia, where it is generally credited with exacerbating the civil war, crippling the economy, and producing a work-shy generation of living zombies. In many areas government offices do not function after lunch because of the effects of khat.

In 1980, a United Nations report linked prolonged use of khat to numerous dental and gastric diseases, cirrhosis of the liver, hypertension, migraine, and cerebral haemorrhage. Since then it has been banned in Switzerland, Italy, Saudi Arabia, Morocco, Finland, the United States, Canada, Finland, Norway, and Sweden.

Like Britain, the latter five countries each have sizable Somali communities, but here the Home Office has declared that the drug is not 'a significant social problem' and has allowed its use to remain legal.

Many Somalis find this distressing. A few years ago, khat was considered a weekend luxury among the first Somali refugees to arrive, but with unemployment rates in excess of 90 per cent, many of the men (tradition dictates that women don't indulge) soon turned to the drug as a form of escape, often chewing non-stop for fifteen hours at a time, four or five days a week.

This increased usage has led to increased problems. Although khat is cheap at just £4 per bunch, with one or two bunches required for a full chewing session, this is a heavy burden on family finances for those relying on state benefits.

'Our families are broken,' says Sadia Musa of the Somali Education Project. 'Our men spend all their money. They chew all night and sleep all day. They are useless. Khat should be banned.'

The drug's legal status has also led to another, unforeseen problem.

Over the last three years, London has become a major clearing house for illegally transporting khat to expat Somali communities all over the world in a trade estimated to be worth at least £50 million each year.

There are at least eighty syndicates in London and the home counties which control the shipment of the drug, often employing naive young couriers who are 'conned' into carrying suitcases stuffed with khat, unaware that the moment they step on to a plane they are breaking the law. The smallest syndicate is said to have a turnover of £100,000 per week.

Each morning, just under a ton of freshly harvested khat arrives at Heathrow. Within a few hours, the bunches, wrapped in banana leaves to keep them moist, have found their way to distributors and greengrocers across the country who openly sell them alongside other vegetables. Speed is of the essence as the drug is active only for forty-eight hours after picking.

But only a proportion of the khat that arrives ends up on sale in Britain. Within hours, at least half a ton has been packed into suitcases ready for illegal smuggling to Europe and America.

The trade is highly lucrative. For example, a single courier travelling to Norway where khat sells for up to £35 per bunch will carry up to three hundred bunches in two suitcases. Even after accommodation, flight and other costs have been deducted, a single trip can generate a profit of £8,000. In America the price is even higher.

Advertisements for couriers have been known to appear in

magazines and newspapers including *Loot* and *TNT* and have also been found in numerous job centres close to Heathrow.

The couriers are strictly controlled. They must have British passports, be white (ethnic minorities have too high a chance of being stopped) and have no criminal record. It also helps if they have no idea of what they are letting themselves in for.

In early 1994 Joanne and Raymond Edwards, both unemployed, visited a housing agency in Hounslow to enquire about renting a flat. They explained that they didn't have enough money for the deposit, and one of the staff said he knew of a man who had some work available.

They were contacted by a Mr Deol who owns a number of properties in the Hounslow area. He offered them £50 each to take 'highly perishable goods' on a day trip to Norway.

Their first trip was uneventful. On their second they were caught. More than twenty-five khat couriers were apprehended during the first six months of 1994. At first they were simply held for thirty days and then deported, but now the government has cracked down on the problem, imposing six-month sentences for all those held.

Another young British courier was caught in Seattle in March 1994 after British khat barons, one of whom had a conviction for heroin smuggling, attempted to open a new distribution chain there.

She was eventually released after the authorities realised that she had not intended to break the law. Back in England, she later received an offer of £8,000 not to give the police the names of those in the syndicate.

The couriers are recruited by middle-men working for the Somalis. When I called one, an Australian named Andrew operating from the quiet suburb of Muswell Hill, I was offered £150 to fly to New York at one day's notice.

'You'll be picked up from home, taken to the airport and put on the plane. Once at the other end, you'll be met, given a place to stay and then taken back to the airport the following day,' he said.

Other couriers are supplied by a former Special Branch detective sacked from the Metropolitan Police because of business links with a convicted IRA terrorist.

Each stalk of khat contains tiny quantities of its active ingredients – cathine and the stronger cathinone – in the same way that individual coca leaves contain tiny quantities of cocaine.

The next big fear is that Somalian and other criminal syndicates will turn their hands to large-scale extraction of cathinone. The implications could be dramatic.

In a letter to *The Lancet* in December 1987, Professor A.J. Goudie of Liverpool University wrote that: 'cathinone has a potential for abuse at least as great as that of cocaine and probably greater than amphetamine.'

Extracting the active ingredients from khat is said to be extremely difficult, yet there has been at least one recorded example of it being achieved in Britain and dozens more in America.

In New York, an even more startling trend has emerged. Seizures of a substance known on the streets as 'cat' are increasing. The drug is methyl cathinone, an artificial khat substitute, and the seizures show that the country's underground chemists – the first to spot any new trend – believe there is a market for the drug.

These seizures were instrumental in moving khat up the American drug classification ladder. Previously, under Schedule 4, a courier would simply be deported and banned from entering America ever again. Now, under Schedule 1, a courier with a suitcase full of khat will be treated in the same way as a courier with a bagful of heroin. The maximum sentence is twenty years.

Khat is particularly interesting because it is the perfect example of the problems caused by unilateral legalisation. Amsterdam has become the major clearing house for cannabis entering Europe for the same reason.

The Home Office is undoubtedly in a difficult position. If

khat remains legal, the use of the trade as a cover will grow. However, if it is banned, the price in London will simply rocket and the economic pressure on the Somali population could force them into crime in order to feed their habits.

And in a classic *Catch-22* scenario, drug experts believe a ban could be just the catalyst needed to launch khat in the wider community. For Somalians, already in the midst of a bitter civil conflict, this is yet another war that no one can truly win.

The Racketeers

For forty-five years, the tree-rich streets of Rathmines, Dublin's neat inner-city suburb, were home to two Martin Cahills. One was an amiable non-drinking, non-smoking car fanatic with a wicked sense of humour; the other was a legendary gangster who, during twenty years of armed robbery, kidnap and art theft, amassed assets in excess of £20 million.

The first Cahill was best known as an unemployed, soft-hearted father of five who spent his days travelling between the homes of his wife and mistress to dote on his children, and his evenings frequenting the city's top nightclubs.

The second Cahill was better known as 'The General' – a proficient and ruthless gang leader who once nailed an associate to the floor for ripping him off; a man who delighted in humiliating the gardai and who would often turn up at a local station to have his driving licence verified while the rest of his gang carried out a robbery, thus ensuring the perfect alibi.

On 18 August 1994, Cahill's double life came to an abrupt end when a man posing as a council worker shot him at the wheel of his Renault 5 as it passed through Ranelagh. Fittingly, two organisations rushed to claim responsibility.

Forty-five minutes after the shooting came a call to a Dublin

radio station from a man representing the Irish National
Liberation Army, the ultra-ruthless republican splinter group,
claiming responsibility for the murder.

An hour later, however, a man using a recognised IRA
codeword told the same station that *they* had 'executed the
crime-lord Martin Cahill' and that the claims by the INLA
were false. Later still, a fresh statement from the INLA claimed
that while they had been planning to murder Cahill, the IRA
had just beaten them to it.

The General was every inch a mainstream organised criminal,
but his death underlined the unique overlap between terrorism
and criminality in Ireland. According to the IRA's official
statement, Cahill was executed because he had expanded his
empire to include drug dealing, an activity classed as 'anti-social
behaviour' by the Provisionals.

Indeed, in the Catholic enclaves of West Belfast, the IRA
has fulfilled a community policing role ever since the troubles
began and, thanks to the work of their 'punishment squads',
the area's joyriders, burglars and other petty criminals now
have a vocabulary of terror all their own.

There is 'breeze-blocking', in which bones are shattered by
flagstones dropped on joints; the '50–50', where the victim is
forced to touch his toes while a bullet is fired into his spine;
the 'six pack', where a single shot is fired into each knee, ankle
and elbow; and the 'bar beating', where the victim is forced
to roll over several times so that his legs can be broken from
every side with blows from crowbars.

Punishments are meticulously scheduled to prolong the
agony – the victim is told several weeks in advance exactly
where and when the attack will take place. Persistent offenders,
particularly joyriders, have on occasion been kneecapped several times.

Surprisingly, such brutal tactics derive widespread support
from many locals who believe that the real enemy is not the
British Army but the city's increasingly wayward youth.

'You have to live here to understand what it's like,' says

one social worker whose home is in the notorious Divis Flats estate. 'The hoods break into houses and beat up whoever they find living there, even eighty-year-olds; they steal your car and set fire to it or try to run you down with it; they hang around in empty flats then jump out and mug people. The police are useless. If it wasn't for the IRA, the hoods would run this place.'

Officially, drugs are particularly frowned upon. One night in April 1994, one man was murdered and a further sixteen shot in the legs in a mass IRA crackdown on dealers operating in Belfast. But in recent years such incidents have increasingly smacked of hypocrisy: a Sinn Fein councillor convicted on drugs charges was allowed to retain his post.

Thanks to a crackdown on other sources of income, the true equation, say the hoods, is that the IRA won't allow you to deal drugs unless it gets a cut of the profits.

The IRA has always denied this in the strongest terms: 'The orchestrated propaganda offensive that seeks to link the IRA to criminality and particularly to drugs-related crime is a transparent and cynical attempt by the British to damage republicans' is a typical statement.

But increasingly, evidence to the contrary is emerging. After alleged Newry drug importer Jim Halliday was shot three times in the stomach and twice in the back as he sat in a café in February 1993, he claimed it was because he had refused to pay the IRA £10,000 in return for permission to distribute drugs.

As for Cahill, many of the remaining players in the Dublin underworld believe the real reason for his death was his long-standing refusal to pay protection money for a 'safe dealing' patch, and his reluctance to buy his cannabis resin from IRA 'authorised' suppliers.

While the Provisionals shy away from dealing drugs directly, other paramilitary groups prefer a more hands-on approach. The loyalist Ulster Defence Association and Ulster Volunteer Force and the (now disbanded) republican Irish People's

Liberation Organisation have all been linked to large-scale drug dealing despite publicly denouncing such activity. There have even been cases of some members forgetting their political allegiances in order to work together in the name of profit.

The dichotomy continues across the water. One little-known consequence of the IRA ceasefire that came two weeks after Cahill's death was a sudden rise in attacks on young, streetwise and ostensibly unemployed men living among north London's sizable Irish community.

Scores of dealers expelled from Ireland by the IRA ('Be gone in forty-eight hours or you're dead') have found that what is unacceptable in one part of the world is all but encouraged elsewhere. Selling drugs to fellow Irishmen may be anathema but touting them to the hostile people of an occupying country was seen as a justifiable, if low-level, strategy towards the greater good.

Thus families like the Bakers – a formidable criminal dynasty led by a merciless matriach who were banished from Ireland in the mid-eighties – currently run a major heroin ring based in Kilburn, and pay hefty amounts of protection money to IRA agents to ensure that their numerous couriers are undisturbed.

But in the weeks after the ceasefire, other gangs began attacking the Baker couriers at every opportunity, checking to see if the IRA protection was still in place. They did not have to wait long for confirmation that indeed it was. As any good villain will tell you, politics is politics but business is business.

At the height of its campaign, the IRA required between seven and ten million pounds a year to bankroll its political and terrorist activities. At best, donations from sympathetic groups such as NORAID brought in a mere £150,000, leaving a considerable shortfall for the Army's 'procurement operations department' to make up.

Listing the department's favoured money-raising schemes

over the last two decades blurs the distinction between political and commercial fundraising even further, being almost indistinguishable from a list of enterprises enjoyed by men like Martin Cahill.

Armed robbery, extortion, fraud and smuggling have all been used to swell the IRA's coffers in recent years. Such activities must be 'authorised' by High Command and are most often directed against targets that will ensure that the group maintains the support of the community. Hence while supporters in West Belfast would baulk at the idea of a break-in at the local bank, extorting funds from business outside the immediate area is deemed acceptable.

In the past the Army (or more accurately renegades within its ranks) dabbled in kidnapping, though not always successfully. Besides the fiasco over the kidnapping of top racehorse Shergar, the IRA also bungled the snatching of Canadian-born multi-millionaire Galen Weston from his Dublin home in 1983.

Weston was at a polo match when the men struck and the gang were arrested. A little later that year one of Weston's executives, Don Tidley, was kidnapped and a ransom of £5 million demanded. He was freed twenty-two days later when a joint army and police patrol stumbled across the kidnappers' camp. In the ensuing shoot-out, a soldier and trainee policeman were killed and the gang got away, but without their unharmed hostage.

In the best Mafia tradition, the construction industry has long been another key area. Each time new works begin, paramilitary labour brokers make the site managers an offer they cannot refuse: hire our crews and enjoy a trouble-free life or hire your own and be constantly watching your back.

The workers are picked from a pool of idle foot soldiers (who continue to collect dole and pass a cut of their wages direct to the controlling group) and extra funds are generated by the addition of a few 'ghost' workers to the payroll.

Higher up the scale, the construction company itself will be targeted by a team of extortionists with the threat of the work never being completed unless money is paid. The going rate is currently around £10,000 per million pounds of contract.

(Such is the acceptance of racketeering that some bankers are said to cost paying protection into financial appraisals. Furthermore, many of the area's self-employed claim that Inland Revenue inspectors accept accounts showing payments of hundreds of pounds per week to the paramilitary organisations.

One unidentified Belfast builder told Radio 4 that, while the government had called on business people to examine their consciences and refuse to support terrorism by complying with the extortion demands, the practice was all but legalised by the attitude of the tax office.)

Smaller businesses and retailers are subject to a more basic form of extortion. In the past men would simply appear from time to time and demand money, but now accountants will visit and look over the books of the business to decide how much the owner is able to pay. Payments are due quarterly and failing to pay is tantamount to inviting violent reprisals.

Many businesses have to pay money to both republican and loyalist groups. Anecdotal evidence suggests that the rivals share information so that the business ends up paying the same amount to both.

Thrice-cursed are the local Chinese community. According to the National Criminal Intelligence Service, they pay not only the rival paramilitaries but also the local Triad gangs.

Belfast's 300-odd black-taxi drivers are somewhat more willing victims, paying over a weekly licence fee to the republicans in order to stay on the road. The demand for their services arose only after the IRA began a bombing campaign against Belfast buses in the seventies, and the arrangement has existed ever since.

Another terrorist mainstay has been the running of clubs and pubs across Northern Ireland. Bar sales and receipts from gaming machines would be drastically under-declared, diverting hundreds of thousands of pounds to the paramilitaries. Being a cash-intensive business, the bars were also ideal for laundering money from other sources.

After a crackdown in 1991, the accounts of one north Belfast club used by republicans showed bar takings up by £100,000 and receipts from gambling up from £3,000 to £17,000. Overall, the Royal Ulster Constabulary and the Anti-Racketeering Unit at the Northern Ireland Office estimated that the terrorists had been denied £1 million.

The gaming-machine scam had also extended across to the mainland. One ring, busted in November 1990, revolved around hundreds of video poker machines, the income from which was not being declared for VAT purposes. Around £2 million was thought to have been diverted.

Because of this and earlier clampdowns dating back to 1989 on these 'traditional' sources of income, the hunt for money has moved into other fields. Art theft has emerged as one lucrative area, with the IRA and loyalist groups regularly linked to paintings stolen from Ireland's numerous collections. One set, stolen by the IRA from the Beit collection, were first offered to the yakuza and then passed on to the supposedly rival UDA.

There is also increasing evidence that the IRA is linking up with major international organised crime figures to work abroad. In November 1993, three men, two of whom had previous convictions for IRA-linked activity, were arrested in New York after a $7.4 million raid on an armoured-car depot.

Five months later, a FBI inquiry into a £150 million US bank fraud uncovered further IRA links. The Army had assisted in the setting up of a bogus bank run from a disused caravan on an American Indian reservation and then used fake documents issued in the bank's name in a string of fraudulent business deals.

Letters of credit authorities with the fake bank and with face values of up to £3 million surfaced across Europe as the IRA attempted to purchase hotels and pubs in a bid to establish a legitimate business base to generate permanent income.

The IRA were also involved in attempts to launder the proceeds of the £292 million City of London bonds robbery (see Chapter One). One parcel of bonds was intercepted at Heathrow Airport on its way from Dublin to Miami. Another, containing £71 million of bonds, was recovered on its way from Miami to Peru having been couriered by a man giving an Irish name.

Irish-Canadian Stephen Orr and his colleague Duncan Rapier were filmed meeting undercover FBI agents in Miami in June 1990, six weeks after the robbery. Asked who was holding the bonds, Rapier is heard saying that they 'belong to the IRA'.

Throughout his trial, Orr denied any link to the Provisionals, but it emerged that he had a previous conviction for selling fake Ivomec, a popular livestock treatment and another mainstay of IRA fundraising frauds in years gone by.

By 1993, the IRA had been identified as dealing in shares on the London and South African stock exchanges, enabling it to invest 'dirty' money and receive 'clean' cash in return in the form of dividends. One company, identified as an IRA front, was believed to have laundered up to £30 million over eight years.

The move into these more upmarket areas coincided with the discovery of even newer methods of fundraising. Hundreds of thousands of pounds were being generated from the sale of antiques stolen south of the border and, according to the RUC, the IRA have also expanded into the counterfeit business, producing fake perfumes, jeans and video tapes for sale at car boot sales and markets.

In April 1994, more than 1,000 police in England and on both sides of the Irish border carried out their largest-ever series of raids aimed at smashing the IRA financial network by 'severing its umbilical cords'.

Operation Maradonna, based on American anti-Mafia methods, led to the recovery of thousands of pounds' worth of cash, drugs, stolen property, bankers' bonds and other documents, but the key target, the IRA's Dublin-based financial controller, managed to evade capture.

The man, in his late forties and ostensibly a wealthy business-man, co-ordinates all the Army's money-making activities from drug trafficking to car theft. His interest in the IRA is said to have far more to do with personal financial benefit than with any commitment to republicanism but, because of his efficiency and business acumen, this is happily tolerated.

The need to spend millions on weapons and explosives may now have subsided but, even with a ceasefire in place, vast amounts of money are still required for the welfare of hundreds of IRA prisoners and their families. As for the members involved in running pubs, clubs and other money-raising operations such as video pirating, to wind up these enterprises would involve throwing scores out of work and make the emergence of violent splinter groups all the more likely.

Theoretically, all the money earned by the procurement division is directed back into the war effort. In practice, a number of crimes committed in the name of the IRA simply provide a superior living for a small number of operatives.

And that the pure criminals within the ranks of the IRA had no intention of allowing the ceasefire to curb their activities was graphically demonstrated in November 1994, when fifty-three-year-old postal worker Frank Kerr was shot dead during a £100,000 robbery in the border town of Newry by what police described as 'a very well-organised, professional, ruthless gang'.

A statement issued shortly after the killing admitted that 'IRA volunteers acting on instructions were involved in this incident' but said that the operation was not sanctioned by the IRA leadership.

Security service sources claimed that the raid was a locally sanctioned fundraising operation, masterminded by a senior brigade commander, an opinion backed up by the IRA's own statement which blamed a 'problem with the army's chain of command'.

Such incidents were predicted long before the 1994 ceasefire got under way. Sir Hugh Annesley, the RUC's Chief Constable, told a news conference in July that, in the event of a cessation of violence: 'I do not believe the loyalists would stop involving themselves in crime and neither do I believe the Provisionals would stop involving themselves in crime.

'The bulk of what we all define as terrorist violence will broadly stop and I think the people within those groupings will turn to crime, organised crime, drugs, money laundering, intimidation and blackmail.'

And those with the most interest in crime will undoubtedly continue to forge links with the London underworld, even going so far as to settle other people's scores, if the price is right.

A former UDA officer, known as the 'window cleaner killer', who was expelled from the organisation for unauthorised drug trafficking, is believed to have been behind at least two contract killings carried out in the capital.

Using the tempting offer of easy money, he has lured UDA colleagues over to the mainland to carry out the murders. Brendan Carey, a forty-seven-year-old former armed robber shot five times with handguns by motorcycle assassins while drinking in a north London pub in 1990, was believed to have been one victim, while former police informer David Norris, shot outside his Kent home in 1992, was another.

Meanwhile, UVF operatives are believed to have joined forces with established London crime families in order to smuggle vast quantities of LSD, amphetamines and Ecstasy from London to Ulster, where they feed the growing teenage rave scene.

Such activities earn the terrorists millions of pounds and help keep the logistical back-up of the now-dormant active service units in place. Even if the paramilitary commanders at the highest level try to shut these operations down, they couldn't guarantee to do so. Up to 30 per cent of the IRA's members, for example, are believed to have opposed the ceasefire, and there is a real fear that they could form a breakaway faction.

The history of Northern Ireland is littered with the emergence of ultra-violent, ultra-ruthless splinter groups, and one that concentrates purely on the bank balance rather than on the bullet or the ballot box could be the most formidable of all.

The NBT

From all across London, they come for the freshly cooked lamb kebabs, the blithe company, and the chance to dance beneath the trees they have decorated with their kaleidoscopic bunting. But most of all, whenever the sun dares to shine, they come for the view.

Every Sunday during the summer up to 2,000 Turks, Kurds and Cypriots leave the bustle of the metropolis behind and head for Thorndon Park on the outskirts of Brentwood. There, they enjoy picnics, circumcision parties, festivals and, whenever they look south across the flat landscape of the lower Thames Valley, a scene strongly reminiscent of the Turkish countryside.

A still picture of the gathering looks like a page torn from a Turkish holiday brochure and is wholly representative of the way in which the community has managed to retain its own identity without being ostracized by the rest of society.

Ever since they began arriving in Britain during the early seventies, the Turks have skilfully avoided the discrimination that has befallen the Asians and West Indians, yet are no less entrenched: large areas of Haringey and Stoke Newington are all but dominated by specialist shops, banks and barbers, as well as community centres and cafés.

But the fact that, until recently, the community had also managed to avoid the kind of criminal associations that haunt virtually every other ethnic group is testimony only to its reluctance to allow anyone to peer behind the idyllic public mask.

In reality, Britain's Turkish community is not only being torn apart by an internal political conflict, but the criminal minority hiding within its ranks is rapidly becoming *the* underworld force to watch, not just in London but nationally, if not globally.

To borrow a tag favoured by the music industry, the seemingly obscure, underrated yet remorseless and highly skilled Turkish mafia are, in world crime terms, the NBT: the Next Big Thing.

Over the last five years, while the headlines have been dominated by tales of Yardies, Triads and Colombian drug cartels, the Turkish syndicates have quietly taken control of more than half the massively lucrative European heroin market, totally usurping the position of the former front runners, the Sicilian Mafia.

In Germany, their principal centre of operations, Turk and Kurdish syndicates smuggle in an estimated 1.5 tonnes of the drug each year. In Holland around 200,000 illegal Turkish immigrants compete fiercly with the Triads for control of Amsterdam, Europe's drug hypermarket.

Before his death in 1992, the renowned anti-Mafia judge, Giovanni Falcone, identified the Turkish mafia as 'one of the great crime syndicates in the world'. Indeed, at the time of writing, three of Interpol's 'ten most wanted' Euro-villains are Turkish, the highest number from any one country. All are wanted for murder and drug trafficking and at least one, Yasar Avni Musullulu, has been spotted in the UK and could still be hiding here.

His colleagues, based in the major Turkish stronghold of north London but also in Hull, Birmingham, Manchester and Brighton, currently control an estimated 70 per cent of Britain's heroin market, dwarfing the efforts of Asian and Chinese syndicates, play a significant part in the underworld arms trade and, more recently, have begun dealing cocaine, cannabis and amphetamines.

They run prostitution and illegal gambling rings, arrange

the transport of scores of illegal immigrants from Turkey and the former Soviet Union, and extort millions of pounds from a wide range of businesses

According to the National Criminal Intelligence Service, the best-established syndicate is led by a single man (with links to the Turkish terrorist group the Grey Wolves) assisted by around twenty associates, and holds regular meetings at two north London venues, both of which purport to be simple community centres.

In keeping with the rest of the community, Turkish criminals have managed to avoid clashing with the underworld at large, acting as brokers and suppliers for those needing drugs or guns rather than as direct rivals.

But in recent years the latest additions to the community melting-pot – Kurds fleeing the guerrilla war being fought against the Turkish state over their claim to an independent homeland – have been accused of rocking the boat, raising the level of tension, and disregarding the accepted tenets of behaviour.

Where once there was harmony, now there is imbalance; where once there was order, now there is chaos; where once there was an uneasy peace, now there is the making of a war.

By all accounts, Mehmet Kaygisiz knew the name of the men who were on their way to kill him. So did many of his friends: get out of London, they told him; hide, start a new life, anything. But Kaygisiz was convinced that whatever he did, he would be found.

In the early evening of 17 March 1994, while playing backgammon at a Turkish café in Islington, north London, Kaygisiz's grim prediction came to fruition. A man appeared at the doorway, sought out his target, then ran inside and shot him once in the chest before making off in a waiting car.

The murder took place a few months after the Metropolitan Police had set up an undercover unit to investigate allegations of violent political extortion throughout the Turkish community, and at first it seemed that this would provide the key.

The allegations had first surfaced two years earlier when dozens of owners of Turkish and Turkish Cypriot kebab houses and sweatshops began to complain of systematic harassment by representatives of two terrorist groups – the Kurdish Workers' Party (PKK) and the anti-government Dev Sol – claiming to be 'collecting' money for the cause.

Annual fundraising drives by both groups had become an accepted part of life for many of those in the Kurdish community, with the vast majority happy to pay the going rate of £100 per worker. Care was always taken by the collectors to ensure that demands were not excessive so that sympathy for the group was maintained. Dev Sol would even issue receipts.

But the targeting of Turks and Turkish Cypriots that began in 1992 was something new, as was the fact that anyone who refused to pay found that either their business premises were mysteriously burnt to the ground or that they became the target of an even more personal reprisal.

Selahattin Yatman, a prominent Turkish restaurateur, first came across Dev Sol in October 1993 when he was approached to buy copies of their magazine, *Struggle*, to sell to his customers. Having heard on the grapevine that those who agree are subsequently approached by the same men for a weekly protection levy of up to £2,000, Yatman refused outright to have anything to do with the men.

'They were extremely intimidating, just like gangsters,' he explains. 'I asked them what they would do if I didn't give them money and they hinted I would be getting a return visit.'

Yatman ignored the threat and threw the three men out. As they left, one turned and told him they would have to 'consult their superiors' before deciding what course of action to take.

The following day, as he returned to his Hackney home after work, he was jumped by ten masked men. 'I know it was the same men who attacked me because they said "now you will pay" before setting about me with the iron bars.' He suffered a fractured skull, broken nose, and fractured cheekbone.

Soon afterwards, dozens of other Turkish businessmen across the country began discussing equally horrific experiences, though virtually all refused to talk to the police. One man in Hull confided how he too had been beaten by men with iron bars after refusing to pay £2,500 to Dev Sol.

Another described how his workshop had been destroyed in an arson attack a few days after he insisted to a PKK representative that he could not afford to contribute to their party. He further explained that many of his worried colleagues were buying guns and making enquiries about hiring vigilantes to protect them.

Other extortion rackets cropped up among the ranks of those running fast-food vans. One Reading-based victim told how, after refusing to pay, he was visited by a man with a gun — a Heckler and Koch G3 military automatic rifle like the one he had used in the Turkish army.

Meanwhile the undercover officers assigned to the Stoke Newington area, the heart of the émigré community, came across evidence that at least six Turkish girls had been kidnapped and then subjected to 'horrendous rapes' by Kurds. Ransoms had been paid and the girls had eventually been returned, but their families were so ashamed that they all refused to press charges.

For a time it seemed that Kaygisiz, who shortly before his death had been complaining of pressure from unknown sources who demanded money in order to 'protect' his business, had simply paid the ultimate price of defiance.

But this simple, convenient theory simply doesn't stand up. Speak to Dev Sol representatives and they will patiently explain that, while people who refuse to contribute to their cause deserve to suffer, they have never used violence other than against the Turkish government.

Likewise the PKK denies all links to the extortion gangs,

claiming they are merely part of a smear campaign organised by the Turkish Secret Service and the British government.

In fact the extortion campaign is being run by Turkish and Kurdish criminals, using the names of the political groups as a cover. As for Kaygisiz, delve deep enough and you eventually discover that his death was not the first – two of his business associates had also been murdered in the same year.

Together, the three were part of a major smuggling syndicate, specialising in arranging the transport of illegal immigrants to Britain, an increasingly lucrative and popular enterprise with the number of Turks attempting entry through Dover alone having risen tenfold since 1990.

Kaygisiz charged each 'client' around £3,500 for a package deal that included travel to Britain (usually hidden in the back of a cramped truck) and instructions on what to say if caught in order to be able to claim asylum.

But what cost Kaygisiz and his colleagues their lives were their attempts to expand into dealing with a different kind of cargo were the profits, along with the stakes, are far higher.

In early 1991 the head of every national drugs squad in Europe gathered at the Interpol headquarters in Lyon for an emergency meeting on one topic – the vast amount of heroin flowing into the continent from Turkey.

Between the 1930s and the late 1960s, Turkey was one of the world's largest producers of illicit heroin and opium. Then, in 1971, under intense pressure from the United States which had identifed Turkey as the source of the vast majority of the drugs reaching its shores, poppy cultivation was outlawed.

Amazingly the ban succeeded, but rather than taking early retirement, the *babas*, as the godfathers of the Turkish mafia are known, simply reorganised themselves, making use of their highly efficient smuggling, refining and distribution network to broker Golden Crescent heroin from the frontier areas of Afghanistan, Pakistan and Iran on the underworld's behalf.

The gangs next rose to prominence during the late 1970s when several Turks (including the fugitive Yasar Anvi Musullulu) were found to have been instrumental in the running of the infamous 'Pizza Connection' heroin ring.

Raw opium would be smuggled into Turkey across the country's thousands of miles of porous borders with Bulgaria and Iran, then processed into high-grade heroin in hundreds of primitive, mobile refineries based around eastern Turkey and Istanbul.

Since then, the gangs have fine-tuned their operations and forged even closer links with the Sicilian Mafia and their satellite organisations, the Camorra and the 'Ndrangheta, retaining their premium position in the trade thanks to the sophistication of their smuggling techniques.

One method, popular until customs officers became wise to it, targeted innocent British holidaymakers who had taken their cars abroad.

An 'accident' was arranged in which the tourist's car was deliberately crashed into, causing a considerable amount of damage. The driver of the other car – generally a well-dressed, well-spoken businessman – would apologise profusely and offer to have the car repaired at his own expense while the tourists continued their holiday.

The damaged vehicle was then taken to a special mafia-run workshop where the damaged body panels were replaced with new ones filled with heroin. A couple of days later the car, looking as good as new, was returned to its owners who headed back to Britain unaware of their lucrative cargo.

Once safely home, the owners were approached out of the blue by a British-based member of the same drug ring who offered to buy the car for an attractive price. In most cases, in view of the car having recently been damaged, the owner agreed to sell. More often, a copy of the key was made while the car was in the workshop and the vehicle simply stolen. Either way, the gang managed to bring up to a dozen kilos of heroin into the country at virtually no risk to themselves.

Larger consignments enter via sophisticated concealments

in TIR (*Transport Internationale Routière*) lorries. These vehicles, used to transport perishable goods across Europe, are specially sealed with bonds that enable that to speed through European borders without being checked until they reach their destination. Luckily for the Turkish mafia, more than 200,000 TIR trucks begin their journeys through Europe from the country each year.

In November 1993, just such a truck carrying a load of tomatoes was followed by customs officers as it entered Britain at Dover and then made its way to Liverpool (where the legitimate cargo was unloaded), then back down to the Scratchwood service station on the M1 just north of London for a rendezvous with the smuggling team.

More than 200 kilos of heroin worth around £20 million were found, almost half the amount uncovered during the whole of the previous year and the largest-ever heroin seizure in the UK. Concealed in two special compartments fitted beneath the loading bay, the drugs took nearly a day to find.

Yet despite such a large seizure, London-based Turkish syndicates showed no sign of slowing their activities. A series of busts the following year demonstrated just how sophisticated their operations were becoming.

Once safely inside the country, the drugs are stored in safe houses, watched over by specially hired couples who will have no previous convictions. For a fee of around £200 per week, their job is to live as normal a life as possible, ensuring that at least one of them is always in the house to guard the drugs.

Every few days or so, members of the gang drop by to check the stock or pick up a few kilos for resale. They also employ couriers (often working for Turkish mini-cab companies) to ferry packets of drugs around the country as they are needed. Representatives of leading organised crime groups including Mafia and Triad bosses may be invited direct to the houses to check the purity of the goods and place their orders.

In April 1994, two safe houses belonging to one smuggling

gang were raided in Hackney and Hendon. In all, 100 kilos of the drug worth £26 million were discovered.

Because of his connection with the trade in illegal immigrants, Kaygisiz is believed to have helped other dealers to find 'mules' to bring their drugs into the country. According to sources within the Turkish community, he is believed to have been in direct contact with Farok Koroglu, convicted in June 1995 of importing £7 million worth of heroin into the country, a few months before he was murdered.

Farok, who ran the drugs syndicate from behind a mobile phone 'front company' is said by detectives to be a 'major player' in the Turkish mafia stakes.

Eight years after he fled to England from Turkey, Osman was running his own clothing company with a six-figure turnover, the proud father of two young sons and a happily married man. Two years later he was divorced, broke and forced to work for a mini-cab firm.

His downfall began innocently enough. Homesick, culturally divorced from mainstream society and too shy to make new friends, Osman, like most other first-generation male Turkish émigrés, gravitated towards the café scene.

There are an estimated 140 such premises in London alone, ostensibly ad hoc community centres where men (women, like foreigners, are not encouraged and rarely admitted) can drink coffee, gossip, and play a little backgammon.

They aim to recreate the village life the immigrants have left behind. Many who frequent the same café will know each other from the motherland and, to strengthen bonds further, many of the cafés will be named after local Turkish football teams.

'When I first got here,' says Osman, 'I couldn't speak the language so the only places I could really relax would be the clubs. At first I just watched the games, then I'd take over hands when friends had to leave. Eventually, I just got hooked.'

Anyone who has seen these sparsely furnished buildings up

close will wonder how it is that they can make a living. Although they are usually quite busy, there appears to be little more than a few friendly games of poker going on. This, it emerges, is the key to it all.

'If you ask the owners, they'll tell you that people only play for pennies, but that's just not true. Some weeks, I'd go to the clubs every night and spend at least three hundred pounds a time. At weekends when they were busier, I could easily lose up to eight hundred pounds. In ten years, I believe I lost a total of three hundred thousand pounds.'

Playing cards for money between consenting adults in private is not against the law. It only becomes so when it is seen to develop into a commercial enterprise with levies or table money being charged. In the spielers, owners take at least 5 per cent of the money staked on each game and can easily make profits of £5,000 per week, of which very little is ever declared.

And with the spieler proprietors profiting from each game, the pressure to continue playing, even if you're on a losing streak, is intense. Coffee and sometimes hot meals are provided free of charge, but only to those gambling. This prevents them having to go out of the café for refreshment – they might not come back.

'If your luck runs out early on, the owners are happy to lend you money interest-free to keep you in the game,' adds Osman. 'It's normally only to people they know well so there is no problem, but if you don't pay it back they have men with sticks who will come round and beat you up.'

The cafés also serve other purposes. Dogan Arif, south-east London's Cypriot-born godfather figure, used those based in the Old Kent Road to plan his robberies and drug deals away from the prying eyes and ears of surveillance squads.

Major drug dealers will often divide up supplies in back rooms late at night, while court cases involving Turks accused of handling stolen goods almost always include accounts of robbers visiting the cafés to offer lorry-loads of wares.

Yet at present, the authorities are virtually powerless to act against them. In the early days, according to one community policeman of long standing, it was a different story.

'They would leave all the money on the table and the evidence that they were involved in illegal gambling was very easy to get. They were being raided all the time. But now the money is kept hidden. It is all given to the owner and the people play for points, sharing out the money at the end.

'It's more professionally run and more organised,' he says. 'These people are involved in big money games but getting the evidence is almost impossible. All we ever see is a man going into a café, giving the owner a hundred pounds, sitting down and playing cards for an hour then walking out with nothing. Where's the offence? What can we do? Nothing.'

For the past four years, British and European police officers have received intelligence reports claiming that the PKK are massively involved in heroin dealing, a charge they have always denied.

In 1993, the PKK commander Cemil Bayik admitted that he had considered smuggling drugs to finance the movement's increasingly violent separatist war. 'There has been pressure but we always resisted it,' he told the world's media.

However, during that same year, a total of four tons of heroin were seized in Europe and 70 per cent of those arrested were Kurdish. The Turkish government and police force back the PKK's involvement in the trade, but this can too easily be dismissed as anti-Kurd propaganda.

Towards the end of 1994 a major heroin seizure in Amsterdam allegedly uncovered documents linking the haul to the PKK, while a Kurdish smuggler detained in France a short while earlier admitted transporting 300 kilos of heroin for the PKK during the previous three years.

These revelations, along with intermittent campaigns of fire-bomb attacks against Turkish targets, including those used as meeting places for London-based representatives of

the Grey Wolves, are beginning to disturb the delicate balance
of rival factions within the community.

Whether the PKK are involved in the drug trade or not,
they are increasingly coming into conflict with those who are.
And as others have recently discovered, politics and gangsterism
simply don't mix.

Bibliography

Beckford, George, Witter, Michael, *Small Garden ... Bitter Weed*, Maroon, Jamaica, 1980

Black, David, *Triad Takeover*, Sidgwick & Jackson, London, 1991

Booth, Martin, *The Triads*, Grafton Books, London, 1990

Bresler, Fenton, *Interpol*, Mandarin, London, 1992

Campbell, Duncan, *That was Business, This is Personal*, Secker & Warburg, London, 1990

Campbell, Duncan, *The Underworld*, BBC Books, London, 1994

Clutterbuck, Richard, *Terrorism, Drugs & Crime in Europe After 1992*, Routledge, Chapman & Hall, New York, 1990

Collins, Larry, *Black Eagles*, HarperCollins, New York, 1992

Constantine, Peter, *Japanese Street Slang*, Tengu, New York, 1992

Cornwall, Hugh, *The Hackers Handbook*, Century, London, 1989

Cornwall, Hugh, *Datatheft*, Mandarin, London, 1990

De Grazia, Jessica, *DEA – The War Against Drugs*, BBC Books, London, 1991

Eddy, Paul, *The Cocaine Wars*, Century Hutchinson, London, 1988

Ehrenfeld, Rachel, *Evil Money*, HarperCollins, New York, 1992

Falcone, Giovanni, *Men of Honour*, Fourth Estate, London, 1992

Fiennes, Ranulph, *The Feather Men*, Bloomsbury, London, 1991

Freemantle, Brian, *The Fix*, Michael Joseph, London, 1985

Fry, Colin with Kray, Charlie, *Doing the Business*, Smith Gryphon, London, 1993

Gage, Nicholas, *The Mafia is not an Equal Opportunity Employer*, McGraw-Hill, New York, 1971

Gillman, Peter, *The Duty Men*, BBC Books, London, 1987

Goodman, Jonathan and Will, Ian, *Underworld*, Harrap, London, 1985

Green, Timothy, *The Smugglers*, Arrow, London, 1969

Gurwin, Larry, *The Calvi Affair*, Macmillan, London, 1983

Headly, Victor, *Yardie*, X-Press, London, 1992

Herridge, Roy, *Believe No One*, Little Brown, London, 1993

Jennings, Andrew, Lashmar, Paul & Simson, Vyv, *Scotland Yard's Cocaine Connection*, Cape, London, 1990

Joseph, Joe, *The Japanese*, Penguin, London, 1993

Kaplan, David E and Dubro, Alex, *Yakuza*, Addison-Wesley, UK, 1986

Kochan, Nick & Wittington, Bob, *Bankrupt, The BCCI Fraud*, Victor Gollancz, London, 1991

Lacy, Robert, *Little Man*, Little Brown, New York, 1991

Lavigne, Yves, *Hells Angels*, Lyle Stuart, New York, 1987

McAlary, Mark, *Crack War*, Robinson Publishing, London, 1990

Morton, James, *Gangland*, Little Brown, London, 1992

Morton, James, *Gangland 2*, Little Brown, London, 1994

Nicholl, Charles, *The Fruit Palace*, Heinemann, London, 1985

Pearson, John, *The Profession of Violence*, Grafton, London, 1985

Pileggi, Nicholas, *WiseGuy*, Corgi, London, 1987

Robinson, Jeffrey, *The Laundrymen*, Simon & Schuster, 1994

Ruggiero, Vincenzo and South, Nigel, *Eurodrugs*, UCL Press, London, 1995

Shannon, Elaine, *Desperadoes*, Viking, New York, 1988

Short, Martin, *Lundy*, Grafton, London, 1992

Silverman, Jon, *Crack of Doom*, Headline, London, 1994

Sterling, Claire, *Crime Without Frontiers*, Little Brown, London, 1994

Sterling, Claire, *Octopus*, Norton, New York, 1990

Whittaker, Ben, *The Global Connection*, Cape, London, 1987

Index